Awaken the Dawn

A true story of travel, adventure, danger and faith.

Anne Baylis Bland

Onwards and Upwards Publishers

3 Radfords Turf, Cranbrook, Exeter,
EX5 7DX, United Kingdom.
www.onwardsandupwards.org

This first edition published in the United Kingdom by Onwards and Upwards Publishers (2018).

ISBN: 978-1-78815-680-6
Typeface: Sabon LT
Graphic design: LM Graphic Design

Printed in the United Kingdom.

About the Author

Born in England, Anne Baylis Bland first worked as assistant to her father in her family's building construction business. After marriage, she went to Canada, then to Africa with a Canadian mission. Six years later, altered circumstances meant she and her husband became self-supporting so they could continue their Christian work, which lasted another twenty-three years.

Mother of three and grandmother of seven, she now lives in England but still visits family in Zambia. Upon her return, alone, to England, she first worked as a school cook, then as a scheme manager in sheltered housing. Since retiring, she has served her local church for sixteen years as a deacon and house group leader, seven of those years also as church administrator. During these years, she also ran the church's ALPHA courses, then Christianity Explored and Discipleship Explored groups. Currently, she hosts a weekly prayer group and one-on-one Bible study/mentoring sessions.

To contact Anne, please write to:

annebland34@btinternet.com

Acknowledgements

I want to acknowledge and thank some very special people – loving and faithful friends, both past and present – for their unfailing support and encouragement: Irene, Joan, Pauline and Terry (especially for technical assistance), Jean, Sian, Bob and Deirdre. May the Lord greatly bless you.

For Joanna, Duncan and David

with my love and blessing.

Have mercy on me, my God, have mercy on me,
  for in you I take refuge.
I will take refuge in the shadow of your wings
  until the disaster has passed.
I cry out to God Most High,
  to God, who vindicates me.
He sends from heaven and saves me,
  rebuking those who hotly pursue me –
  God sends forth his love and his faithfulness.
I am in the midst of lions;
  I am forced to dwell among ravenous beasts –
men whose teeth are spears and arrows,
  whose tongues are sharp swords.
Be exalted, O God, above the heavens;
  let your glory be over all the earth.
They spread a net for my feet –
  I was bowed down in distress.
They dug a pit in my path –
  but they have fallen into it themselves.
My heart, O God, is steadfast,
  my heart is steadfast;
  I will sing and make music.
Awake, my soul!
  Awake, harp and lyre!
  I will awaken the dawn.
I will praise you, Lord, among the nations;
  I will sing of you among the peoples.
For great is your love, reaching to the heavens;
  your faithfulness reaches to the skies.

Psalm 57:1-10

Contents

FOREWORD

In the summer of 1989 I did what many college and university professors do: I responded to a request to teach summer school at an institution other than my own. This particular summer took me to Regent College in Vancouver, British Columbia to teach psychology to a mixed class of lay Christians and seminarians training for ministry. The details regarding my class and my students have since faded into a pleasant blur (Vancouver and the west coast of Canada being anything but a hardship posting in the summer), but one incident stands out in my memory quite vividly. Sitting in my office one afternoon preparing my lecture for the next day, with doors and windows open for the breeze, I suddenly heard a most unscholarly scuffle of large and small feet proceeding down the hall. Looking up, I saw framed in the doorway of my office a large, bearded bear-like man in his thirties with a toddler in his arms and two children not much older hugging his sides.

"You're Mary Stewart Van Leeuwen, aren't you?" he began without preamble. "I need to talk to you. I'd like you to come and have dinner with my family and me. My name is Flynn Ritchie, and I became a Christian at the Blands' farm in Zambia, just like you."

Despite my surprise and puzzlement over how he had accessed my conversion history (he had, it turned out, seen one of my books which I had dedicated to the Blands), there was never any question that I would accept his invitation. For as readers will discover in reading Anne Baylis Bland's book, the farm was a place uniquely touched by the Holy Spirit, for the extraordinary mix of people, varying in age, sex, education and national origin, who passed through its ever-open doors were a testimony to the creative ways in which God can pursue those he has chosen for himself.

Those two decades, as the reader will be reminded throughout the book, were ones of great political and economic ferment in sub-Saharan Africa. In 1965, when I first went as a Canadian volunteer to teach high school in Zambia, the country was celebrating its first year of independence, the price of copper was high, and Zambia was jokingly referred to as the "richest pauper in Central Africa". When I returned in 1970 to collect data for my doctoral thesis in social psychology (the same year I met the Blands), students' pre-independence revolutionary spirit had quieted, the economy was still stable, and the University of Zambia had opened its doors to provide me with a research base. The national mood was upbeat, both in Zambia and elsewhere in Africa, and 1965 through 1975 was consequently a decade during which many European and American young people (and even the not-so-young) came to the continent to spend weeks, months or occasionally years in search of adventure, in the idealistic pursuit of service or, more often than many of them would admit, in search of their souls.

Coming from North America, with its history of acrimonious tension between anti-intellectual fundamentalists and post orthodox liberals, I had come to thoroughly dislike the human-centred theology of the liberal churches in which I had been raised, but had concluded I could not become an evangelical Christian without putting my mind in permanent cold storage.

I discovered how wrong I was when I began to visit the Blands' farm between rounds of data gathering in Lusaka and elsewhere. Here was a place where, despite modest levels of formal education, God was worshipped with their minds as well as their hearts, and the beauty and complexity of God's creation was deeply appreciated. Moreover, they practised in their extended family life a kind of healing hospitality, which was at once an affirmation of the created goodness of ordinary life and a dim foreshadowing of the great banquet of the Lamb pictured in the Book of Revelation. It was a place quietly saturated in prayer for each person who passed through, and at the same time unpretentiously immersed in the practicalities of raising farm stock and developing part of the property as a conference site. Its atmosphere of spiritual nurture combined with the invitation to help run a farm in the ruggedly beautiful Central African bush was just what many of its visitors, myself among them, needed to bring them face to face with the Christ of both creation and redemption.

As this book also describes, the second half of the 1970s was a time of much greater uncertainty in the countries of Central Africa. Not only was there the spill over to Zambia of the independence struggle of what was later to be Zimbabwe (the former Southern Rhodesia), there were also the problems of falling copper prices in Zambia, rising oil prices everywhere, mounting foreign debt and internal political corruption in countries less than perfectly prepared for democratic nationhood. Yet despite – or perhaps because of – these accumulating "dangers, toils and snares", the church in Zambia and its neighbouring countries grew, not just institutionally, but by means of creative and dedicated small outreaches such as that exemplified by this farm. The ministry of its hospitality is a testimony to what God can accomplish when people cling to a vision of a unique ministry despite often uncertain financial resources and many spiritual, political and psychological challenges. All of us have God's treasure in earthen vessels and all of us live brokenly and imperfectly in this time of "the already, but the not yet". God in his mercy separates the gold from the dross of our efforts, and his Kingdom thus continues to grow. That was the case also at the farm near Lusaka in Zambia, and may be yet again as a younger generation has returned to work the farm.

All of this was confirmed as I shared my dinner in Vancouver with another graduate of that farm whom I had never met until then. There was so much about our subsequent histories that was uncannily parallel: both adult converts to the faith, we had married "cradle Christians" – he the daughter of American missionaries to Japan, I the son of Dutch Calvinist immigrants to California. Both of us had entered specialized Christian vocations – he as editor of an urban Christian newspaper, I as a professor in a Christian college setting. Both of us were active leaders in our respective churches, with all the passion and grumbling that inevitably accompanies such a commitment. Both of us had been educated in the vocation of parenthood and prayed daily for the spiritual growth of our children. Each of us was, and is, a simple gatekeeper in the house of the Lord. But take this and multiply it by the hundreds who passed through that Zambian farm, and the Kingdom of God is much enriched as a result. The author's account of that ministry will give a glimpse into God's ongoing narrative of redemption in one corner of the world and is one that will richly repay any reader's attention.

Mary Stewart Van Leeuwen Ph.D.

"...if I settle on the far side of the sea, even there your hand will guide me, your right hand will hold me fast."

Psalm 139:9-10

CHAPTER ONE

The Far Side of the Sea

Inky blackness threw the pale reflection of my face back through the window as the train thundered on towards a destiny I could only guess at and a meeting for which I had waited five long months.

The previous week had been a heady mix of emotions and exhilaration as I embraced new experiences, having said farewell to my family, crossed the Atlantic to Halifax in Nova Scotia, Canada and boarded the train that would take me to the prairies of Saskatchewan and my new husband.

Tired after the transfer from the ship and the immigration formalities, I had boarded the train and subsided in my compartment feeling a bit numb as the train rumbled past the backs of innumerable wooden houses until it finally left the town and picked up speed stretching for open country. As darkness fell I dozed on and off to the rhythm of the train until sleep finally overcame me.

Brilliant sunshine greeted me next morning, bouncing off an endless white landscape, an ever-moving vista of frozen land, trees and lakes. It was a three-day journey. How is it, I thought, that I had already come so far yet felt my journey was barely beginning? It felt more like a lifetime, not barely three years, since I'd stood on the bridge over the canal near my home in England longing and praying for something to change.

As I stood on the bridge looking down, an unexpected gust of wind blew my long hair across my face and snatched at my hair ribbon. My hand was too slow to catch it and from my perch I watched the strip of blue silk float down to the dark water below and settle among a scattering of autumn leaves. For a moment I lingered, reluctant to return to the stifling monotony of my office, which was built alongside our family home only a short distance away.

Overhead an aircraft roared into the sky from the airport barely two miles away. My eyes followed it out of sight and I sighed as I turned away. Would it ever be my turn to take off into the world? The summer was over and winter loomed. Would it be better next year?

Despite a good education to age sixteen, I had not been encouraged to continue my education nor train for anything because my father insisted I come into the family business – a building construction business that had been handed down from father to son for many generations. My brother, three years my junior, had to finish school and do his National Military Service before his turn came. With the pressures of failing health and financial difficulties that had built up during the war years, my father was adamant. Two attempts to strike out on my own, to try and find employment elsewhere, failed dismally. Without training it was extremely difficult and in the end, I could not resist the family pressure.

My brother left school and joined a man's world. While waiting to do his National Service, he began his apprenticeship in the family trade but his natural aptitude as a potential craftsman was far stronger than his desire to be involved in office work and the management side of things.

However, things were about to change for me. An introduction from a new mutual friend brought a young man into my life. Gordon was in the Government Agricultural Service working in Africa and subsequently an enthusiastic pen friendship developed over the next eighteen months. We shared many interests and it came as a welcome surprise to me that here was an opportunity to get to know someone whose life was so different and it also opened a door to meet other interesting people. Our shared Christian faith made the acquaintance even more acceptable. In the midlands of England, I was as lonely as he was in Nyasaland. From time to time this friendship was bolstered by opportunities to meet some of his Christian friends who were home on leave or passing through.

The eldest of five children, he was born on the mission field in Bolivia. The family returned to England and moved around quite a lot since his father was first a curate, then a vicar in the Church of England in several locations. He graduated from agricultural college but not wanting to stay in England joined the Colonial Agricultural Service in 1948. Many years later, when we first met, he had left the service and was managing a group of large farms in the central province of Nyasaland.

In the 1950s a group of Canadian missionaries arrived in the district and were directed to the local bwana for assistance and advice as they sought for somewhere to live while they built their first mission station. He offered them the use of his guest house and they gladly accepted his offer of hospitality. He knew the district and the people very well and spoke their language fluently; thereafter, he spent a lot of time assisting and translating for the two young Canadian couples and their friendship flourished. Years later he made the decision not to renew his contract with Kikuyu Estates but to take up the Canadians' suggestion that he enrol in their mission's training college the following year. So at the end of his contract, he came to England for an extended visit until it was time to go to Canada.

By this time I had been working in the family business for more than seven years. There was little opportunity to get out. My brother had commenced his National Service and my father's health had deteriorated. The business was plagued with financial problems and the resulting stress was hard on us all. The best thing that came out of that period was what I learned and absorbed about business in general, together with many practical skills. But I had no way of knowing then how great an asset these skills would prove to be in the life I was destined to live.

I was a willing assistant to my father because I loved him and understood the family predicament. Nevertheless, my situation seemed more than ever to be without choice or advantage and I had no social life. From childhood I had never questioned the presence of God and grew up enchanted by his creation. My most enjoyable times were when I was able to escape from the tedium of my working week and take my dog walking for miles in the surrounding countryside. We lived right on the edge of farmland backed by bluebell woods through which small streams ran and, of course, there was always the canal where one could walk for miles and miles along the towpath enjoying the wildlife, waving to the passing barges which throatily *putt-putt*-ed along, though many of them were still horse-drawn. It was the Grand Union canal, at 110 miles long, the longest canal, built to transport goods from the industrial midlands to the River Thames, London and out to the world. Even in winter there was always something interesting to see. It was glorious to be out there as the cold months gave way to spring and the land awoke from its winter sleep.

Through years of attendance at St. Nicholas Parish Church at Elmdon in Warwickshire, and from what my father had taught me, I had attained one thing of great value: the consciousness of loving God, a God who was there. A neighbour, Mrs Brown, invited me to a Youth for Christ rally in Birmingham Town Hall when I was seventeen. It was there, for the first time, I saw the transforming Spirit of God light up a human being and, in the grace of God, understood that marvellous fusion – the possibility of that most precious relationship between God and individual people. I had already realized that several things I read in the Bible were true of me and therefore thought it reasonable that other truths I found in the scriptures must also be true. Now my own conviction of sin and a desire to have that gift drove me to my feet and drew me forward in response.

Before I left the building that night I had embarked on a new life. Everything I knew and subsequently learned from God's word rang true and I began to think differently. Sometime later when the Browns' twenty-one-year-old daughter died of polio, their sorrow was something of a milestone for me also, for I witnessed in that family a depth of faith that was truly impressive in its strength and peace. My own budding faith was deepened and the assurance that a fearless future was possible took a firm hold on my life.

The long months when my friend from Africa was on leave deepened our relationship and we became engaged. Finally, we married at Elmdon and spent our honeymoon at Capernwray Hall in Lancashire and the beautiful Lake District. The only thing that cast a cloud over that time was my father's continued ill health. It was causing great anxiety. How I longed to go to college and study with my husband, but there was no spare money. I had no savings and only a tiny wage. Our wedding was very modest and by the time he had paid for his passage to Canada, his train fare across Canada and his first year's tuition, there was nothing left. Indeed, he could only afford passage on some Greek immigration ship flying under a 'flag of convenience'. So we took the decision that I would stay back and follow in a few months and hopefully join him in college the following term. Expecting to be in Canada for at least three years, we had elected to officially immigrate, so there had been a sprinkling of formalities to see to. Being unsure when I would be able to join him was disappointing but I was resigned.

So off he went while I waved my little damp hankie on the Southampton dockside. When the ship was nearly out of sight, I trailed back home to wait and work. My father's health continued to deteriorate and we decided Mother should apply to get my brother released from the army. This request was finally granted on compassionate grounds with the help of the Church Army. By this time I had managed to book a ticket on the Cunard Liner 'Sylvania' which was new and promised a far more pleasant trip than my husband had experienced. And so, early in the following March, I finally set sail and allowed myself at last to feel excited about the future.

It was very early and still dark when my train pulled in to Saskatoon. An icy cold wind was hurtling across the prairie, intent on giving me a real artic welcome, but my husband was there muffled to his eyebrows in a quilted car coat, snow boots, gloves and woolly hat. I was not so well equipped but he bundled me into the wonderfully warm restaurant and sat me down, and introduced his companion, a friend who had driven him to meet the train, explaining we still had a three-hour journey ahead. We began our drive just as the sun was coming up. Fortified by a wonderful breakfast, my first delightful tasting of pancakes dripping with maple syrup and lovely strong coffee, I was ready for the next step.

Life in a small college town on the prairies that was still in the firm grip of winter proved to be an exciting experience. Our small basement room introduced me to central heating, which, along with shopping in a supermarket, was a revelation. These things had not yet come to the part of England where I had lived. There were only two other married couples in the college that year and they also lived out so we were invited to visit their modest quarters quite often, and from them I learned how to initially start a one-pot stew on top of a pot-bellied wood-burning stove at night and how to keep it cooking, with no further fuel, in a hay box so the meal was ready when required next day. The college staff members were very hospitable and it was in their homes that I first tasted strawberry shortcake, six-inch deep Angel food cake, potato salad and root beer, and our meals at the student canteen introduced me to wieners and sauerkraut. It was a wonderful new world but after a few days I fell ill. Now whether that was a result of the rich, very different food or the altitude, I don't know – maybe a combination of both – but suddenly I couldn't stand up or even wield a hairbrush. I was prostrate, but before medical help was summoned a group of my husband's student friends gathered round and prayed for me and the condition left me as abruptly as it had arrived. Thankfully, we were then able to think through our situation and make some important decisions.

There were still several weeks to go before term ended and the Bible college was due to close for the long summer break. According to custom many of the students dispersed to earn money for the next year's fees; some went to a church or a summer camp in order to gain valuable experience. It seemed that most of the students already had plans but we did not. Our money was almost finished and we needed a car to get around this vast rural area so we decided I should look for a job straight away and we hoped we'd find direction by the end of term.

I found a job in the Town Clerk's Office and happily spent the next few weeks typing out utility bills and the like. At lunchtimes, I explored the town and was amazed to see the dramatic seasonal change that heralded the spring: the arrival of the Chinook. Frozen roads were transformed overnight into seas of glutinous red mud that rolled up on the car tyres and generally gave a good impression of slimy soft toffee. No wonder the land grew such wonderful grain.

One of the things that fascinated me about the prairies was the almost total absence of trees and the way that, driving around, we could see faraway grain elevators standing tall like huge posts on the horizon. Then, as we drew nearer, we could see the town's name in huge lettering on the towering elevator and lastly the town spread out beneath. Some of our new friends took us to the hills for an outing one weekend but the 'hills' were actually ravines that lay below the level of the surrounding prairie.

The end of term drew near. Icicles dripped and then disappeared with the last snow and the college buzzed with a new energy. Happily sharing their plans, the students prepared to leave for the long break. Just when we thought we were the only ones who didn't know where we were going, an opportunity came up for us in Western Alberta to assist with four country churches. By now we had enough money for a second-hand car and we found a sturdy 1949 Pontiac. So when the time came to leave, we too were part of the general exodus.

With high hopes and real excitement we set off, speculating on the summer before us and talking over plans for me to enter the college in the autumn. It was my first experience of driving hundreds of miles on a straight road. The melting snow draining off the rolling prairie had collected in triangular pounds alongside the roadside. These 'slews' were full of wild duck. It amazed me that occasionally we would have to pull over when we passed a tractor pulling an entire house along. Here many farmers built a basement and foundation for their house on the farm and another on a plot in town for the long winter, and moved their house between the two as the seasons dictated.

About fifty miles west of Red Deer, a town roughly midway between Calgary and Edmonton, we found the small town of Eckville and turned on to a dirt road that led to Diamond Valley. Here the pastor looked after four small country churches. He lived in a wooden house built alongside the largest of these churches and he wanted us, under his direction, to look after the two smallest, which were also the farthest away. The house beside the church at New Raven was occupied at the time, so we were offered a cabin on a nearby cattle ranch in return for my husband working on the ranch during the week.

I coped quite well with having to chop my own wood, cooking on a wood-burning stove, also a first for me, and having to carry all our water from a distant pump. I even coped with the rats that ate holes in my best dress, but my pioneering spirit wavered when I realized that the toilet was across the yard next to the bull pen. Trekking across the yard in all weathers was no real problem, but I never could get used to the bull banging, huffing and blowing through the somewhat wide chinks in the log wall.

Our chief responsibility was the larger of these two outlying churches, New Raven. Music was provided by a local guitar-playing ranch hand called Slim. There was a large number of Danish people in this congregation and once a month a Danish circuit preacher took an additional service for the people there. It wasn't long before the little log house beside the church became vacant and we moved in. We had also been asked to take services at the smallest of the four churches, in the tiny settlement of Sundre, more than an hour's drive farther west, though sometimes we didn't have the petrol to get there.

There had been no salary offered for any of this; we just had whatever was in the offering bag each Sunday, but there was very little cash offered. The people were accustomed to supporting their pastor by offering their produce. Sometimes the local dairy farm gave us milk and a few eggs but the problem was that our small congregation's gardens would not be yielding a great deal until later in the summer. We needed some cash.

Once again I went in search of a job and found one, as the laundress in the small hospital at Eckville, some twelve miles away from New Raven and, of course, there would be petrol needed to get there and back. It only paid $90 per month but it did get us some petrol, groceries and a quantity of preserving jars to take care of the surplus donated vegetables because, when their gardens did begin to ripen, our people were very generous. When I was first asked if we would like some rhubarb, I happily said yes, expecting a few stalks, but was staggered when they brought a full wheelbarrow to our car. Would we like some peas? A bucketful appeared together with sweetcorn by the sack.

Living in this rural setting was lovely. Both lovers of the countryside and wildlife, we revelled in being on the edge of the wilderness. We could see the foothills of the Rockies in the distance, we often saw bears on our drives to and from the outlying church and as the summer progressed the hedgerows bloomed with masses of wild roses. We were invited to church picnics, barbecues and even rodeos but all in all, though we loved it, we did get tired sometimes. Late one evening, as we drove home from one such gathering, we talked about how we were going to get back to college, but as usual we had no solution and we fell silent. I was half asleep in the passenger seat when my husband swerved violently off the road and the car shuddered to a halt partway down a ditch. He said he had swerved to avoid running into the flock of sheep standing in the road. But there were no sheep; he'd fallen asleep at the wheel. We were fortunate that, before too long, another late driver, a farmer in a heavy truck, came across us and managed to tow us back on the road. But now our car, though still running, was damaged.

Time was getting short and the uncertainty was a pressure on our minds. Just what were we going to do? My job as laundress at the hospital was soon coming to an end as I had only been hired for the summer while their regular lady took a long leave. But I had really enjoyed it. Not having done such a job before, I was nervous at first, not sure if I could handle it, and had only applied because I couldn't find anything else at the time. The person who interviewed me for the job had assured me it wasn't difficult, only washing machines and ironing. I didn't dare tell her I had never used a washing machine before, so I turned up on my first day with some trepidation. But I need not have worried. It was very straightforward and before long I got used to arriving at 7.30 am to find the shoulder-high pile of dirty linen on the floor beneath the laundry funnels that came down from the wards and operating theatre above. I enjoyed a daily sense of real satisfaction as I surveyed, at 4.30 pm, its transformation to sweet-smelling piles of pristine linen stacked on the long shelf that ran the entire length of the laundry, and I loved it that the diapers that came from maternity were of soft muslin, pink and blue – so different to the ubiquitous white terry towelling used in England.

The laundry was in the basement with only very narrow slit windows near the ceiling showing very little daylight so I got used to working in artificial light in this big, cavern-like space. In no time at all I mastered the huge roller washers, dryers and irons and the intricate art of hand-finishing the nursing sisters' uniforms and caps. Break times were interesting because of the many nationalities represented in the workforce. The most dramatic thing that happened that summer was a violent electrical storm during which a horse, grazing in the field just outside the laundry, was killed by lightning.

Our hopes of returning to college seemed to be receding. All along we had thought that, surely, by the time I finished work early in September, we would be in a position for at least my husband to go back to school, if not both of us. And by this time, I admit, I was already half expecting I'd have to find another job that winter and my dream of going to Bible college just wasn't going to happen. We had prayed about this many times but our circumstances had not changed. If college was closed to us, what then? Could something else be on

God's mind? My fledgling faith was finding the uncertainty increasingly difficult.

Chapter Two

The King's Business

Toward the end of August, a student friend invited us to his home in Banff in the Rocky Mountains for a weekend. We had a great time and we loved the journey and the magnificent scenery we saw on a day trip farther into the mountains on the Saturday. In his home church that Sunday morning we were greeted warmly and, to our surprise, invited up to the platform. The pastor, obviously cued in by our friends, asked us how we felt about returning to Africa once our studies were complete. We replied we were ready to go whenever the Lord called – a reply we were to be reminded of a great deal sooner than we could have dreamed.

After our return home, we grappled again with the cold facts. School started in a few weeks and we had not been able to save enough money for even my husband to return. It was now a matter of urgency and prayer. Arriving home from Sundre on the first Sunday evening in September, we found a note from the Diamond Valley pastor pinned to the door. It said, "Please call this (a Winnipeg number) urgently."

We were mystified. Yet as we made our way over to the nearest neighbour we knew of with a telephone, we could not help speculating. Winnipeg was in a different time zone. We didn't know anyone there. So how come someone there knew us? Was it a mistake? What was it all about?

Once connected, the situation became clear. It was a summons from the founder of the mission to which my husband's friends in Africa belonged. The mission was faced with an emergency in Southern Rhodesia. This pastor and his wife, herself a veteran missionary who had served in China, had been praying for an answer to their problem for some time. They needed to find a replacement for their man in Bulawayo as quickly as possible. His extensive work could not be left without a supervisor. His mother lay very ill in Canada and he was long overdue for leave.

Apparently, earlier that day they had shared this need with two other missionaries, home on leave and passing through. Hearing this, over lunch, the two from the same territory told them about a Mr Bland, whom they had met out there, and who had attended their Bible school. They suggested it might be worth contacting him. Though they didn't know his present situation, they did know of his desire to return to Africa as soon as possible. Of course, the founder of the mission had never even heard of us and was full of questions. The upshot of all this was that, being people of great faith and a certain godly boldness, they placed the call to Diamond Valley later that same day.

I clung to my husband's side during this call trying hard to catch what was being said on the other end. My husband relayed snippets to me from time to time and finally he asked them to hold while he spoke to me. It seemed that there was a suggestion that we should go to Winnipeg to talk about a possible return to Africa.

It was a considerable shock to be asked such a momentous question out of the blue. After a long conversation, it was agreed that both parties should think some more and pray on it that night. It was arranged that they would telephone the pastor's house in Diamond Valley at noon the following day, and that we should be there to take the call.

Monday. We arrived at the Diamond Valley manse ready to take the call at noon as arranged, still full of questions and feeling excited and apprehensive in turn. Too much speculation and conjecture with intervals of prayer had meant we hadn't had much sleep. We had thought of all the pros and cons, not least of the increasing likelihood of a closed door to college, and what a possible earlier return to Africa would mean. But even so, we were thinking in terms of the next few months or even the following year. So we were considerably shocked when we learned of the proposed timescale.

The call came through from Winnipeg on time and we were asked how we felt about the suggestion that we should go out to Bulawayo to care-take the work there while their missionary took some much needed and overdue leave. My husband replied tentatively that, in principle, we were willing and could be available. A confident response came down the line. After a night of prayer, the mission founder and his wife had been put in mind of a passage of Scripture from the First Book of Samuel in the Old Testament[1]. "The king's business is urgent, Brother Bland," he said. "Can you get here by the weekend?"

We found ourselves suddenly flooded with confidence and agreed. Then we had to figure out how that was possible. It's probably a great understatement to say that our departure from Alberta was hurried, but everyone accepted our decision. The calm understanding of the situation by both our mentor and the congregation at New Raven helped enormously. Though we were confident in our decision, practical matters took some organising. Still expecting to have some time in Winnipeg to prepare for such a momentous undertaking, we stopped ourselves from too much surmising and concentrated on the task in hand.

Tuesday. Finding that our old suitcases were damaged, my husband took off for Red Deer to purchase new ones while I laundered all our stuff ready for packing. He came back that afternoon with cases, but now we didn't have enough money for the train fare to Winnipeg. The pastor at Diamond Valley had got the word round quickly and the whole congregation threw a farewell supper for us that night. The whole of our train fare was raised, together with the gift of a shirt for my husband and a blouse for me. No one questioned our decision, everyone expressed their wholehearted acceptance and blessing, and the evening ended in prayer and praise.

Wednesday. Thinking that we would be in Canada for at least three years, maybe much longer, we had a good supply of winter clothing and this had been left at the college awaiting our proposed return. Since there was hardly anything in it that we would need in Africa, and the Canadian Pacific Railway via Red Deer to Winnipeg did not go through Saskatoon, we sent a message to the college dean suggesting that our things could be distributed to any needy students. Then we had to think about what we owed the local garage for car repairs. The garage was pleased to take the car, after our departure, in lieu of the debt. In a

---

[1] 1 Samuel 21:8

whirl of activity, every problem was dealt with and by bedtime we were ready.

Thursday. We said our last farewells at New Raven and our mentor drove us into Red Deer. By noon, and in the grace of God and in his provision, we were aboard the transcontinental train going east. We had not had the money for sleepers so we stayed in the day coach, alternately dozing and talking through the night. And late on Friday afternoon we reached Winnipeg where we were met and warmly received.

Throughout that busy week we had supposed that in Winnipeg we would have time to prepare for our new position and, hopefully, procure the things we would need for such an undertaking. It was not so. Our gracious and very loving hosts were on fire and plans already in place. Over dinner that evening, it was all explained to us. First, the position in Bulawayo had become even more urgent as their man's mother was extremely ill and they wanted him to get back to Canada to be with her before it was too late. The work in Bulawayo was extensive so it was also important that my husband arrived in time for proper handover. The work spread over a ninety-mile radius of Bulawayo: work in five rural schools, a prison, a new church-building project and a couple of other meetings that involved both African nationals, Europeans and Indians. Therefore an air ticket had been booked for my husband, for very early on that Monday morning. They regretted that their funds did not stretch to me going with him. I would have to wait.

Apparently, while we were whizzing round at New Raven, the mission founder had been in communication with their other missionaries in the British Central African territories and with colleagues in Canada and it had been agreed that despite his not having finished at the Bible college, they would recognise his contribution and assistance to their people in Nyasaland and therefore he should be given the recognisable authority his new job demanded.

The speed with which events had developed had left this church without sufficient funds to send us together, but, they hastened to say, they had no doubts whatsoever that the Lord would supply what was needed. So the plan was for me to stay with them, with the remainder of our luggage, until such time as a passage by sea could be arranged.

Saturday was spent in more talks, shopping for some things my husband needed and with me trying to get my head round it all.

Fortunately, there was no problem with immigration because my husband had residential status in those territories. He also spoke two of the main African languages in those parts and all this had weighed very favourably with his suitability for the position. While his year at Bible school and, moreover, his experiences out there had given him many skills suited to his new position, I was totally unprepared for the role of 'missionary elect' that had so precipitously been thrust upon me. My inner conviction that this decision was right for me also, nevertheless, vied with my awareness of total inadequacy. I had never spoken in public and was extremely nervous of being asked to do so. It seemed as if every time I turned round, it was only to face another challenge. And those challenges were coming at me thick and fast.

Events had swept me along, but on Sunday afternoon while my husband was being briefed, I had a real panic attack. Alone in the guest room, attempting to sort our things out for packing, I was becoming more and more distracted by thoughts of the enormity of what we were about to do. Tears ran down my face, blotching my glasses and I found myself slumped on the floor totally overwhelmed. I felt then much as I think the woman who'd bled for twelve years must have done as she pushed her way through the crowd endeavouring to touch the hem of Jesus' garment[2]. I was desperate for some restoration of peace and assurance. All of a sudden, it seemed to me that Jesus was in the room saying quietly, "Fear not, my child," and immediately my anguish gave way to a real sense of peace. It was as if a spring of warm water gushed up in my innermost being and washed over me and its ripples reached all the way to my fingers and toes. The room was flooded with a marvellous light – very, very bright, but which did not hurt my eyes. When I got up off the floor, I was surprised to note I had been there almost an hour.

That night at the end of the evening service, it was the custom in that church to gather at the altar rail for prayer. I went forward also and almost immediately was swept into a very similar experience as I'd had that afternoon. The presence of the people round me faded as again this brilliant soft light engulfed me and a joyous spirit of praise took over. Like a drinking fountain, the warm sensation of bubbling light grew from the centre of my being and spread throughout my body,

---

[2] See Matthew 9:20-21

rippling down to every extremity. I was not conscious of talking but apparently, as I was told later, I did in a heavenly language. Someone asked if I had been baptized and when I only admitted to an Anglican christening, she asked if I would like to be. When I said yes, people ran to arrange it then and there and before the night was over, I had been baptized in water in the church's basement baptismal tank. My overwhelming sense was one of a great inner peace and my worries and questions about our situation and the future were gone.

Monday dawned and in the pre-dawn chill my husband flew off on the first leg of his journey, and I was left praying I would be strong enough for all that was now required of me. Alone with the old couple, I eagerly waited to see how things would work out. In the days that followed, I was to learn many lessons that stayed with me about faith, trust, a whole new way of living and what it meant to be part of God's family. As we had driven back from the airport, my host had said, "Now we will see how the Lord will provide for you, my dear." To my knowledge, they had made no specific appeal for money, though obviously their own congregation knew of the need. They appeared to be a church with a careful budget and an extraordinarily high percentage of their income was invested in the mission.

Winnipeg was the home church of the man in Bulawayo and this was the reason for their high degree of involvement. Despite the apparent lack, I sat day after day with my hosts at breakfast-time and watched them open their mail. Dollar bills dropped out of letters, cheques and money orders littered the breakfast table. With the letters came messages: "We felt you had need of this," or, "We are not sure what the need is, but became convinced we should send the enclosed," etc. With love, with prayers and with blessings, cash flowed in from near and far. Together with a special offering that very next Sunday, I had my fare in little over a week. There was enough over for travel expenses and even for the purchase of a sewing machine. Though I didn't know it then, in that same week a single gift had been received in Bulawayo to provide us with a very good, almost new car. That wonderful week taught me, in so many practical ways, such a lot about faith and God's provision and care – spiritual truths and lessons that have stayed with me ever since.

Accordingly, I took the train to Montreal, then travelled to England by sea. As the ship steamed down the St. Lawrence Sea Way towards the Atlantic, I felt the excitement of those few days gradually settle into a calmer mood of expectation mixed with a sober resolve to do my best in this emerging situation. But on arrival in England I encountered a new setback.

It had been planned that I should take a short break of two or three days to be with my family before sailing to Beira in Mozambique where I would take the train to Bulawayo. However, my letter, posted from Winnipeg advising my family of these new plans, had crossed with their letter advising me of my father's continued decline in health, so I knew nothing of his present state until I landed. I arrived the day before he was due in hospital for major surgery. My mother was in some difficulties with the business and she asked me if I could stay a bit longer until they were over the crisis. So I sent a telegram to my husband and to the people in Winnipeg and all agreed I could stay for a while. The people in Winnipeg were totally supportive and they suggested that when I was ready, I should exchange my ticket and fly the rest of the way to save time. They even sent me extra money to cover this period. Truly I was blessed in their care.

So, in no time at all, I was back in my office almost as if I had never left. Sadly, the day after my arrival, my old dog, the companion of my youth, was run over and killed in front of our house. My father rallied but it was plain to us all that he was struggling. I sent our heavy luggage on by sea and prepared to fly out by the middle of November. The day of my departure dawned and the whole family came with me to the airport and there we waited... and waited.

Apparently, my plane for London originated from Manchester and it was stuck there with an oil leak. So I missed my connection in London. It was a Saturday and there seemed little the staff could do. They offered me a seat to London the next morning but couldn't get me on a plane to Africa. They suggested I get myself to London, then present my ticket and explain what had happened and see what could be done for me. It was a major anti-climax.

We trailed home. I sent a telegram to my husband explaining the delay but couldn't give him an alternate ETA, though when I did get there, some thirty hours late, it was to find that the message hadn't been delivered anyway. Typically, my husband didn't worry; he just told me when we finally met that, though disappointed at not finding me on the expected flight, and in the absence of any sort of message, he'd just decided to keep turning up to meet flights from London until I, or a message, did show up. Just as well everything was alright then! The next morning my brother drove my mother and me to the airport but the mood was very different. My dad wasn't up to coming again and sombrely we'd said our goodbyes at home.

CHAPTER THREE

Land of the Midnight Rainbow

I had been advised by my husband not to come to Bulawayo, but to book my ticket to Ndola on Northern Rhodesia's Copperbelt, because he would be attending a conference near the town of Kitwe about an hour's drive away. I planned to be there as the conference closed in order to be introduced to the other missionaries before they dispersed but I missed them by a day. The rainy season was getting underway. That territory, having twice the rainfall of the Bulawayo area, was already lush with verdant new growth and steady daily rain could be expected. It was wonderful to come from frosty, foggy England into the warm velvet air of tropical Africa. To me it seemed like perpetual summer at first and it took me a long time to recognise the changing seasons. The richness and colour of this new land and people absorbed me and I was very happy to be reunited with my husband again.

Among the seasonal changes was the presence of flying ants. Triggered by the coming of the rains, they rose out of the ground in hordes. In town, attracted to the glow of street lamps, they swirled like a snowstorm round the lights, leaving the confetti of their discarded wings to litter the pavements. They were a hazard when we drove anywhere, as attracted to headlights, they threatened to choke the car radiator, leaving their squashed bodies to smear the windscreen and clog up the wipers. The rain was not constant but regular, sudden and hard, often announced by electrical storms which were more common at the beginning of the rainy season. Town roads were built with deep gullies and culverts on each side to accommodate this volume of water.

On the corrugated iron roof of the mission house, the noise was deafening and when the rain stopped, usually as suddenly as it had begun, the earth steamed.

Those first few days in Ndola flew by with so many new things to taste, to see, people to meet and a new kind of church to sample. Our hosts were the two young couples whom my husband had originally befriended in Nyasaland. While we were in Canada, they had relocated with the aim of planting churches in each of the eight Copperbelt towns. It was my first experience of the exuberant African church and their joyfully noisy services that ran practically all day. Women sat on one side of the church and the men on the other. All through the proceedings people got up, walked about, chased toddlers and fed babies. About midday they paused to eat and drink right there, and then people regrouped and settled down again. There was an ecstasy in their praise and a very evident hunger for God.

Then it was time to go home to Bulawayo. The journey south, of about eleven hundred kilometres, was a revelation. The new fully tarred road had only recently been completed and proved to be a wonderful introduction to the Rhodesias. The road stretched to the horizon. There was not much light traffic, just a few private cars, most of which had a canvas water bag slung in front outside, but plenty of huge heavy goods vehicles from the mines. Within a couple of hours, we left the heavily forested north and were running through lighter *miombo* woodland characterized by anthills and candelabra trees. Very large anthills had been a feature all over the Copperbelt. They were so high and wide that many houses, where they occurred in the garden, had their water tank built on the top of these to give a gravity fed supply to the house.

Slowly the thickly wooded north gave way to more open country. The sun beat down as we dropped to the Zambezi valley and after passing through the Northern Rhodesia border post, we stopped on the bridge that stood very high above the river to take a look at the green swirling water rushing beneath us. It was high noon and swelteringly hot. We returned to the car and crossed into Southern Rhodesia.

There had been no rain in the Zambezi valley for seven or eight months and the road was an anvil under the hammer of the sun. In this heat the road in front of us appeared to float in what seemed to be streams of trailing mist. I saw my first elephant, alone and standing motionless under an acacia tree near the roadside, beside what looked like a dried-up waterhole. The constant sound of the Christmas beetles, *cicadas,* in the trees reminded me of frying eggs. As we approached the end of the flat, we had to cut our speed to allow a trio of ambling elephants, this time with attendant tick birds riding pillion, to leave the roadside, where they miraculously seemed to fade into the bush.

We wound our way up the southern escarpment to Makuti to take a break and stretch our legs. At the café perched high above the road, we sat on the shady veranda gazing at the endless panorama spread out before us. To my husband, this was already commonplace, though well appreciated, but that day I fell in love with Africa.

Taking to the road again, we pressed on, passing roadside vendors who patiently sat waiting beside piles of watermelon or tomatoes. Occasionally, we would see a bullock cart trundling along, often with a giggling child or two perched on top of the load. Later, when I saw some tall sacks propped up beside the road without any attendants, I asked about this. He slowed down and pointed to some huts, barely visible among the trees. "See there," he said, "can you see? If you want to buy, you just honk your horn and someone will come running."

As we drove he regaled me with tantalizing stories about the territory that fired my imagination, making me anticipate my new life in this wonderful land even more. For instance, he promised me a visit to the Victoria Falls on the Zambezi at the earliest opportunity. "Do you know," he said, "you can see the cloud of spray rising above the falls several miles away as you leave the little town of Livingstone, and," he went on, "the sunrise colours that cloud salmon pink, peach and lemon. It's extremely lovely and up close you can see the gloriously brilliant rainbow. But what is fascinating is the pale, ethereal and exquisite night-time rainbow created by a full moon. The Africans call the great falls *'Musi-o-tunya'* ('the smoke that thunders')."

The sun was sliding down the western sky as we pulled into Salisbury, the capital of Southern Rhodesia, and made our way to the home of the mission's presbyter whom I hadn't met yet as he'd left Kitwe before I arrived. As our car drew up, he appeared on his front veranda grinning from ear to ear, with his Norwegian wife at his side. Gripping my hand, he roared out a typical greeting: "Welcome, welcome! Have you got the victory, sister?"

It was all a bit overwhelming and at first I didn't understand what he meant. I was unsure of myself and a bit nervous in the face of so much exuberance and experience. But they were kindness itself and I warmed to them immediately. During our overnight stay, I learned a lot more about the mission and the country, and early next morning we set off on the last leg of our journey home, some four hundred and twenty kilometres south through little settlements clustered amid the ubiquitous mango trees, each with its grain stores and cattle markets. The country was now all rolling, richly developed agricultural land; huge beef ranches, irrigated crops, orchards and tobacco farms.

At last we arrived in Bulawayo with its very wide streets, planned at the turn of the century to allow carts with their twelve span of oxen to turn easily, and lined with jacaranda trees which were scattering their deep mauve flowers on the city's pavements. It was the territory's second largest city and home for that first year was to be in the suburbs, at 14 Flamboyant Avenue.

My husband was already familiar with our task, but I was surprised when I grasped the extent of our responsibilities. First, there were the five rural schools spread out in a ninety-mile radius from the town, and that meant at least one monthly visit each, to view progress, facilitate supplies and pay the teachers. Each Sunday meant a very early visit to Khami Jail, the maximum security prison on the outskirts, to take a short service with the prisoners. This was always a favourite with me, for although I was not allowed inside, we would park the car under a shady tree right close to the prison gate where I could hear the sound of hundreds of wonderful male voices raised in song, clear and beautiful, that floated on the warm morning air.

Then back to town for another fairly short service, alternately for the youngsters at one of two boarding schools, then on to take a service in the new, though as yet uncompleted, town church. After a late lunch at home, we sallied forth again by four o'clock to another suburb, where there was a large Asian community, to lead a home group with an Indian family. At this time, this meeting only attracted about five or six adults and when the children saw our car approaching they used to run and hide in the garden. Sometimes during the service, we would catch a glimpse of them peeking round the doorway, but if we attempted to get their attention they would scuttle away giggling. Little did we dream then that one day one of these children would grow up and become a prominent Christian leader in that land.

We were grateful for the generous tea that was laid on for us here after the meeting ended because we still had another, mainly European, home group due to start at about seven o'clock, on the other side of town. Time flew by. I developed a keen appreciation of all that our bachelor colleague had accomplished and the workload it had entailed. About three months into this, we received an invitation from one of the couples from Kitwe to accompany them on a brief visit to Durban in Natal, South Africa. And it was there that I discovered I was pregnant and our joy was complete.

All went well, and by the time the child was due, word had come from Canada that our colleague was preparing to return to Bulawayo in October. Indeed, he arrived just a week before the arrival of our little daughter with the good news that he was going to get married in the very near future, to our presbyter's daughter, also a missionary. His timing was excellent, freeing us to concentrate on the baby's arrival and prepare for our next move.

Headquarters wanted us to go to the Copperbelt and assist in the work there as one of the two resident couples was due for long leave. This time, we would have to share a home with the remaining couple at Garneton, a few miles north of Kitwe. The work would be quite different: eight different churches, established in the eight major towns strung out across the copper fields, services in several vernacular languages and, unknown to us at the time, an opportunity to work with Billy Graham's organisation.

Before we left, we paid a last visit to all the schools in the company of our colleague, partly to hand over and mostly for us to say goodbye. On average it took two or more hours to reach each one and because they were all in different directions, we could only visit one at a time. They were all on farms, fanning out roughly south-south-west of the city and once away from town, the countryside grew more arid the farther we went. Grazing seemed very poor and verging on stony semi-desert. But these farms, or ranches, were vast and did support huge herds. Everywhere we went there were numerous gates to open and then close again and in these very hot, dry conditions I was thankful that often there were ragged urchins who came running at the sound of the car to open those same gates. It was here that we found a use for many second-hand Christmas cards sent to us by ladies' groups. This had puzzled me at first but with brief gospel stories or simple texts copied on to the blank backs of the pictures they made ideal little 'thank you' tokens and the kids loved them.

Finally, we would arrive at the school, a thatched one-room building built of lime-washed mud brick, standing in a clearing of swept, bare ground shaded sparsely with an acacia tree or two together with a couple of mango trees. As the car drew up, the teacher would appear from the dim interior to greet us. Inside, light and air were provided by a simple gap, about shoulder height, on three sides beneath the eaves. The pupils, of various ages, sat on long, rough wooden benches, girls on one side, boys on the other. We were led to the front and given places of honour beneath the blackboard. Then we were treated to songs and chanted lessons. After a short address, the children were dismissed and the men would settle down with the teacher and do business.

On these farewell visits, I would return to the car at this point to attend to our daughter. I found it disconcerting at first, getting used to breastfeeding with the car completely surrounded by curious children, jostling and giggling, all vying for a closer look. Seeing a woman with a baby at her breast was no novelty to them, but as a white woman doing it, I was.

At the beginning of November, blissfully unaware of all the challenges that would confront us, we duly packed up our stuff and, with our precious three-week-old baby tucked in her pink carrycot on the back seat, we set off and took the road north. This was the hottest time of the year and as the day wore on and the heat increased, I got a bit worried. As a first-time mother, I was anxious about how the baby was coping and all the way through the Zambezi Valley I was continually hovering over the back seat watching her for signs of distress. But apart from a little crop of minute beads of perspiration on her tiny button nose, she was fine.

The aim of these workers had been to establish a church in each of the towns on the Copperbelt: Ndola, Kitwe, Bancroft, Kalalushi, Chingola, Mufulira and Luanshya. This vast copper-bearing area extended over the border, to Katanga in the Congo. The two Canadian couples believed that the churches should become self-supporting from the start and we agreed with this principle. Once the township plot was secured, the work on the building only advanced as the people were willing to give and to work. Progress was therefore slower than perhaps it may have been had the mission provided everything and did it all, but this policy produced steady and enduring growth. The churches were small with corrugated iron roofs and little or no furnishings but they resounded with joy and genuine fellowship.

Early in 1960, Billy Graham visited both Rhodesian territories. There was great interest among the churches and missionaries. These were the first multiracial meetings held in the territory and there was much prayer. During the week before he was expected, there had been some unrest and a spate of hold-ups, and this was a concern for us all. It came to a head when a European woman was stopped on the Kitwe-Ndola road, dragged from her car and murdered. Everything was blanketed in prayer and the unrest did not escalate. The atmosphere quietened and the Christian community steadily continued their preparations. A huge marquee went up on the outskirts of town while teams from all the churches consolidated their follow-up plans.

When the meetings began everyone was on tiptoe. Just in case there was any disturbance, there was a row of police lining the inside of the marquee, and a similar line encircling the outside. We attended with our baby stowed in her carry-cot under my seat. All was well, so much so that the extraordinary peace attending the meetings was the talk of the town among Christians and non-Christians alike. There was a great spiritual harvest and my husband and I took on the follow-up work with a group of new converts at Mwekera, a nearby government forestry station.

The momentous event later that year was the Congo uprising. We were barely sixty miles from the border and witnessed this exodus. Vehicles came pouring over the border, some shot up, people fleeing for their lives. Hastily, signs were erected all over the Copperbelt, with indicating arrows. They simply said, "TO THE SOUTH." Those who were able to travel onwards were fed and given fuel and sent on. We heard many harrowing tales. Local residents gave what aid they could and we met some people at this time who later became our friends for life.

All this time, we had been thinking about what we should do and where we would live at the end of that year when our colleagues returned. There was a suggestion from our colleagues that we should stay on to reinforce their team and we could see the sense in that as the work was growing apace. But it was essential that, if we were to stay, we should have a home of our own, and this was to be the test as we sought God's will. Consequently, we actively began our search for a suitable place and searched all over the area in the following weeks. We knew that whatever we found wouldn't be a financial problem because, according to custom, it would become the property of the Canadian mission. And we knew they would gladly accept our decision. If the aim was to open up a new work or extend the existing, their policy was to give credence to the missionaries' own calling.

But our efforts were in vain and by the time another annual conference was called, this time in Salisbury, we were no further forward. When the time came, we were struggling financially and it would mean having to leave a week before our allowance was due. As the day of departure drew near, it was hard not to feel anxious about how we would manage the six-hundred-mile journey. But we had also resolved that we must look to God for the provision, not advertise our need and not borrow. If we were to continue to work as God's representatives in this country, it stood to reason that it had to be *his provision and his alone* that enabled us, no other. Our colleagues left a few days early in order to visit friends on the way. We waved them off and returned to the house to wait.

CHAPTER FOUR

A Handful of Change

Since arriving in Africa, we had been on the same basic allowance with no extra for the baby. Our total income was $150 per month to cover everything. We were totally dependent on the car, which was essential given the long distances we travelled in our work, most of those on rough gravel country roads, so the cost of maintenance and fuel always took out a big chunk to start with. True, we didn't pay rent because the house belonged to the mission, but unlike many of our colleagues, we did not have family or a home church contributing extras from time to time.

We would always first set aside enough to cover the baby's needs for the whole month, and now, a full week before our allowance was due, we were low on groceries and low on petrol. So low, in fact, that even if we set off then, we could only hope to reach Kitwe, but with scarcely enough fuel to get back. Of course, we could SOS our presbyter in Salisbury for some emergency financial assistance but it wouldn't really solve anything as we would have to pay it back and therefore it wouldn't change a thing.

All along we had planned to leave on the Thursday before the conference because it was a two-day journey and we had planned to have the weekend with our hosts before meetings started officially on the following Monday morning. Since we didn't have enough money for our needs even if we cancelled and stayed home, that wasn't the answer, and in any case, we had already instructed head office to send our next allowance to Salisbury so we would have cash for the journey back. So it was crunch time.

We decided that as we were legitimately working and it was our duty to be at the conference, either our God would meet our need or he would not. And if that were the case, we were possibly wasting our time and mistaken in our calling. We decided to put our faith to test and begin the journey and see what God would do for us.

Early on that fateful Thursday morning, we drove in to Kitwe knowing full well we didn't have the wherewithal to go back. On board were our suitcases and everything our baby would need plus some basic camping gear to enable us to spend the night on the road. Maybe there might be some money in the post; we couldn't think of anything else. This at least was a contact point, if someone had it laid on their heart to contribute. The fact was, we were so unsure what to expect, but to expect nothing didn't make sense either.

We reached town and parked near the centre. My husband went to the Post Office to check our post box. There was nothing. Baby needed changing and feeding, so we moved the car to a small riverside park on the fringe of town. My husband was restless and decided to walk around a bit. Noon came and we ate a little picnic I had brought, then decided to return to the town centre. He said he'd try the post box again.

Nothing. Now he began to feel a bit despondent. Returning to the car to check on us, he decided to walk around again. As he crossed the road he heard a shout and looked up to see a Christian acquaintance waving from a nearby shop front.

"Hi, bro, what are you doing here? I thought you'd be away by now." A beefy hand shot forward in jovial greeting.

With no intention of confiding in him, my husband shrugged a vague answer about delays and prepared to move on. But the man beckoned him in.

"Not to worry, man! Come in, come in!" and with great good humour expressed in a broad Afrikaans accent, the butcher coaxed him into the shop. Minutes later he shoved a small parcel of prime steak at my husband and, grinning, plunged a hand in his pocket and drew out a handful of cash. He laughed, "Not a lot, my friend but," he shrugged, "go with God." And with a hearty backslap he waved farewell.

Back at the car we considered the gifts, bemused but considerably relieved and thankful as it was an obvious answer to our prayers and, seemingly, confirmation that we were meant to go on. But now other questions arose.

The money was not enough to get us to Salisbury. What should we do? Should we attempt to go on knowing we did not have enough to take us all the way, and just how far would it take us? The butcher, whom we knew to be a generous giver, could have given us more had he raided his till but he had not. Had God laid a restraining hand on him for a purpose? Prayerfully, we considered our options.

A little under halfway, between Kitwe and Salisbury, lay the town of Lusaka. It was destined to become the new capital when the territory became independent and it represented the farthest we could expect to get with the money we had. Having the faith to go on was one thing, taking chances with a baby was quite another. However, we had everything she would need and she was safe with us in the car even if we had to sleep beside the road. We decided to go on.

It was nearly two o'clock in the afternoon when we left Kitwe and headed south. That night we camped beside the road just north of Lusaka and entered the town early the next day. Though we knew no one there, we were growing in confidence that the town somehow held the key to our future. We had travelled through it twice before and had a general idea of the layout so we drove to the post office, which was central. Uncertain where to start and not knowing what to expect, I stayed in the car with baby Grace while my husband went off to explore. I bought a local newspaper and settled down to wait.

When he left the car, he had no idea where to start. Thinking about our year of living in someone else's house in Bulawayo, then sharing a house in Kitwe and our fruitless search for a place on the Copperbelt, it occurred to him that finding a place to live was still our most pressing need. He knew that mission headquarters would probably be happy to have some workers in this very strategic town. Living in a town was anathema for him but fortunately his work, mainly in translation at that time, did not specifically require us to do that. It was only a short jump from these thoughts to wondering, "If this is the way ahead, how and where will we live?" He looked around and seeing an estate agent's office, he walked in.

He cast his eye around and the agent asked him what he was interested in. With nothing to lose, he described his dream: a nice little place, out of town, with a bit of land and – oh, yes, it must have good water. The agent produced a handful of colour snapshots, saying he'd only received them that morning and had therefore not yet catalogued them. It was a small cottage, about ten to eleven miles from town, twenty-seven acres freehold, £5000. A vast sum for a penniless missionary!

"Nice," Gordon murmured, "but out of the question." He expressed his thanks and walked out.

Nevertheless, when he came across another estate agent later, he went in and was astonished to find himself caught up in the same routine. The agent fished in a desk drawer and brought out another selection of coloured snapshots of the same place. He read off the card to which they were clipped. "This might suit, sir. The owner came in first thing this morning. Nice little place, about ten or so miles out on the west side of town."

By now my husband was struggling with reality and tried again to put the agent off: "A bit too grand... Not quite what I had in mind..." *Oh, but it's exactly what I had in mind,* he thought.

He turned to go but the canny agent had correctly read the expression on his face and, pressing his advantage, offered to drive him out there to see the place. By now, feeling a little more buoyant, my husband was incapable of refusing and arrangements were made for two o'clock that same afternoon.

"You'll not believe what's happened." His slightly breathless voice at the car window had my immediate attention. "We're going to look at a house."

"What?" Though I had long given up expecting even the obvious, this was astonishing indeed. But I also had something to impart. "Look here," I opened the newspaper I had been reading and pointed to the middle pages and the church notices for the coming weekend.

He took the paper and scanned the page. "Here's a familiar name. Now, who was it that told us about this man?" His finger stabbed the page as he turned to me. I peered over to look and indeed the name was familiar.

"Look, why don't we try phoning this number they've given? It's probably the manse," I suggested. "We've nothing to lose and it might be useful."

Having agreed that is what we'd do later, we hastily had a snack from our meagre supplies in the car, tidied ourselves and made the baby comfortable. Just before two o'clock we drove round to the estate agent's office and followed his car out of town taking the road west of the city.

The road wound through an area known as Botha's Rust. Originally a very large tract of land, it was settled at the turn of the 20th century by Boer farmers who came up from South Africa in covered wagons. The area south of the road had several natural springs dotted all over it, and had been divided off and was part of a large cattle ranch.

Our destination was about eleven miles west of the city where, along a small river, several smaller plots of between five acres and twenty acres had been divided off by the original owner. He had kept the choicest piece of land at the head of this little river for himself. It was a plot of some twenty-seven acres and the spring that gave rise to the river was on this land. Now he wanted to sell and take his pregnant wife to South Africa.

The agent's car turned off the main road to the right, followed a narrow dirt road and finally entered a gateway. The drive sloped gently downwards and as he approached the house, he slowed right down so that we could absorb the first impact. There in front of us, against a backdrop of wild bauhinia trees covered with white blossom and set among extensive lawns, was a large pink-washed thatched *rondavel* with honeysuckle-covered walls.

The agent drew the car to a standstill alongside a hibiscus hedge. As we got out of the car, we saw the sun glinting off water at the bottom of sloping lawns. The agent indicated the way round to the main entrance and we followed him along the short path leading to a flight of half-circular steps on our left, that rose up to a curved shady veranda running the width of the house. From these steps we could see the whole panoramic view of the garden below us. In the centre, at the foot of the terraced lawn, was a curved natural waterfall sparkling in the sunlight. Quite bemused we followed the agent to the open doorway where the owner and his wife stood ready to greet us and, still a bit awestruck, we followed them inside.

They were kind and expressed an interest in our baby, who obliged us by going off to sleep while they showed us round. Radiating from a small oval hall were two triangular-shaped bedrooms and a bathroom, roughly half the total area, and a large, much wider three-sided sitting room overlooking the curved veranda, all arranged round a central stone fireplace. A small dressing-room extension had been added alongside the master bedroom and a long narrow kitchen extension had been built on adjacent to the bathroom, but the surprise came when we were taken up a short flight of steps immediately to the right of the front door: we found a large rectangular room with a wooden floor and picture windows on three sides which gave more views over the far reaches of the flower garden, as well as the small kitchen garden and a distant orchard. Then we were taken back out of the front door to another flight of steps, leading downwards, close built against the side of the upper room wall, hitherto not noticed by us. Wending our way, we found a guest room and bathroom with French doors opening straight on to the lawn, this room and the room above being a double-storey extension allowed by the sharp drop in the land.

In the garden the only mature trees were indigenous though there were several newly planted jacaranda and *nande* flame trees. When we tasted it, the river water was pure and, they told us, it was bilharzia-free. In addition to the land that went with the house, there was a considerable area, nearly seven hundred acres, on the other side of the river. This lightly wooded, undeveloped land rose gently so what we were looking at was a tiny valley of surpassing beauty. The owners told us that with the purchase of the house came the option to purchase this area also, the "remaining extent" of the original holding, for a very much lower price.

By the end of our tour it was apparent that the owners were anxious for a quick sale. She was pregnant and they wanted to be resettled in South Africa before the birth. As we returned to the house, my husband and I managed a quick whispered consultation. We knew we had to reveal our true situation, and knowing that by now we were far too interested to just walk away, we had to test what was possible. To our surprise, the owners were not dismayed. Seemingly, they had taken a shine to us and our baby, and were willing to wait until we could talk to our presbyter, so we promised we would visit again on our return north in about eight or nine days' time.

When we finally tore ourselves away, we were both exhilarated and very tired. It was nearly sunset and darkness fell swiftly at this latitude. Our excited minds were full of visions of how such a lovely place could be used. Could it be a centre for young people, a place for missionaries or other needy people to rest, or maybe it could be a Christian guest house? We could not tell yet. But we knew that, in principle, once this year's commitment on the Copperbelt was completed, we were free to form a new ministry according to God's leading. My husband's translation work, if it continued, didn't require him to live in town, so the way was open for God to reveal his intention.

By the time we reached town, darkness was falling. Soberly we took stock. Because we had enjoyed refreshments at the cottage, the edge was off our hunger and we made do with the odds and ends left from the trip. We did have baby food and so, after stopping at a garage to wash and brush up and fill our water container, we drove south out of town a mile or two before pulling off the road. There was a township not far away and some pedestrian traffic, so that night we slept in the car.

Early next morning we were back in the centre of town, parked outside the post office on the main street. We telephoned the pastor whose name and number we had found in the newspaper. It was Saturday.

What a welcome! The pastor's family was very generous and their children took over the baby. From the first cup of tea, we felt we had found real friends. Indeed, we were destined to become very dear and close friends over many years. Their invitation to stay for lunch led into the afternoon. After teatime we were encouraged to stay for supper and that was followed by an invitation to stay the night. Of course we were grateful, but genuinely enjoyed their fellowship. While we did not reveal all of the true extent of our need, these people were very discerning and not slow to recognise the signs of need in fellow Christian workers.

We accepted their kind offer to stay overnight and, in response to their invitation to accompany them to their church the next morning, we said we'd love to but absolutely must leave after lunch. The pastor then made two suggestions: first, that my husband might like to say a few words from the pulpit that morning; and second, that we might find it useful to telephone the hotels in town offering a ride for the three-hundred miles to Salisbury upon some payment towards fuel. This was quite a regular practice at the time in those territories, so my husband promptly did this. Gratefully, we slept well and enjoyed the Sunday morning service.

But our problem was still unsolved when we sat down to lunch and we couldn't help feeling a little anxious. Yet once we were all served and the children settled down, the pastor handed over a small cash gift for my husband, a small contribution as a "visiting speaker". It was still slender for our proposed journey but we were thankful and, seeing it as the earnest of God's provision, were vastly encouraged. And then, while dessert was being served, the phone rang in the hall and our host hurried out to answer it.

"We really should be going," I whispered across the table.

"OK but…"

His reluctant reply was cut off by our host's reappearance in the doorway. "There you go, folks. That was the Grand Hotel to say they've got someone wanting a lift to Salisbury and only too happy to pay for the all petrol needed. I said about a half-hour; he'll be waiting for you in the lobby."

"Great! Thank God for that! I'll get the cases, you get Baby ready."

In a moment my husband was on his feet and all bustle. In twenty minutes, we were packed, stacked and, after a flurry of affectionate farewells, driving away. It was ten minutes to the Grand where we found a young traveller who promptly handed over enough money to pay for the entire journey.

Late that Sunday evening, we thankfully pulled up into our conference host's drive, having dropped our passenger off as we passed through the city. We had quite a story to tell. We had more cash in hand than when we had started out, we had arrived on time, owing no man and we had seen the cottage near Lusaka.

During the course of the conference we had time to sit with the mission presbyter and fully explore the Lusaka question. It was the custom of the mission board back in Canada to buy the missionaries' houses and our ideas were received favourably. The leaders approved of a plan to open a work in Lusaka which was very strategically placed in the territories and which was being spoken of already as the likely capital when Northern Rhodesia would become independent. So they were happy to endorse the proposal and, after their exchanged messages with the Winnipeg office, we were told we could go ahead. Naturally we were very pleased at the outcome and began to look forward to our return journey and the opportunity to visit the cottage again with such encouraging news. Our next allowance had arrived as arranged and so, when the conference ended, we set off north in a most happy mood.

Our second visit to the cottage at West Lusaka was lovely and the owners expressed real pleasure at our news. But we knew there was still a lot to do before everything could fall into place before we dare begin to think of it as "our place". While our head office gave us permission and expressed their pleasure, it transpired that they were not able to send any money in the foreseeable future, though the promise to do so as soon as possible was made. But we couldn't wait indefinitely as the owners needed the sale to go through so they could move down south. So to make our dream come true, the onus was on us to produce a deposit and arrange a mortgage. With no collateral, we had no idea how this could be achieved, but faced now with a tantalizing half-open door, we prayed as we sped north, trusting that God would not allow it to shut and therefore would indeed provide the answer.

On our return we told our friends about our journey and the place we had found in Lusaka. To our delight one of our friends, a Christian businessman on the Copperbelt, came forward within a few days and offered to guarantee a bank loan so we could proceed – and so it was arranged.

Unknown to us at that time, events had taken place in Canada that had complicated the mission's position, events that would have far-reaching consequences for us. In Winnipeg the much revered but elderly founder of the mission who had personally recruited us had become very frail and died a few months later. A much younger, dynamic man was subsequently appointed to take his place, and it would swiftly become apparent to all that he had very different ideas.

Over those same weeks, while we were completing our commitment in Kitwe and waiting for our colleagues to return from their leave in Canada, we paid several short visits to the cottage in Lusaka. Like the rest of that area, there was no mains electricity, but we were fortunate in that this property was connected to its nearest neighbour who had a generator and so each evening, for a very small fee, the house had electric light from 6-10 pm.

Though we couldn't do much to the house until we were living there, once the former owners had departed, our new neighbour kept an eye on the place, and when we visited we would camp relatively comfortably in the unfurnished house. We took long walks over the property dreaming and praying about the future, asking the Lord to make clear to us what specific purpose he had in mind for this special place.

It was during one of these brief visits that a missionary couple, who had fled the Congo earlier, arrived. They were making their way down to South Africa and an uncertain future. Someone had told them we were to be found on our property that weekend so they had come to meet us and see for themselves. We shared some food and talked a bit but they were worn out and only wanted some peace and rest. They had arranged to sleep in town and now, having found us, they just wanted to gently walk or sit by the river; it seemed that's all they needed. And in this small way we saw, by faith, some indication of what God would do there.

Finally, as soon as we could be spared, we left Kitwe and moved to Lusaka. We were full of hope and confidence, happily looking forward to establishing our own home at last and eager for our future to unfold. The car comfortably took all we possessed, including the baby and newly pregnant me. We had no furniture, no bank balance and no idea of the trials to come, only determination and an unshakeable faith in our Lord's protection and guidance.

Chapter Five

Pieces of Pie

It was heaven to get up in the morning with the wind gently swishing among the treetops and the birdsong counterpoint to the sound of the waterfall. For as we explored, we began to discover more, all sorts of interesting things that seized our attention and delighted us. We could hear the waterfall from the house and could go to sleep at night to its music. The river ran all the year round and had never been known to run dry.

From its birth spring near some bottle palm trees, it burbled over a stony bed and fell through a rocky ledge covered in maidenhair fern. This dainty but luxurious fern got squashed down as the annual torrent of floodwater tore down at the end of the rains, only to raise its feathery head again as the water subsided whereupon it would flourish all through the dry season, with the water eventually only trickling through its roots at the height of the seven-month dry. The banks were heavily wooded, lush with reeds and ferns, and in the depths of the sparkling water were swarms of jewel-like tiny fish. But the 'cherry on top of the cake' was the discovery of a family of otters living between the ancient tree roots on the riverbank, a delight we hadn't seen before on any of our previous visits.

Just before leaving Kitwe, we had taken the long road trip east to Nyasaland to Gordon's former home to collect a few items of furniture he had left there. We'd also discovered a second-hand furniture store in town so very soon we were comfortable, if still sparsely furnished. Turning our attention outside, we speedily tidied up the small kitchen garden and extended it, and also came across another area, where another small spring kept the ground moist all year round giving sustenance to tall clumps of feathery reeds, and right on our south boundary we discovered the site of an old dam, though the wall had been damaged. The whole hollow area was covered in a veritable field of these same tall reeds and they were home to a variety of birds including flocks of snowy egrets.

A local man was hired part-time to keep the grass slashed down, especially near the house, against the danger of snakes. A troupe of *vervet* monkeys living in the riverside trees often played on the lawns, while very near the house an owl was raising a family in the hollow of a tree where a bushbaby lived in the upper branches. And all the time, while we soaked up the peace, we prayed for guidance and a definite indication of some specific purpose to be revealed. In the meantime, we set about meeting our neighbours who lived on plots along the river below us, as well as some of the Christians in the town, where we found more good friends and fellowship.

There was so much for this *'muzungu'* (literally 'long nose' – any white person, all classified as Europeans) to learn. The local people were cheerful and well mannered, with many of their customs almost opposite to ours. For instance, when coming to my door they would herald their approach by calling out softly their customary *'odi'*, then with polite patience would stand quietly waiting however long it took until someone in the house would notice them and come. When entering, they would just as politely sit on the floor just inside the door until invited to stand and come forward. A gift would be received with both hands and a small 'bob curtsy'. They had a delicious sense of humour and would laugh at the least pretext. Falling over or putting one's bike in the ditch had them cracking up even while they hastened to help.

My first experience in taking a village meeting was memorable. It was while we were on another visit to our presbyter. He and his wife took us out to one of their preaching points and gave me a translator. I stood facing about fifty intent faces and completely dried up. As I sat down again, I felt the tears of total inadequacy welling up. My husband took over with a small humorous remark that had everyone smiling and then proceeded to give a fluent message in the vernacular. What won my heart was that at the end of the meeting they surged forward and, with characteristic politeness, they smilingly thanked me for coming.

One and all they gripped my hand in the typical African handshake, palm to palm, the thumb gripped, and then again palm to palm. The men nodded and the women curtsied. I was charmed by their kindness but nevertheless came away with a sneaking feeling that somehow preaching in the villages was not going to be my forte.

Gordon was still doing a little translation and other work in support of our colleagues on the Copperbelt and elsewhere. Gradually we explored various villages that lay to the west and began regular visits to a few of them.

"Muli bwanje?" the village headman would greet us. ("How are you?")

"Ndiri bwino," we replied. *"Kyino?"* ("We are good, and you?")

"Bwerani," came the hospitable reply ("Come.") and we would be ushered towards a central place in the shade. Out would come a couple of carved stools and we would be invited to sit down. All gatherings commenced with polite general enquiries after health, crops or cattle. Only after these civilities had been observed could we get down to the business of talking about the things of God.

The weeks flew by and we still prayed and wondered about the future, sensing that these visits to the villages would not be our primary concern. There were several other missions working in this part of the Central Province and in many of the sprawling shanty townships surrounding the city. There had been no word from mission HQ regarding our house purchase and we were beginning to seriously struggle as we endeavoured to make the monthly interest payments on the mortgage out of our set allowance, which had not altered since our arrival despite our efforts in keeping that office informed regularly of necessary expenditure. And our gut feeling, that some important thing was yet to be revealed, persisted.

We chose the name for our home from the passage of Scripture in Jeremiah 17 as those words seemed to express the ambiance of our small valley. Later an artist drew for us a stylized tree and waterfall that would become our logo. We continued to pray over every acre and share ideas about what it might be used for. The existing orchard was mostly guavas and *naartjies,* the Afrikaans name for a fruit similar to tangerines and mandarins. To these we added a small plantation of bananas and a few orange, grapefruit and lemon trees. I set out to learn about which varieties of vegetables would grow best and when. By trial and error Israeli varieties were found to be best suited to our climate and latitude and although when I'd first come to this territory I'd felt it was summer all the time, I soon became familiar with the signs of the turning of the seasons and found a deep satisfaction in this new way of living close to the earth.

We were fortunate that our small home already had a party telephone line. Our small enterprise had grown to include a dog and two hens. The hens had been a sort of housewarming gift from a friend and the eggs were most welcome. With the property we had inherited an old two-stroke petrol engine that pumped water from the river and filled a tank behind the house. Moored on the riverbank, it was mounted on a raft that rose and fell with the seasonal volume of water, though at flood times it had a distressing tendency to suck up an unwanted amount of sand and on one occasion it even sucked up a couple of tiny fish that flopped into the bath in a gush of brown, murky water. The water tank also fed the 'Rhodesian boiler', our only source of hot water. The boiler was a 44-gallon oil drum on its side, elevated on a brick stand which stood at the side of the house with outlet pipes to the kitchen and bathroom, and where every afternoon a log fire was lit under the tank. In the kitchen we had a stove and a refrigerator which ran on paraffin.

Someway into my pregnancy, I fell down the flight of kitchen steps that led down to the garden. To my great relief the fall didn't appear to have damaged my unborn child and the hurt to my back seemed to ease after a while, so once the bruises healed I dismissed the occasional twinge. But my back had been damaged and that was to have long-term consequences.

The time of our annual missionary conference came round again, about a month before the baby was due, and was to be held in Nyasaland. My husband went off, leaving me in town with some American friends. He returned a week or so later and we went back home. Our first son was born about three weeks later.

The day I came home from the hospital, two of the local African ladies called on me. They offered me small gifts with giggled greetings: a few small eggs in a reed basket and some tomatoes on a banana leaf 'plate'. It seemed I had attained some new status; as the mother of a son, I was now being called 'amayi Stuart'.

It was while I was with our American friends that I met their weekend guests, an American lady evangelist who was visiting the territory with her son. I was fascinated by her somewhat flamboyant personality and very strong southern accent. The first day, at breakfast, she announced her intention of "popping downtown for a few little necessities" and I imagined her buying a newspaper and perhaps a forgotten toilet article. But whatever small things she may have bought, she also bought a brand-new car.

When we had settled down with the new baby and the lady evangelist had completed her tour, she and her son were again the guests of our friends and had a day or two to spare before flying back to the States. One afternoon we invited them out to our place and, hearing the car arrive, we went out to greet them. As soon as her wiry, red-headed figure skirted round the hibiscus hedge, she called out to us, throwing her hands wide in apparent enchantment. And once she was ushered inside, her admiration knew no bounds. "Oh, Anne," she cried in her high pitched southern drawl. "Oh me, oh my, your rooms are just like pieces of pie!" And looking up, she exclaimed, "And all under a grass roof too!"

With a toddler and a new baby, my days were full. We couldn't really afford help but employed one man to do the heavy work in our enlarged garden and to keep the grass down, especially around the house. Because there were many tasks that took me out of the house, my attention was often divided and I was always worried about what the children were getting up to, especially with so much water around.

At the back of the house, across a small patch of grass, there was a small brick-built garden tool shed. From this an adjacent hedge ran along the driveway almost to meet the wall of the children's room, an extension of our bedroom. The little room had stable doors which opened out onto this small area set neatly between the house, the hedge and the shed. This small lawn was shaded by a large tree so we filled in the gaps in the hedge and, setting out a little table and small chairs, made this into a safe play area; by locking the hall door to the rest of the house, the children could freely run in and out the bedroom/bathroom part of the house safely.

On our eastern boundary our neighbours were not tilling their plots nor did they plough firebreaks. This grass grew up to twelve feet high and was allowed to grow unchecked through the dry season – seven or sometimes nearly eight months – so it was a constant danger, especially as the prevailing wind blew from them toward us. In the dry season, local lads would often deliberately start a fire to trap small mammals, but even a piece of discarded broken bottle could ignite and cause a blaze that could jump the road and cause havoc. So we got used to fighting fierce grass fires along our boundary in the dry season months.

At such a time, whenever smoke was seen to be rising above the trees, all the neighbours would despatch their gardeners and in a very short time a whole gang was on the spot to help. So as the season approached, we got used to keeping lots of 44-gallon oil drums filled with water, strategically placed, each with its pile of feed-sacks alongside. Though the locals tended to bash at the flames with tree branches, we found wet sacks more effective even if we had to get a little closer to combat the flames. Throughout the season, we did our best to keep the undergrowth down on our side, but often extra men and tools, together with some pretty smart footwork, was needed when the wind changed direction. As we got to know our neighbours better and began to work with them in maintaining our mutual access road, my husband was able to arrange and undertake the annual ploughing of strategic firebreaks with a borrowed tractor.

Five years had passed since leaving Canada and our allowance had not increased despite the changes in our family and the strain of keeping up the interest payments on our mortgage. I had taken a couple of jobs during that time, one as a secretary at the Dairy Produce Board for a few months, but the job wasn't permanent. A few months later I did the annual stocktaking at a big garage and car showrooms in the town. Had we not been repeatedly assured that the purchase money would be coming, we would have rethought the whole situation. Each month we hoped it would come, and each month ended in disappointment and a growing anxiety.

But no matter how difficult it was in general, there were many pleasant surprises and small delights. A few of the women's groups in the Canadian churches took an interest and sent us a parcel or two each year and we were grateful and encouraged by the arrival of these tokens of their support. Among the first were gifts of baby clothes and cot linen and later a patchwork quilt for each of the children and some very pretty kitchen towels. But for the most part, the parcels consisted of packet foods, powdered soft drinks, teabags, sewing notions and toilet articles, all very, very welcome. Then, on one particularly difficult and needy day, a stranger came to our door and handed us a large box of groceries. He turned and left abruptly before we could properly express our thanks or discover who he was. Certainly, however hard it was, we were left in no doubt of God's love and the inner knowledge that these conditions could not possibly continue indefinitely.

We carried on as best we could. A Sunday school was established at our house with neighbourhood children joining ours. This led to more contact with the neighbourhood and I formed a group of local African ladies; they demonstrated their crafts while I taught them sewing, told Bible stories and prayed. My husband took care of our openings in the surrounding area when petrol allowed.

Time passed and our concern grew concerning the purchase of our property. It was the one vital matter we needed to bring to a conclusion and, at the same time, the one in which we were most powerless to act. Every enquiry we made to the mission office was met with reassurances, but they didn't explain so we had no means of knowing the full background story, nor did we dream that this seeming procrastination was the outworking of God's will.

Christmas came around and we shut up our house and took off for the Copperbelt where we would spend the holidays with friends, a young couple we'd met when they were forced out of the Congo a couple of years before. Like several of their colleagues, these missionaries had not left Africa but had taken a job to wait out the emergency, hoping to return someday. Our friends had taken over management of the Kitwe schools' hostel. Grace seemed a little below par that morning but not really sick, yet by the time we'd gone the first hundred miles, her condition was rapidly deteriorating. When I lifted her quilt-wrapped body on to my lap, even though I didn't have a thermometer with me, I could tell her temperature was obviously climbing because the quilt was hot to the touch.

Now thoroughly alarmed, we went straight through to the hospital where she was admitted and initially thought to have meningitis. Badly frightened, we took it in turns to look after little Stuart while they did a lumbar puncture; then, after a long anxious wait, we were told it was only pneumonia. *Only pneumonia?* I thought as my knees nearly gave way. But she was in good hands and recovered swiftly, and we had a good Christmas.

At mission HQ the board was financially stretched, having a lot of workers out in the field. They were sincere in their support but the bottom line was that we were not Canadian and had no local church backing us. Having been sent out to the field in answer to an emergency meant that we were not necessarily going to be offered the customary year in Canada to do deputation work, nor guaranteed any sort of future with the mission. So the problem hung over. By now we had been with the mission for nearly five years without a break.

Matters came to a head. Our four-year-old daughter was unwell and I was humiliated and ashamed when the doctor diagnosed "poor nutrition". I had done my utmost to see the children's needs came first and they had first call on the eggs, vegetables and fruit. Nevertheless, it was increasingly clear that we couldn't go on like this. Something had to give.

Gordon was reluctant to take a job. He felt the mission's policy would not allow him to work and he was plainly not about to leave the mission. This attitude hurt and annoyed me and we argued. I thought it was nonsense for him to say he couldn't supplement our allowance when our need was so great. I doubted God would honour a man, a husband and father, who did not consider the welfare of his family. I was already washing clothes in the river because our money hadn't stretched to soap powder that month. I really couldn't see why the mission would object to him taking a part-time job. Heaven knows, a lot of the time we couldn't afford the petrol to visit the outlying villages anyway.

"But we're not supposed to have another job; you know that." His face took on a stubborn look.

I snatched a bill from the desk. "Look at that!" I raised it in my clenched fist and shook it in his face. I was trembling and my voice rose. "Look at this red warning on the third reminder to pay for our last car repair! It brings no honour to God, and I doubt if it does much for our witness if we can't pay a debt for something so necessary. What do you suggest?" I flung the offending final notice back on the desk in my fear-driven anger.

His eyes shifted away from mine and he mumbled, "God will provide. We should pray…"

I broke across his words impatiently. "God *is* faithful. He *has* answered so many of our prayers. He *has* provided so many times, but don't you see? Surely, he expects us to be sensible and responsible, not live like weak and feckless children. Money won't float down from the nearest cloud! This situation has been going on for far too long. You know we are failing in the work because half the time we can't get around. On top of our mortgage interest payments and car expenses, food and things for the children are necessities." I found I was shaking. I had just found out I was pregnant again and beginning to doubt we would ever find the true purpose for which God had brought us here – and I certainly did not want to miss it.

He ambled over to the window and stood staring at some bird on the patio.

I stared at his back and strove to be calm. I tried again, quietly. "Doesn't it bother you that we are in this situation, dependent on handouts, limping from one financial crisis to another just to keep going? If we are in his will, he *will* provide, though not necessarily by cash trickling down from the nearest cloud! For five years, every month, we have sent the obligatory reports back to head office, truthfully accounting for every penny and charting our needs, and nothing has changed. Doesn't that tell you something?"

"Well, what?" He half-turned from the window but kept his eyes on the bird.

My shoulders slumped. I was tired, despondent, frustrated and, by now, frightened of the added pressure a third child could place on our slender resources. I tried again. "Right now, I don't think it matters what the mission leaders think. I'm not talking anything major, not switching careers, maybe something part-time; just something to tide us over while we wait for the answer to come from Canada about our house purchase – anything that would help us pay our bills so we wouldn't have to struggle so much. Maybe," I added carefully, "maybe it's time for you to just be the man and work to take care of our needs."

I stopped. He was silent, still staring out of the window. I waited.

"Right, then! If you won't do that for us, you look after the children and I'll find something." I turned and left the room and he let me go without another word.

What I found was one day's work per week, book-keeping for the ranch owner on our southern flank. She had extensive holdings and it was but a short drive to her homestead. She invited me to lunch with her on these days and we became good friends. I became very interested in all aspects of her farming methods and her prize-winning cattle. The small amount of cash she paid didn't make a lot of difference but I guarded it for the children's needs and temporarily it satisfied my deep-seated need to be doing something. As my pregnancy advanced it was all I could manage anyway.

Then another near disaster struck. We could not afford the dental treatment I needed and halfway through the pregnancy I suffered an abscessed tooth and landed in hospital with septicaemia. I recovered but was only partially reassured about the safety of the baby I carried. Nonetheless, as soon as I could, I went back to my little job although I was badly pulled down and struggled through the rest of my pregnancy, and the birth was difficult. Baby John was born with respiratory problems and developed pneumonia immediately. He suffered recurring bouts of pneumonia, ear infections and dental problems throughout his early childhood.

Just before going down with the abscessed tooth, I had put my one good pair of shoes in to be repaired, only to find weeks later, when I was well enough to remember them, that they had been sold to "defray expenses" as the cobbler did not expect me back. This relatively small incident seemed to sum up all my frustration.

We decided it was time to apply for some overseas leave, not only to get some rest but also to see our families, and also in the hope that it would give us the opportunity to speak directly to the mission board. Moreover, perhaps a visit to Canada might allow us to bring our work to the attention of the churches on the mission's circuit and help generate more support for the future.

By the time their reply came, we had been in Africa for almost six years. In England my father's health was failing and I very much wanted him to see my children before it was too late. It was a considerable surprise and disappointment to learn that we were not being invited back to Canada. The new head at mission headquarters reasoned that as we were British and had no connections in Canada, we should take a three-month break in England for which they would pay for our return sea passages from Cape Town and our allowance would be sent to us for that time. Nothing extra was sent for any travel incidentals and, more importantly, nothing for the journey from Lusaka to Cape Town, nigh on two thousand miles to the south by road, and the same journey back. And, again, there was no mention regarding our house purchase.

When the shock wore off, we were forced to make contingency plans. We advertised our house to let for three months to cover the mortgage interest payments. Gordon looked for a job and the only casual work he could find was at the Lusaka abattoir, a most miserable, bloody and cold job but he gamely coped as it was only going to be for a month or so. But disappointment wasn't done with us yet.

When I told a friend I had two lovely dress lengths sent to me in a Christmas parcel but not yet made up, she, knowing I was busy sewing for the children, offered to make them for me so I'd have something nice to wear on our forthcoming trip. I was so thankful and spent a delightful afternoon at her house discussing patterns. But the pleasure didn't last long. Within a few days she had withdrawn her offer and although the dresses had been cut out, I was not able to finish them in time. It transpired that her husband was manager of the abattoir and autocratically forbade her to dress-make for an employee's wife.

John was nearly seven months old when we set off finally in April 1964. All our personal stuff was locked into the smallest room and a Christian acquaintance and his wife were happily installed as our short-term tenants. The bank had been pressing us to improve our arrangements but we had talked them into deferring any changes until our return. We didn't have any real hope now that things would be any different then but badly needed to put this question aside and concentrate on our journey, and we hoped for respite. It never occurred to us that our position could get worse and we were too tired to imagine how God might be about to deal with the situation.

Our departure was plagued with delays. Because of handing over the house, packing the car and so on, it was well into the afternoon, so we just drove to our farmer friend where I'd worked on the books, having accepted her offer to stay there for two nights. The full day in between was needed to tend to a car repair and get it ready for the long journey. After breakfast Gordon drove off to the garage in town and I went to fold laundry and finish the packing in the bedroom. Then my mother's 'sixth sense' kicked in and I realized it was too quiet; there were no little voices from the veranda where I'd left the two oldest playing. Sure enough, there was no sign of them and after a somewhat fraught interval I tracked them down to the far side of the farmyard where they were happily playing in the pond, floating Grace's new white shoes as boats.

Shortly after lunch I was in the bedroom settling the baby down for a nap when I heard frantic shrieks coming from the garden. Rushing to the window, I saw Grace and Stuart cowering against the wall. There had been a pet monkey chained to a pole in the yard and somehow it had got loose. I could see Stuart's leg bleeding and guessed he'd been bitten. But before I could move to his aid, the monkey jumped through the open bedroom window right into the baby's cot and snatched his feeding bottle. Without thinking, I snatched a nappy and swiped at the animal in an attempt to drive him off, but chattering furiously, it leapt on to the dressing table sending everything on it crashing to the floor. The uproar brought the indoor staff on the run and after a lot of sweat and shouting, the monkey was ousted. Clutching the screaming baby, I rushed out into the hall where I found the terrified duo, brought inside by the housemaid, still shaking and sobbing.

Our hostess was away for the day and my husband not likely to return until late so it wasn't possible to get the child the twenty or so miles to a doctor in town. Prayerfully I washed, disinfected and bound the nasty gash on his leg and put him to bed, hoping all would be well. However, in the morning he had a slight fever and what looked like heat bumps all over his body. It was obvious that although we must begin our journey early that day as planned or risk missing the ship, it was imperative we seek medical advice. Because we couldn't leave at dawn as planned, we accordingly breakfasted at the farm before heading for town to arrive just as the surgery was opening.

The doctor didn't seem unduly worried and advised a plentiful application of calamine, some baby aspirin and plenty to drink. So after a visit to the chemist to stock up, we put our doleful little one to sleep in the car and after nearly half a day's delay, we set off. But he was so distressed that we stopped in the small town of Gwelo in Southern Rhodesia and tracked down a doctor. Unfortunately, he didn't have anything different to suggest. We repeated the story that it was a monkey bite but it didn't seem to signify. We were now so late we dared not stop in Salisbury overnight as planned but phoned them and pushed on. We arrived very late at our colleague's house in Bulawayo and fell into bed hoping it would be better in the morning. But it wasn't, and once again we were forced to seek medical advice before continuing our journey. The third doctor had nothing new to add, so we stocked up again on calamine and aspirin and drove on. Strangely, although the wound was healing well, the bumps were now turning into blisters.

After Bulawayo there was no time to stop overnight again if we were to reach the ship before she sailed. Our Chevrolet Coupe Imp was ideal for this kind of travel. We had taken out the back seats and on the revealed platform behind the front bench seats we piled blankets, quilts and pillows, added a few books and toys, and piled the children in. It was a two-door car with an extended open back designed to take a half-ton load so happily it took all the luggage, spare tyres and a selection of car tools, a food box and a large water container.

We had calculated three days to reach some friends in the wine-growing area near Cape Town. The plan was that we'd spend the night before sailing, leave our car with them and they would drive us to the ship which was due to sail at midday. They would also meet us on our return. But by now we were so delayed we had to push on.

We picnicked as we drove and only stopped to fill up with petrol or make toilet stops. Just before sundown, we would pull off the road at a designated picnic spot and let the children run about while we shook out the blankets and quilts and remade their bed in the back of the car. After we fed the children, we filled a large, shallow bowl with water from our big container, which was lukewarm from the sun, and one at a time sponged them down completely and put them back in the car dressed in their nightclothes; then we drove on again.

One by one the children fell asleep and a couple of hours later we pulled into a motel where, while an attendant kept an eye on the car, we ate a hot meal and had our Thermoses filled with boiled water for Baby's feed, then washed and tidied ourselves, refuelled the car and replenished the water container. In an hour we were away again and took turns driving through the night. We passed through customs, crossed the Limpopo River into South Africa and pulled into Messina for lunch and to top everything up, and pressed on. There were plenty of designated picnic spots along the road, which was lined with white and mauve cosmos. It was open country rolling away to distant blue hills. Then Pretoria fell behind us as we drove down the map on the verge of the great Karoo desert, through another night – on and on until at last we saw the vast wine-growing lands and mountains of the Cape.

Finally, on the last morning, we pulled into Worcester and our friend's home where they were waiting, anxiously concerned over our delay. We still had seventy miles to go so after hasty refreshments, the transfer of our luggage to their vehicle and attending to Baby, we were off on the last leg of our momentous journey, sharing prayers of thankfulness as we went along. We made it to the ship with only a little over an hour to spare.

Our poor toddler had weathered the journey reasonably well and as soon as we sailed we consulted the ship's doctor. He had nothing new to offer though, so I just kept him in soft, loose cotton clothes and did everything I could think of to keep him comfortable. Although his temperature had returned to normal, nothing else changed.

My brother met us at Southampton and drove us to Solihull and we were at my mother's doctor by 5.30 pm that same day, but that visit was no different. Seriously worried, we battled on for another three weeks until, on a visit to some missionary friends who had lived in the Congo, we confided in them and asked for their prayers. They wholeheartedly agreed but they also suggested we might like to consult a herbalist, which we did the next day. To our huge relief but utter astonishment, the herbalist suggested a remedy that only cost a dollar and when we tried it the blisters dried up and healed within a week. A year or so later, we shared this experience with a veterinary friend who had some knowledge of what happens to zoo animals who became stressed when transported. He told us that the dangerous secretions in the saliva of an excited monkey could be lethal. Once again, we marvelled at God's protecting hand.

CHAPTER SIX

A Box of Matches

The letter from Canada arrived just before Stuart's third birthday, late in May. We were being asked, since we were British, whether we would consider remaining in England. They advised us that their financial support would cease after the current three months as they were overextended financially. The letter didn't refer to the house purchase at all; it concluded with their hope that we would find this acceptable and ended with their good wishes.

As the shock waves receded, we thought back over the years of procrastination and found we were not really surprised. It was too early to feel confident in the assumption that God had some great alternative in mind though. We were faced with a serious dilemma and needed to make some quick and practical decisions. As to the three-month grace period, we were already partway through that. Our desire had always been to serve in Africa and we had started a work there in good faith. Moreover, we had committed ourselves in buying the house so we had to either extract ourselves from our responsibilities at long distance or go back and sort something out.

Not least of these problems was Gordon's real reluctance to give up everything we had achieved so far in Lusaka. He didn't want to stay in England where he would have to find a job and housing and, whichever way we looked at it, there was going to be no money to re-establish ourselves. It was all very distressing in the light of our conviction that Lusaka was where we were meant to be. We decided to go back.

Setting sail once again in the S.S. Cape Town Castle, we reached Cape Town towards the end of July. It had been a good trip and as everything needful was included in our ticket, we managed to hang on to our small amount of cash on that leg of the journey. Our friends were on the dockside to meet us in Cape Town and we spent that night with them. Our car was ready, serviced and fuelled and resolutely we said our goodbyes. When they'd understood our predicament, our friends had been kindness itself, waiving the cost of getting the car ready and they had sent us off with a generous picnic hamper. We had landed with only about thirty rands[3] and we faced a journey of almost two thousand miles. Either we had interpreted our situation correctly in the light of our faith and what we knew of our God, or we were completely wrong and would come badly unstuck. We were about to find out.

We headed north knowing that Gordon would have no problem finding a job in Northern Rhodesia if we could get back there. It was now mid-winter in South Africa and the wind coming off the mountains had a bitter edge. We slept the first night in the car and the second on mattresses on the garage floor of a very small town manse we came across. And although our hosts hadn't had space inside their house for us, they had done their best to make us comfortable and gave us a hearty breakfast. Our sturdy car, second-hand though in pristine condition when purchased, was now nine years old, and our extensive mileage on consistently rough roads was taking its toll.

A few hours short of Johannesburg, the car broke down and we were forced to seek the help of a small town garage. We were still a thousand miles from home and had no money for repairs so we had to explain our situation and ask them to trust us and wait for payment. This was not as extraordinary as it sounds. At that time it was still possible to charge an account anywhere in the Rhodesias, Nyasaland and South Africa as there was a huge amount of ex-pat traffic moving through the territories. When we came back a few hours later to claim the car, we discovered that the garage proprietor was a Christian. He called us into his office and told us that he'd noticed a bible in the car, so we explained our position in more detail. Cordially, he waived the bill as his gift and sent us off with a blessing.

It grew bitterly cold as we climbed the high veldt to Johannesburg. Again we found a church and begged a night's shelter at the manse but

---

[3] South African currency

we were so cold, we slept fully clothed in one bed with the children huddled between us. The next day, we reached Messina, which was thankfully warmer, and slept in the car in the town's central carpark, which had the advantage of an open toilet facility. Early the next morning we crossed the Limpopo River and once over the border, felt we were on home territory and could look forward to a rest at our friend's house in Bulawayo, and to spending the next night in Salisbury. We were nearly home!

The people we stayed with in Johannesburg had given us a cash gift, enough to take us to Lusaka. We were so thankful. All along, our God had supplied us sufficiently so the children lacked nothing and we never ran out of fuel. But what we didn't know was that somewhere along the way our baby had contracted measles and, needless to say, the other two children would also become ill over the next few weeks.

It was no easy task we had set ourselves. First, we had to find some money to live on while we regrouped, and it was our good friend the lady rancher who came to our aid and lent us enough to live on that first month. Immediately after our arrival, Gordon went job-hunting. His whole experience was in farming but he needed something local. He found the vacancy for an assistant manager in the milk-bottling plant of the Dairy Produce Board in Lusaka and was able to start immediately. Due to his experience in dairy farming, he quickly assimilated the necessary other skills, and we were over the first hurdle. I also considered taking a job but when the children went down with measles, one after the other, I was grounded and threw myself into extending and preparing the kitchen garden ready for the coming rains.

It was an enormous relief to have money coming in but the job meant a lot of adjustment. Gordon began his day shortly after 4 am in order to start work at 5 am when the first milk tankers from the outlying farming regions would begin to arrive. It meant we had to purchase a second car so I would have transport for the children, shopping etc., so it was a considerable blessing when, only a few months later, the bottling factory manager left and Gordon moved into that position with its higher salary. But he still had to begin work at the same time each day and his new responsibilities meant he also had to sometimes go in at the weekends if there was a breakdown of any sort.

During the preceding months, N. Rhodesia had been gearing up for the celebrations that would usher in the new independent nation of

Zambia. There was an air of great expectancy abroad in the country and by early October, rehearsals for the ceremony at the city sports stadium were in full swing. Thankfully, the children were all well again by then but, all unsuspecting, we were about to experience our own terrible drama.

By mid-October we were busy preparing to receive friends from England, a couple with four children aged two to seven years old whose father was coming to manage a poultry franchise a few miles east of the city. They had been warned that although they would have a car immediately, their accommodation was not quite ready, so it was arranged they would come to us for a couple of weeks in the meantime. To make room for this family of six, we cleared the bedrooms in the main house for them and we moved downstairs to the guestroom. They duly arrived and were installed, and for five days we enjoyed renewing our friendship and catching up with the news from England while the children settled down and had a fine time together. But turmoil was just around the corner.

Early on Monday morning, October 19th, after dropping Gordon off at the milk factory, our friend Tony drove off to his new job. About 8.30 am I took our car into the city to have it serviced and to shop while this was done, leaving Tony's wife Jean to take care of the seven children. Near the tiny church we'd built at the edge of our property, a small African boy was playing with a box of matches and laughing as the grass verge caught fire. His amusement turned to terror as the fire ran along and ignited the church, a simple building made of wooden poles and thatch. After several months of completely dry weather, everything was combustible and in minutes the entire little building was destroyed and the wind had caught up the burning thatch, carried it over the ploughed firebreak and dropped it squarely on our thatched house.

When Jean realized what was happening, her first thought was for the children. In the next several frantic minutes, she located them all and pushed them out the front door with instructions to run down to the river. By the time she had scooped up the seventh child, our precious baby, the ceilings and curtains in that room were alight. Our only worker had come running and it was not long before our neighbour's gardeners and workmen were already on the scene. But little could be done; the whole house was consumed and only the remnants of the badly damaged kitchen extension and part of the children's nursery remained. That there was anything left at all was because those two rooms had been roofed in corrugated iron which, though badly buckled, had nevertheless afforded a little protection.

When the smoke rose above the trees, it was spotted by our nearest neighbour, who first despatched her gardeners, then drove over and took Jean and the children to her house. None of them were burned nor injured although they were in a considerable state of shock. She telephoned the dairy and Gordon immediately phoned Tony at the hatchery. Gordon's managing director threw his own car keys at him, saying, "Go, go, we'll manage here," and on the far side of the town at the hatchery, Tony threw himself into his car and roared down the Great East Road, arriving only minutes behind Gordon – but there was little they could do. The house was a smoking heap of debris, everything both families owned destroyed. The whole scene looked strangely odd because the trees which grew all around the house had contained the flames completely and everything outside that tight circle was untouched, still verdant.

Leaving Tony in charge, Gordon went back to town looking for me. At the garage he found the car still not quite ready and my shopping deposited in the manager's office. He guessed I'd gone off in search of a cup of tea while I waited. At our usual café, I looked up and saw him enter. I felt a brief moment of foreboding when I saw his face and could only think he'd lost his job. Time seemed to stand still as he took a seat opposite me, obviously struggling to find the right words to tell me something dire. My expression must have conveyed my anxiety for he swiftly reassured me of the children's safety before he informed me of the morning's events. It took a few minutes for the news to sink in, but I'd latched on to the fact that the children were unharmed which was my chief concern. We went to the milk factory to put them in the picture and returned the borrowed car, then collected our own and very soberly drove back to what had been home.

Tony and the soot-covered workmen stood around in a state of sweaty exhaustion; they had done all they could. Some brought more water from the river to thoroughly douse the kitchen area and a few others willingly stayed on to keep watch in case anything reignited. Everyone was very subdued as we viewed the ruins. Small tendrils of smoke arose here and there but amazingly, although the breeze had carried bits of debris and a little ash across the garden, nothing outside the house's encircling trees had been touched by the fire. The rafters and floors of our house had been made from old railway sleepers, beautifully crafted and polished to a deep chestnut colour, but it was all this wood that had contributed to the swiftness of its demise and now only parts of the outer walls remained.

It was barely lunchtime and once we felt it safe to leave, the three of us drove over to our neighbour to check on Jean and the children. They were fine and being looked after well. There was no sign of injury on any of the children save for an insect bite on Grace's forehead, but they had all been extremely frightened. We sat around, shocked and spent, while our neighbour kindly prepared lunch for us all. Well aware that we couldn't just check into a hotel in the city, mainly because we couldn't afford it, we talked through our predicament and decided that Jean and the children should stay where they were for the time being, while the men, after calling their respective employers with an update, left to go back to our place.

I went to town for supplies. We needed eleven of everything – towels and wash cloths, toothbrushes, basic toilet articles, soap, washing powder and First Aid stuff – also a four-gallon bucket for carrying water from the river, a smaller one to hold drinking water, and a large shallow enamel bowl for washing and for bathing the children, a basic change of clothes for everyone, a camp stove and pot for heating water, plastic drinking cups, food, blankets, baby food and diapers. Fortunately, we already dealt with a good general store and they were happy to extend us thirty days' credit. Tired out, I steered the heavily laden car home in the late afternoon to find the place had become a hive of activity.

Gordon's general manager had sent us his large, six-bed family holiday tent and the men to erect it, and that was already being done on one side of the garden. Our men had cleared the floor of the small, open-sided barn-cum-shed we had adjacent to the tool shed, and someone had brought bundles of clean straw which had already been strewn on the barn floor. Other neighbours had sent paraffin lamps, some hot food, milk, blankets, pots and dishes. Before sunset we had created some sort of order. Tony went to fetch Jean and the children who had all bathed at our kind neighbour's house. The rest of us managed a wash, changed our clothes and then we all had something to eat and drink. We were tiredly thankful that all our children were safe, which fact had done much to cushion the shock. Nightfall, which comes suddenly in the tropics, found us all bedded down – Tony and his family in the tent, while we, with our children between us, slept in the barn.

The next day was baby John's first birthday. Both men went to work but assured us that they would make it a short day and be back early. Jean and I went down to the river with a huge pile of laundry, glad that at this season the weather was hot, and afterwards we organised a temporary kitchen in the tool shed next to the barn. Exploring the ruin of the partly demolished kitchen, we pounced happily on our paraffin fridge and found, though the outside was damaged, there seemed nothing to prevent it from working, so we cleaned it up and had it moved over. Likewise, our paraffin stove, once the jets and pipes were cleared of ash, we judged as also useable. We were very heartened by these discoveries and sent a message over to our neighbour to phone Gordon, telling him to buy new wicks and a five-gallon tin of paraffin before he came home.

While Jean looked after the children, I attempted to make a better job of our makeshift shelter and sorted through some donated clothes. The next couple of days were interrupted several times by visits from people bearing more gifts. Someone from the Baptist church in town came with a gift of two bibles for Gordon and me, and shortly afterwards a friend drove out with a cake, loaves of fresh bread and some toys for the children. Two mattresses arrived, which greatly improved our bedding arrangements, followed by the Telephone Company van. Because our fire had knocked out the district party line, the telephone company sent men to investigate. They immediately replaced our telephone and installed it on the tool shed wall.

Our rancher friend sent a truckload of useful odds and ends: tools and various bits of equipment, clothing and a large basket of fruit, a box of tinned goods and a gallon of fresh milk. Our next-door neighbour who had the generator came over and rigged up one bulb in the tent, one in the barn and one in the shed/kitchen. And finally, we received a gift that thrilled me from one very thoughtful person: an old treadle sewing machine in good working order, together with a bag of sewing notions, cottons and some scissors. Now I could make the best of much of the donated clothes.

On the first day after the fire, Tony came back from work with the news that his head office had assured him that they would speed up the work on their house and indeed would hasten to complete one wing so he could move his family in within the next few days. That night, after supper, we had a time of thanksgiving, praise and prayer. We were profoundly touched by all that had been given to us by friends and neighbours, even by some who hardly knew us. In the circumstances, any gift was welcome, but we marvelled in the variety of the gifts, so many of them minutely tailored to our personal needs. Surely the hand of God was in that.

Our sleep was disturbed by thunder rumbling and a glance outside revealed ragged flashes of fork lightning in the sky to the north, a sure sign the rains were coming. Very conscious of the coming storms, we had to give some thought to how we might protect our living space. The first storms of the season tended to be heavy. Jean knew that it was only a matter of a day or two before her family were in a proper house, but I had no such hope.

We were particularly vulnerable as the barn, as we called it, was merely a roughly thatched extension to the tool shed, held up by four brick pillars, leaving three open sides. Presently, the days were hot and the nights were warm, but when the rains broke, the temperature would initially drop, and if that happened before the other family moved out, we would be hard put to keep the children comfortable or dry. We made barriers along the open sides with some old corrugated iron sheeting, various old boxes and some plastic sheeting, which we also used to cover our stores, and used the space closest to the inner brick wall for our bedding area.

The only piece of furniture to survive the fire was a heavy, square low coffee table. We had taken it out into the garden for tea on the Sunday afternoon. At dusk the men had carried the chairs indoors while we mothers followed along with the children. We were too tiredly content to bother about the table for the time being because we knew it wouldn't rain that night nor was there the likelihood of dew this late in the dry season. And there we found it, on the grass by the orange tree, its polished surface unmarred except for a wisp or two of wind-blown ash.

As the week drew to a close, enough work had been finished on Tony's house and they moved to the hatchery. We moved into the tent and I was mightily relieved. There was still a lot of stuff piled in the barn but it was reasonably secure and protected from the weather. Zambia's Independence Day came and went almost unnoticed. Then, after almost eight months dry, the rains broke. We dug a trench round the tent to channel off the water and prepared ourselves for the onslaught.

Day after day, storms had been building up in towering clouds, heralded by deafening thunder, and lightning frequently lit up the darkening sky. Gradually approaching from the north, the life-giving rain drew nearer. One could hear the rain coming, then feel the change in the air – catch the scent of it on the arid breeze. The first warm, swollen drops would plop on the hard, dry earth to be swiftly followed by the refreshing peppering of massed raindrops until finally the grey blinding downpour arrived.

It was such a relief when the rain came but this year it presented us with multiple problems. The temperature dropped ten degrees in as many minutes and I had my work cut out to meet the needs of the children.

The rain beat down everything in its path, pouring off every surface, rushing down every slope and filling every crevice. Debris swirled in the flooded lane beside the barn and steely rods of water poked through every weak spot in the old thatch roof. It was so difficult to keep our things dry in those first storms. Constantly on the alert for new leaks, we had to move our stores about in the battle to keep everything protected. The children couldn't play out on the drenched grass and it taxed my ingenuity to keep them amused cooped up in the tent. They had to be carried one at a time over the sopping grass and mud whenever a move was necessary.

Nevertheless, after the initial storms it rarely rained all day, and once it stopped, the thirsty land absorbed the moisture very quickly. For a brief time, droplets sparkled on every branch and bush, but soon everything had dried off in the hot sunshine and I could put the washing out, air the bedding and let the children play outside.

Chapter Seven

Running the Race

Time flew by as we engaged in the daily battle to keep the children healthy and secure. Although Gordon had been promoted to factory manager at the milk-bottling plant, we needed more money. I found a job in a small engineering office in the city and day nursery places for the children.

One morning I went to the baby's cot to find him limp as a rag. He could neither sit up nor even suck when I tried to give him a drink. Terrified, I wrapped him up, ran with him to the car and raced to town for the doctor, who immediately admitted him to hospital. The sister in charge of the children's ward was a local pastor's wife, a lady I knew slightly, and she was very kind and reassuring. She knew my circumstances and the difficulties surrounding my job and the management of the other two children round the visiting times, so on work days I would telephone in the morning for a progress report, leave my work a bit early, and pop in at the hospital for a peek, having a quick chat with this ward sister before collecting the other two from the day nursery.

When I eagerly hastened to bring our baby home about a week later, he didn't notice my entrance at first. He was standing up at his cot rail with his back to me, jabbering away at a little girl in the next cot. I tiptoed up behind him and softly spoke his name. His head whipped round and his arms went up in an instant for me to hold him in my arms.

The doctor had no other suggestion to make other than his collapse was probably due to delayed shock following the fire. Our daughter had suffered nightmares for a time and was nervous of any crackling sound, but that was already several weeks behind us. Whatever the cause, it appeared he had suffered a severe anaemia.

In general, the children kept reasonably well in the circumstances. We were longing for the rains to end, when we would have several months of dry weather to look forward to, months when conditions would allow us to start rebuilding perhaps. But that was some distance ahead and in the meantime we made the most of every weekend day when it was fine enough for us to dry out and work in our garden. Gordon had constructed a chicken run for more layers and rabbit pens in order for us to raise more meat, and both of us worked hard at enlarging the vegetable garden.

It was a time of relentless effort that stretched into years. Grace started school in January 1965 and the boys followed her at two-year intervals. I stayed working in town for four years and all through this time we were slowly building. It was hard work because we couldn't borrow money to rebuild and had to pay cash for all our building materials as we went along, but it did mean that in the end we achieved a home the value of which far exceeded its cost.

The stability and peace that prevailed in Zambia throughout this period was a great blessing. In the year or so before Independence there had been only a few relatively minor disturbances, happily a long way away from us. As a former British territory, the political set-up had allowed the country to ease into independence reasonably well and the people's own peace-loving culture did the rest. Regular police patrols on cycles from the police post at Lusaka-West would keep an eye on our area. They would call in at every property with time to stop and talk, allowing us to voice any concerns we had, which they would report. The country's independence became visible in lots of ways such as changed town and street names. For instance, the Copperbelt town of Bancroft became Chililabombwe ('place of frogs'), and one of the main thoroughfares in Lusaka was renamed Cha Cha Cha Road.

Our water was raised from the river by a small two-stroke petrol pump that was already in place when we came to the property. It was aging rapidly and had been damaged by flash floods several times over the years. It was becoming increasingly difficult to keep it running smoothly. During the rains the river water often carried a lot of sand in it so it wasn't surprising that our household linen took on a sandy hue, despite my efforts to sun-bleach it. Care had to be taken to iron everything, most especially the children's things, because of the *putsies.* Putsy flies laid their eggs on damp cloth and if not killed off by a hot iron, the eggs, which were too small to be visible to the naked eye, would hatch on one's skin and the grubs would burrow under the skin to cause an abscess.

As time went on, my hands were often shaking with fatigue by lunchtime but I was in the grip of such determination, a relentless drive to get back on our feet, and a deep-down conviction that somewhere in all this we would find our God-given new purpose. Our day started with the alarm clock going off at 4 am for Gordon to get off to work. Then I would get up, get the charcoal iron going and prepare one set of clothes for each of us, polish the children's shoes and pack three little snack packs. Then I'd go outside and load my car with whatever spare produce we might have: eggs, lettuce, tomatoes etc., to sell round my office and to the teachers at the primary school.

After getting the three children ready and giving them breakfast, we would leave by 7 am and were on the road to town to drop Grace off at school and take the other two direct to the nursery before getting to my office by 8.30. At Grace's age, school finished at 12.30 pm and the day nursery would pick her up in their little van and take her to join her brothers until I finished work. This arrangement cost me a third of my monthly salary, but as the boys also began school at intervals, it included transport for all three from school to nursery, and a proper lunch. It was extremely good value for money as they were safe until I arrived to collect them. Even if a health emergency cropped up, the supervisor would ring my office to inform me, either for me to agree she should call a doctor to the nursery if it was serious, or to advise me to obtain medicine before leaving town that evening. The children loved it there.

In my lunch hour I went out to buy supplies: food for us and our animals, or bags of cement and other building materials. Our sturdy Chevrolet with its extended back had come into its own once more. In time, we would take this trusty vehicle three-and-a-half times round the clock before the bodywork succumbed to the ravages of time, and even then the engine was used to run a generator. Very near my office there was a timber company with a huge pile of discarded lumber in one corner of their yard. I could pull in there and, with their permission, rummage freely. I became quite good at spotting potentially good pieces of scrap wood of one sort or another. Many a time I'd pull out of there with a considerable load all topped off with several sacks of sawdust for our animal pens.

Often Gordon did not get home with daylight to spare. For instance, there were often delays in the arrival of milk tankers from the depot at Mazabuka, a town about eighty miles to the south. Milk tankers and machinery of all sorts would break down and there were often power cuts in the rainy season. These sorts of hitches meant he was often called into the factory at weekends and public holidays. We were not so affected at home. The small amount of electricity we'd previously enjoyed from our neighbour was no longer available so we'd graduated to gas lamps; we replaced our rickety paraffin stove with one that ran off bottled gas and the old paraffin refrigerator was still going strong. We had completed one big room to live in, though as yet without ceilings and doors but at least it was stout and dry.

Long afterwards, I was to look back and realize that it was during this time that Gordon's periodic mood swings and bouts of anger began to surface. As he had done immediately after the fire, he took to disappearing for a day or so without explanation and later, when he no longer worked at the dairy, those random absences grew longer. His discipline of the children was physically very heavy at times which I found extremely distressing, and my remonstrations had no effect. One day he turned on me and actually grabbed me by the throat which badly frightened me. But later, when he asked my forgiveness, I gave it and afterwards things were calm for several months. Nevertheless, I couldn't forget entirely and the shadow of that memory lurked at the edges of my mind; subconsciously, I grew wary, less secure.

The children's welfare came first. They were amazingly resilient – so long as I didn't forget the Jolly Juice, that brilliant alternative to blackcurrant cordial that was fast becoming part of the Zambian scene, fed them regularly, cuddled them often and prayed over them. John had suffered several bouts of pneumonia and ear infections. His teeth were not forming properly and at four years old he had extensive dental work done in order that his jaw and secondary teeth would develop correctly, but he bounced back every time. We had an African worker named Thousand. He could always be relied upon to keep an eye on our youngest and he in turn, would shadow Thousand around, knowing he'd be scooped up and carried when he grew tired or some mishap would make him cry. We became used to this man toting our little one round until he could safely hand him over at the back door.

One of Gordon's duties at the milk factory was to taste-test each batch of raw milk that came in, and he began to go down with some nasty strep throat infections. As these became more frequent and more virulent, he was forced to give up the job, but he quickly found a position with an agricultural equipment company.

By the end of the third year after the fire, we were employing a Zambian builder almost full-time and an extra worker for the kitchen garden. The poultry and garden produce was increasing and I went to working mornings only. Though I still didn't get back until early afternoon, I had more time to spend on what, by now, resembled an English small holding and was able to supervise the picking and packing of produce. In addition to the layers, I bought in day-old chicks to raise so we had more layers and table birds, and ordered several batches of day-old Aylesbury ducklings from a farm near Salisbury who sent them up on the overnight train. We bought a cultivator, and a milk cow, and followed this with the purchase of some week-old calves which we intended to raise and sell on. Along with all this we were steadily progressing with the house and had built some necessary sheds and bought a modicum of needed equipment such as poultry feeders, an egg grader and heavy duty scales to weigh our garden produce. By the fourth year we were producing dressed rabbits and table ducks for a supermarket in the city, all bearing our own brand label, and had developed a local outlet for our surplus garden produce together with a neighbourhood milk round. Whatever was left over was taken in to the city open-air market.

"*Njoka! Njoka!*" one of our workers was shouting as he ran past the house. At the aperture soon to become my new kitchen window, I craned forward to see what the fuss was about outside in the lane. I could hear a bird frantically chattering in the tree opposite. *Ah,* I thought, *she's alarmed. There's a snake threatening her nest.* The cry of "snake, snake" always promised more excitement than hoeing or weeding. And sure enough, our other two workers came rushing to the scene. Excitedly all three danced around the tree throwing stones and gesticulating wildly. Not one of their missiles actually hit the target but the snake gave up anyway and slithered away, while the disconsolate gardeners trailed back to the boredom of weed-pulling.

The road that linked our property to the main road is a sandy track, about a quarter mile long. The aim was to get it graded once a year. Since beyond our gate it linked several other smaller properties, the idea was that everyone on that road should share the cost of such a grade, but it didn't always work out so neatly. When we had first come to live there, we'd had one sighting of a leopard on the road and seen duiker in the bush near the river. But as the population in the district grew, the only evident wildlife were cane rats, mongoose, an occasional monitor lizard and snakes. In addition, we had our lovely family of otters and the troupe of monkeys that lived on the riverside, and ants – lots of ants.

We often saw long columns of soldier ants marching across the road. Red ants were particularly lethal and we learned that if they entered your house, it was best to evacuate while they worked their way through. They ate every living thing in their path: spiders and other insects and even pets if they were penned up and unable to get away. When we first began to keep rabbits, we lost some in this manner and learned to spray circles of ant killer round the base of their pens and those of any other livestock that were shut in. Swarms of red ants in the garden were nasty too because the children would stumble on them and stand screaming to be rescued, while the ants crawled into their sandals and up their legs.

Fortunately, the red ant threat grew less and less over the years, until sightings became much less frequent. Whether or not it was because the ground surrounding our homestead had absorbed so much ant killer that it became a real deterrent, we'll never know. But we were very thankful to see less of them. Sometimes we'd see soldier ants filing across the road but they were not such a threat.

There were lots of beautiful and gentle things surrounding us that made us laugh, such as the monkeys playing on the lawn, the tiny jewel-like fish that tickled the children's toes whenever they paddled in the river and the spotted eagle owl raising her young in a hole in a tree in the calf paddock. There was a myriad of birds and butterflies and, in the rains, exquisite moths and millipedes ('chongololos') which had a dark, hard coat and curled up into balls when touched. Throughout the dry season, we could see Venus, the 'evening star', hanging low in the western sky whenever we drove back after dark, as if guiding us home. High in a tree by our garden gate, a wide-eyed bushbaby would stare at us, its huge eyes shining like twin moons when we shone our torchlights up. In the house we'd catch glimpses of our resident geckoes darting about in the rafters, through the open kitchen door there would be the sparkle of fireflies winking on the lawn, and, loveliest of all, we could go to sleep to the sound of the waterfall.

The troupe of grey monkeys that lived along our river would gambol through our growing orchard and play on our lawn, sometimes venturing very near the house. When this happened, the dogs would get extremely excited. It was a mix of chattering monkeys, loudly barking dogs dashing about and children hanging out of windows or running up and down the patio shrieking with laughter. Of course, there were no casualties as the monkeys easily danced out of the way of the dogs and they, once a few token rushes had been made, retired to flop on the grass, tongues lolling and honour satisfied... 'til the next time.

And what were the children doing? Well, as soon as the monkeys ran away, they were already busy looking into the mysteries of puppies, kittens, frogs or fish... The days just weren't long enough to get round to it all! Where some small natural springs helped keep the ground moist, we had planted a banana grove between the orchard and the river, and this proved to be an irresistible attraction to the monkeys. However, it has to be said, the pleasure we got from these little visitors far outweighed any damage they might do, which was negligible. But if we saw them coming, we'd instruct a herd boy to hover nearby with his catapult handy, and the monkeys caught on very quickly.

For four years after the fire, we did not take a vacation. Our respective employers allowed us to take our holiday pay in cash while we worked on. Although we had properly insured our original house, it was almost a year before a settlement came through, and it went directly towards paying off the mortgage. This meant that although the mortgage was almost fully paid off, there was still no money available for rebuilding. By the end of the next year, we had paid off the balance and had the freehold title deeds in our hands. It was a rare moment!

In 1968 we planned our first real break and took the children down to South Africa for the Easter holidays. Gordon wanted to go to the Rand Easter Show, the most prestigious agricultural show in sub-Sahara Africa, so we booked ourselves into a small guest house on the outskirts of Johannesburg for that, then wandered south to the Drakensberg Mountains and finally down to the sea, mostly camping all the way. We made one short stop at a lovely guest house in the Drakensburgs and then went on and spent a couple of nights in the Four Seasons Hotel in Durban.

It was the children's first glimpse of the sea and they loved finding a small bar of chocolate on their pillows each night. We had travelled the length of Kruger National Park and after leaving the park by the northern gate, we travelled through Mozambique to the sea. The entire journey was full of new scenes but we were particularly fascinated to come across a fishing village. Several gaily painted and decorated boats were pulled upon shore; when we got out of the car and walked down onto the sand, we found they were also *building* boats. Finally, we made our way to Lourenco Marques where we stayed a night in a hotel, ate a goat meat dinner and witnessed the local *fado* singer throw a tantrum because there were so few people in that evening; she didn't want to perform before such a paltry audience. She came back later and treated us to a short programme of Portuguese traditional songs. We spent the next day sightseeing including a visit to the zoo. Early next morning we commenced our journey back through eastern S. Rhodesia via Tete, Umtali, Beit Bridge, Bulawayo and home again. It was a grand time. Three weeks of refreshment and leisure, but it only served to give us our second wind.

Later that year I left my job altogether to concentrate on our growing enterprise. We were now enjoying the fruits of our labours such as sufficient fresh food in addition to a small but steady cash income from the sale of our surplus, but the house wasn't finished yet. It still lacked indoor plumbing, ceilings, decorating or any furnishings beyond the most basic necessities. We were still a very long way from curtains and cushions. Among the gifts that were given to us immediately after the fire was a lorry-load of second-hand metal window frames of various sizes, bought, we were told, from a fire sale. It was a large load and we used them all but it wasn't until we came to install the glass that we came up against a problem. All had warped ever so slightly. We'd measured and ordered all the glass based on the standard sizes but when it came to fitting the glass, a large proportion had to be returned to the glazier in town to be individually and very finely re-cut to fit

For the fifth time pneumonia hit our youngest. I bundled him into the 'poorly' quilt and drove to the doctor in town. This cotton patchwork quilt, one of several sent to us from a church sewing circle in Canada after the fire, was made in a pattern of big plain squares. Each square had been embroidered with simple scriptures such as "He cares for you" and so on, and we'd started the tradition that each child could have this quilt whenever they weren't well. Placed so the writing faced the child when sitting up in bed, we made a game of reading the promises.

Once home and tucked up, his little face flushed and, his blonde straight hair even more on end, he greeted his six-year-old brother with a wobbly smile.

Stuart climbed on the bed and attempted to cheer him up. "Don't worry. If you die I 'spect you'll have the most famous cowlick in heaven."

"It's OK," said our doleful tot. "I'll be able to help God make the butterflies."

Two days before Christmas that year, just as I was decorating an evergreen bough in lieu of a Christmas tree, the telephone rang. It was the news that my father had died. Suddenly overwhelmed with profound sorrow, a desolate weariness engulfed me. England had never seemed so far away.

By the following January all three children were in school but my husband had left his job. Though it did allow him more time to work at home, the loss of his salary seriously slowed us down.

We were still virtually camping out with our beds all at one end and the stove and frig and stores in the section that would eventually become our bathroom, where we'd broken through the old brick tool shed, now situated in the middle of the new house. By the completion of the walls and windows, we had graduated to an L-shaped shell, divided to make a bathroom, three bedrooms, a store room, kitchen and dining room and, at the far end, a sitting room with a fireplace and a curved end wall, mainly window. It was all under a temporary corrugated iron roof so we were weatherproof. We had put down a concrete base and were building in breeze blocks, easier to get than burned brick.

In years to come, I would come to love that curved window and the seat we built beneath those wide windows which gave us such a lovely view of an extended garden. Right now, however, the only reason we had designed the sitting room this way was because in that original load of second-hand window frames was this very wide curved one, and window frames filled up wall space quicker than putting up breeze blocks which we had to buy and then could only transport a hundred at a time.

Cost had governed every decision we made. For our bathroom that overlooked the road we used one odd window frame that we couldn't see fitting anywhere else. It was tall and narrow, and since, in the circumstances, it didn't really matter what shape the bathroom window was, we decided it would do for now; perhaps we'd change it later.

But we didn't change it, first because it was so low down on our list of priorities, it didn't signify, and then because it became too useful, and even a little amusing. The sill was so low that one could easily step over it and many times in the heavy rains we drew the car right up to the bathroom window to transfer luggage, shopping, children and sleeping babies dry straight into the house. Once, carrying our youngsters and a sleeping baby, we crept out of the house this way in the middle of the night to avoid armed robbers. Because it was at the front of the house, this window was covered with a thick, heavy curtain.

On one memorable day, a lady visitor decided on an afternoon bath, unaware that the window had been left open. Seeing the curtain was drawn across, no doubt she didn't think to check. Imagine! There she was enjoying her bath when one of our huge Friesian cows, being herded down the lane, stuck her curious head through the open window and bellowed right in her face. That shock was bad enough but due to the following efforts of the cowman to prod his charge away, which resulted in its horns becoming hopelessly entangled in the curtain, her shrieks could be heard all over the house. We all came running, only, to our shame, to fall about laughing – but our poor guest was not amused.

Some years later, when the new roof went on, we purposefully extended the eaves to provide shelter all around the house so windows could stay open even in the rain. We designed the house to have a front door on to the lane where cars drove up, and a back kitchen door. But one rainy season, early in our building programme, a neighbour's earth dam that had been built on higher ground burst and flooded our house, so we changed the front door to the other side. Thus, the house grew with an entrance directly into the kitchen and another one directly into the sitting-room, both at the back of the house with steps down to the patio, both with stable doors to keep the dogs out and the children in (well, that was the theory anyway), and the paved patio, under the shade of several trees, became our main entertaining area.

Towards the end of 1968, through a friend working at a big mission station in the Southern Province, Gordon heard that their secondary school needed a teacher for their agricultural science programme. They planned to recruit overseas, but in the meantime they hoped to find someone local. Gordon was interested because he had become involved that year in Z.A.G.E.D.A., the Zambia Agriculture and Education Association, a government-backed scheme to introduce the teaching of rudimentary farming practices into the secondary school curriculum throughout the country. The idea was to equip and encourage young Zambians in these basic skills and thereby, hopefully, foster ideas of self-sufficiency. Accordingly, one weekend, we made a trip to this school.

It was a large mission station, about two hours' drive away, and comprised a junior school and a hospital in addition to the senior school. There was a large number of staff, doctors, nurses and teachers together with many auxiliaries, both Zambian and ex-pats. And with all the necessary housing, a church, mechanic's and carpentry workshops, and boarders' accommodation, it resembled a sizeable village. The plan was to create a small mixed farm alongside for the students to run as part of their practical studies.

We thoroughly enjoyed meeting many of the people and their hospitality as well as being taken on a comprehensive tour. At teatime that afternoon Gordon, who had been closeted since lunch with the headmaster, announced he'd agreed to take the job. I stifled an initial dismay; we'd had no time to discuss it. And while I listened to him expand on their plans, my misgivings grew. Because of the distance, the timetable would be amended so all the new agricultural science classes would be scheduled at the beginning of the week in order that he could leave home on Sunday afternoon and return on Tuesday evening. The headmaster, apparently, had warned him that since he wasn't a qualified teacher, there was still a question over salary but he was sure they'd "sort something out".

Despite my remonstration and pleas, he settled down happily into this new pattern and I only found out later that he'd agreed to work for the petrol money for his journeys only. Nothing I said would change his mind and gradually he slipped into leaving on Sunday mornings and began to return late on Wednesdays. It was not only the loss of income, but his being gone for four days out of seven meant I had no help in practical matters or with the children, who missed him sorely. He worked there for five school terms.

A few times he even went back on other days to check on livestock and 'things' while I grew even more troubled about what I observed in his inappropriate behaviour around a young auxiliary who worked there. This unsavoury situation continued despite the presence of her husband and my remonstrations. He remained impervious to every effort I made to challenge him. Once during this latter period, this couple came up to Lusaka and he invited them to stay overnight, which did nothing to allay my fears. In private, my husband ridiculed whatever I said, and I, in turn, was angry and hurt by her mocking attitude and sly wit.

Despite the periodic school holidays when he would be home, his regular absences were a trial. Now that our little farm was our sole livelihood and the children growing, it was hard work on my own. One memorable night I'd sat up rather late but before I turned in, I checked on the sleeping children in the room next to mine. The rooms were still not finished but we were basically comfortable and the weather was warm. To my dismay I saw a snake between the boys' beds, rising up to the edge of Stuart's blanket. In my panic I saw nothing handy to use as a weapon and was too frightened to leave the room to look for one. In desperation I prayed against it in Jesus' name – and watched in fascinated horror as it turned back to the floor, slithered past my feet, went through the door and disappeared outside.

At long last that school period drew to a close and I was desperate for a new start. I prayed for wisdom and calm and tried one more time to confront him and get him to respond. We talked at length. I marshalled all the arguments and pleas I could and finally he expressed contrition and asked for my forgiveness, which I gave. But I was still a little heartsick and disappointed by his overall attitude. In prayer I asked for God's help because I trusted in his power to make that forgiveness real. Yet this problem had exposed a fatal flaw that ultimately would bear a bitter fruit.

One day during his last term, I came home from town and parked, as usual, right close to the house. While the children scrambled out, I went round the back of the car to unload the shopping. As usual the children skipped ahead through the gateway to follow the path round to the back of the house. As Grace started screaming I dropped the groceries and ran to them. There, in front of the three petrified children, was a snake, reared up and ready to strike. For a ghastly moment I thought it had already struck and as my mind scrabbled to assess the situation, our dog rushed up.

As she usually did whenever she heard the car arrive, our dog had raced to greet the children and in a flash got herself between them and the snake. As I frantically pushed the children behind me, I heard her sharp yelp and saw her run off down the garden. The snake slithered away and disappeared in the undergrowth. It took a while to calm the children but after they'd had their tea, I searched the garden for our dog and found her in some bushes near the river. She was dead.

The children were upset when I told them what had happened to our faithful pet but we prayed before bedtime and gave thanks for her bravery. The next morning we ceremoniously laid her to rest and remembered all her funny and endearing ways: her excitement when she chased the monkeys and when she'd found a monitor lizard one day down by the river, and how she used to bark at one of the gardeners every time he wore his bright checked socks. We agreed it had been an honourable end, protecting the children she loved.

In those early years I'd killed eighteen snakes. The children thought this quite heroic especially as my preferred method was to get in close and slice their heads off with one precise blow using a long-handled spade with a sharpened blade which I kept handy. From my experience, many snakes make off when they sense the vibrations from someone's approach, and will only turn and strike if cornered. Puff adders were dangerous because they were sluggish and very slow to move. They would lie low beneath the vegetation and were particularly dangerous to gardeners when they'd plunge their hands in the vegetation when weeding or harvesting.

We had a friend desperately ill for a long time after he had been bitten on his ankle, and one time a motorcyclist on a bush track skidded on a tree root and was thrown off his bike, only to fall right on top of a basking snake. I never had any faith in our workers' way of chucking stones at snakes because mostly they'd slither off and you knew they were still around. I much preferred to lessen the risk, if I could, of that particular snake threatening us again, especially near the house where the children played. Most of my coups were in the first couple of years after the fire, when we had many snakes nesting in the ruined walls.

But we were about to receive two gifts, both of such intrinsic value that they would be remembered ever afterwards with a very deep appreciation for the thoughtfulness that had prompted the giver. The first of these encouragements came in the form of a pair of new armchairs, delivered to us from a department store in town, accompanied with a note from a friend. The other gift was very different – unsolicited and totally unexpected; it was a gift of time and skill.

It was just after lunch one Saturday afternoon. We were hot and tired and struggling to find the energy to get on and do something. The temptation to go and have a rest was strong but one of us had to stay alert for the children. Even to move seemed like too much effort. So we lay slumped in our two new armchairs in the middle of an uncompleted sitting-room that still bore a marked resemblance to a building site. Stacked against the walls were several doors, some for bedrooms and some for the exterior. A toolbox lay ready but it was a daunting job for the unskilled. We stirred at the sound of a car coming down the drive.

"Hello-o," a voice called out. We went out to find a friend from the Baptist church in Lusaka. "Hi, we've come to see if we can give you folks a hand." He slammed the car door shut. "This is George," he introduced his companion and, turning, waved a hand at a tall man heaving a toolbox from the back of the car, "and you know Peter, of course." The third man extended his hand to us both in greeting.

"Oh, this is wonderful," I said trying to control the wave of children and dogs that had crowded round. Peter hefted his toolbox over the threshold and stood looking round, hand on hip.

"This is going to be just great," he said. "Let's get to it."

"Anne, keep the kids out of the way," Gordon said, his face lighting up with renewed energy. I was only too happy to comply and only returned to the scene briefly from time to time with mugs of tea. By nightfall the doors were all hung and we had reached another milestone.

In the following months, whenever doubts and misgivings would crowd in, I kept returning to God's promises. As my hands and feet went from task to task, my mind was continually engrossed in a kind of dialogue. It swung from introspection to the realities that surrounded me, between what I read in scripture and their application to my personal situation, between the theory and my gut-wrenching determination for my faith to work and be as natural and loving as possible. Even on really difficult days, always aware of my God's power and compassion, I knew deep down I was compelled to keep going and not give up.

So through those uneven days, whether bone weary from labour or heartened by hope, I constantly meditated on his word. Gradually it became easier to focus and I became even more convinced of how I must go on. The words lay clearly on the page under my hand; it was as if they spoke aloud. I must run, with as good a heart and with as much determination as I could muster, the race that was set before me. That was the point, it seemed. This race was mine to run, mine to endure and mine to win. As yet, the finishing line was far out of sight, but unseen witnesses would cheer me on. I sensed a battle hardly begun but I knew what I was fighting for and I knew who had won the war. So I wouldn't give up, I decided I would keep going.

CHAPTER EIGHT

The Grey House

It was a grey day. Until well after lunchtime, a steady drizzle had fallen from a dull sky. The cloudy dampness suited my mood. By mid-afternoon I was tired and dispirited. Constant work and the continuing financial struggle were getting me down. By four o'clock the sky had cleared but every leaf still dripped and the grass underfoot was soggy.

I went outside just to feel the air and catch the faint breeze that often came just before sundown. Looking towards the river to the west of the house, there was just enough space between the last wisps of departing cloud and the tree tops for the sun to send its last rays of chartreuse light. Released from the confines of the house, the children were gleefully running about barefoot, stamping in the remnant of puddles in the lane.

Driving the children home from school earlier, I was paying little heed to the bouncing and chattering going on in the back seat until a repeated phrase suddenly grabbed my attention: "the grey house". Suddenly I focussed on what they were saying and realized that the "grey house" was our house, our new home, the new house we were trying so hard to finish.

So when we got home, I immediately took time to look at it from their point of view. The house was finished, the roof sound, the doors were all on and every room had some furniture. Very thankful to have reached that stage, I think both of us had simply turned our attention to all the outside work that needed doing and got on with that.

What I saw was indeed grey – very grey – inside and out. Pale grey walls, darker grey primed doors that waited for their finishing coat of paint, unpainted steel window frames and smooth grey floors. We had built in concrete blocks with a cement plaster finish. The concrete floors, though smooth, were not yet finished. They waited until such time the gallons of old engine oil, ordered but not yet delivered, arrived from a motor repair garage in town. Then the oil would be painstakingly worked into the floors and that would give them their lovely chestnut brown finish. Once the surface was completely dry, this smooth-as-silk surface could be polished with *stoep* polish. It had amused me when I'd first arrived in the territory to see house servants polishing this type of flooring. They used large oval brushes that had a canvas strap across them, into which they simply fitted their feet and skated round the floor.

Before I slept that night, I made a note at the end of my list for the following day: "Think colour, think paint!" And so, without saying anything to the children, I built an interesting pile of tins and tools at the back of the store shed, all ready for the weekend. On Saturday morning I showed this treasure to the children: tins of pink, blue, green and white paint, a collection of old clean cans, brushes, rollers and several old plastic sheets. When I explained what all this was for, their excitement knew no bounds. We hauled it all into the house and the fun began. I let them choose what colour they wanted for their bedrooms. Happily, we sloshed paint all day with great abandon, until by nightfall, their bedrooms were transformed and we were all tired out. There was nearly as much paint on the kids but nobody cared, not even when it took some pretty hard scrubbing to get it off!

They sleepily agreed we'd do some more the next day. Could we even make a start on the sitting room? I wasn't sure about that, there was quite a lot of touching up to do after today's effort, but it didn't really matter. What mattered was that we'd made a memory today; we'd pushed forward to the next phase. It would take time, but I promised myself that while they were at school I'd find time to go on cheering the place up. By the end of that month, the interior doors were painted and the inside of the outer doors, the sitting and dining room walls gleamed white, and I had bought yards of inexpensive cotton and made curtains for the bedrooms. The next month's budget would include bright bedspreads.

The work on the house and garden now took a back seat. In 1969, my mother-in-law, on her way back from Australia where she'd been working, broke her journey to visit us. She was the first family member to come. Since the fire, when the big tent had to be returned, we'd patched up what was left of the original children's nursery and had used it as a bedroom while we were building and we'd also done this with the old kitchen. Now we made a better job of the old nursery to give Nana Bland the best accommodation possible.

Gordon drove down to Durban to collect her from the ship and a few days later, on a Friday, I took the children down as far as the Victoria Falls to meet them so we could spend that weekend sightseeing. We were all looking forward to this little holiday and all the way down the children sang the little ditty they'd made up: "We're going on safari / in the middle of Central Africa / You wouldn't have thought it, would you? Tra-la, tra-la, tra-la." It became their holiday song and featured in every trip we made thereafter for years.

It was a grand weekend though it started badly for the children and me. The plan was that we'd book into our reserved chalets that night and Nana and Gordon were expected to join us the following morning. Accordingly, we arrived at the Falls in time for supper and went to bed early. I settled the children down and went early to bed myself, placing my handbag under my pillow. Sometime in the night I awoke with a start. Everything was very quiet except for the constant background sound of the Falls. I couldn't detect anything amiss, the door was shut, but I just knew something was wrong. I turned my head to look around and instantly realized my bag was gone from beneath my head. That's what had woken me.

Getting out of bed, I hurried to the children. Thankfully, they were unharmed and only our daughter was awake. She said in a frightened whisper, "I woke up, Mummy, and saw the man walk past our beds. I was too scared to call you; I thought he might hurt us." I was glad she hadn't called out; it might have ended badly. But it was frightening to realize how quiet and skilled the thief had been. Still feeling a bit wobbly, I duly reported the incident at the police station next morning, an exercise, I have to confess, I thought tedious and probably futile. But in that I was proved wrong.

It was a grand weekend. Nana Bland was suitably impressed by the Victoria Falls, the lovely Riverside Drive and the adjacent game park, while the children loved having their supper at the restaurant opposite the camp and playing on the see-saw outside while the monkeys swung in the nearby trees.

Apparently, there had been a series of similar robberies around the chalets and at last the thief was caught. The Victoria Falls Tourist Board couldn't afford so much adverse publicity and their staff had been extra vigilant. Some weeks later I was called as a witness at the court case in Livingstone and although that was time-consuming, I eventually received some money back, approximately what had been stolen, as well as all my travel expenses.

Nana Bland was very active. Slim, with long auburn hair pinned up in a bun, she had been working in Australia for a considerable time as a hospital holiday relief sister or sometimes as a deputy matron. In the years running up to this, she had been a private nurse. She ran and played with the children, chased balls and swung on their swing. But when my mother, Grandma Baylis, came to stay, she was very different. She suffered severely with arthritis, but was plump with curly white hair and usually had some knitting or needlework to hand. She told stories, so over the following few months our children enjoyed the best of both worlds.

My mother had intimated that following the death of my father, she would like to come and have an extended visit. Because of the unfinished house, it seemed hardly the best time for such visits but Gordon and I knew we'd always regret it if we'd said no to the mums and another opportunity didn't come. As it turned out, both mothers coped very well with our limitations. Nana Bland had been a missionary to Bolivia in her youth and my mum was an extremely practical person.

The two visits were co-ordinated so that at the end of her stay I drove Nana down to Cape Town to continue her journey to England by ship. I then waited there a couple of days, had the car serviced and new tyres fitted, and then collected my mother at the airport. We had suggested she fly direct to Cape Town so that I could give her a tour of South Africa on the way home, much as I'd given Nana on the way down.

The long journey up from the Cape was a great opportunity for us to relax and talk at leisure about my father and all sorts of other family news. She was a great letter-writer and she recorded the journey, indeed the whole visit, in great detail for those back home in England. We took the stunningly beautiful 'Garden Route' through Swaziland and the Transkei: that is, following the coast from Cape Town to Durban, and from there inland to the high veldt and Johannesburg, before turning north. The Transkei was an experience! It took hours, reduced as we were to a crawl, in a very heavy mist and with sheep wandering all over the fence-less roads.

While I had been down south, Gordon had been working on our new roof and we came home to find it almost complete. The last section, over the dining and sitting-room, took a few more days so we quit that area in the daytime and lived in the garden. The weather was warm so we moved a collection of chairs and a table under a shady tree and picnicked. The kids thought it great fun, of course, and Mum could always stretch out for a nap whenever she wanted as her room was a little distance from the main house. I had a house-help by then – a very large, beefy Matebele named Samuel, who in former years had worked for a posh lady in Salisbury, the capital of Southern Rhodesia. It didn't bother him to temporarily have to wash dishes in a bucket on the lawn or wash clothes in the river. He once paid my mother his highest compliment: "That Madam, she proper Salisbury lady," he told me solemnly.

At last the new corrugated asbestos roof was finished. Most roofing in the country was either corrugated iron or asbestos. It was rare to see a clay-tiled roof since these tiles had to be imported and were therefore expensive. Corrugated asbestos, which was readily available from the asbestos factory a few miles south of Lusaka, was ideal, for it kept cool, whereas iron sheeting got tremendously hot in our climate. Whatever long-term problems regarding health issues were brewing at this time and in the factory, none affected us. We designed all our buildings so we could utilize the 12ft-long sheets and therefore did not have to cut them, save for drilling the screw holes for attachment to the blue gum pole frame.

The last of the mismatched roof covers, put on at various stages of our building, were gone. Now it looked like a proper house, wide and low, already looking good against its backdrop of trees. We knew it would look even better in a year or two as asbestos weathered beautifully. We planned to stipple the outside walls and paint them cream and pick out the door and window frames in black. We still had no mains electricity but we hoped that wouldn't be long now. There was none in our district to date, so our problem was that we would have to pay for the power lines to be laid from the town boundary, some considerable distance, on top of the cost of our own installation. It would be a very big investment but a major step forward.

The grandmothers' visit gave us lots of opportunity to take little trips to show them round. On a trip through the Zambezi valley we came across an elephant right in the middle of the road. Nana Bland was sitting in the front passenger seat and I was directly behind her. We had just seen a new Mercedes-Benz parked by the customs office with its front bonnet crushed where apparently an elephant had sat on it. Gordon braked but we were quite near the elephant before the car came to a halt. He kept the engine running and we sat waiting to see what the elephant would do.

The elephant just stood there. Then it moved a step nearer and Nana frantically wound her window up, at the same time pressing back hard against her seat. Even as we all caught our breath I couldn't help smile at her instinctive action. We waited and I saw a trickle of perspiration creep down Gordon's cheek. He was rigid and his hand clenched on the gearstick ready to slam the car into reverse. I looked at the children squashed beside me and saw their eyes widen with fright and I realized that I too was stiff with apprehension. We sweated it out another few minutes; it was a complete stand-off. Then, with a slow flap of his ears, the elephant swayed a little as it got its feet into gear and casually ambled into the bush and disappeared.

During my mum's stay I was stricken again with severe back pain and was forced to take to my bed. Over the years there had been several of these times and it was patently obvious that the fall I'd sustained when pregnant with my second child had left a lasting problem – and, no doubt, the hard work I'd been doing hadn't helped. As usual, after a rest I got going again, though deep down I knew these bouts were getting worse and lasting longer.

I took my mum to Chobe in Botswana. We drove down to Livingstone and, just before entering the town proper, turned right and took the road to Kazungula. We spent the night with friends and the following morning took the pontoon across the river. This was the first time I'd done this on my own and tried not to let Mum see how nervous I was as I very gently drove the car down the ramp and on to the pontoon. This was where the territories came together – Zambia, S. Rhodesia, Botswana met the far northern stretch of Namibia, the Caprivi Strip – and the river was very wide.

The safari lodge was on the edge of the river and we could sit outside on the lawn and watch fishermen paddling by in their dugout canoes and hear the clarion call of the fish eagles. As the sun went down, African drums throbbed nearby and we watched enthralled as the huge cream-coloured disc of a full moon rose majestically over the water. The following morning we followed a herd of elephant along the river path. Our progress was slow. The elephants, with young, were unhurried and the riverside road was pitted with huge sunken holes where the elephants had trodden in the rains and their huge footprints had baked concrete hard in the dry season.

Mum returned to England and we turned our attention to the next big step. Things were moving along steadily. We had taken up our option and found the money to buy the remaining extent. The following year we managed to pay for the power line extension on to our property and at long last we had mains electricity. It was the most important stage yet and we installed a big new electric pump at the river. The farm complex, including the dairy that supported our growing herd, was wired first because it was our living, and then the house. We were granted the water-rights, forty thousand gallons an hour, so long as water was kept flowing downstream to our neighbours. That meant careful management at the end of the dry season if the previous season's rains were below average. But best of all, it meant we could now bring in irrigation equipment.

As our enterprise grew we had to clear the land. There was no development on it when we took the property over. Pigs were the answer. At first we hadn't thought about pigs, but when it dawned on us that they were the best way forward, nothing was simpler. A relatively small investment in a quantity of electric fencing and a few pregnant gilts paid off handsomely. Sections of land were fenced off and, in rotation, the pigs were let loose to grub up, churn and trample the earth until, in an impressively short time, only the trees remained. Their automatic fertilization of the land paid dividends when we used that land for planting. Their efforts made it easier to level where we intended to build.

A change came about. All through these years, we had been concentrating on building up our livelihood, a natural progression. But I had never forgotten our original purpose, our hopes and our dreams. We had not set out to deliberately create a commercial farm, merely to feed ourselves and rebuild our home. But now, circumstances had brought us to this new threshold. Were we to settle as farmers or was this the God-given platform from which we could specifically re-engage in his work? It was time to find out.

Change came in the form of a beaten-up looking Land Rover limping to a stop outside the house. One tyre was flat and the whole covered in a layer of red dust. A couple of weary young people emerged and gratefully accepted our invitation to come into the house. Hot and dishevelled, they told us that this was their second flat tyre since leaving town. Over the teacups, they told us their story.

They had specifically come to us because they had met an acquaintance of ours and he had given them directions to the farm, saying that perhaps we might be able to help. Only recently married to his American sweetheart, the young man had worked in the Copper mines up north, until he'd been involved in an accident. Now they were jobless and homeless. Not quite seeing what he could do, Gordon drew him out and discovered that their dream was to work in the bush, possibly with a safari guide or hunter, but they had no idea how to go about it.

When Gordon told them he knew a hunter who lived in the Luangwa Valley, they immediately brightened up. Over a meal, we suggested they stay with us while they got their tyres fixed up and had a rest, while enquiries were made on their behalf. They pitched a tent in the garden and left several days later with a letter of introduction to the aforesaid hunter who took him on as his apprentice. The young man did well and they both loved the bush. We kept in touch and they stayed with us whenever they came to town, and both became Christians. After a few years in the safari business, they left Africa to establish a game farm in America.

At the time, we hadn't thought this incident was actually a taste of what was to come, that these needy people would be the first of many. It didn't occur to us that instead of trying to figure out our future and our purpose here, God was already showing it to us; it had already begun. Over the next few months, several others in need of one sort or another found their way to our door. They became a trickle and then a regular pattern began to emerge, and we were forced to take stock and consider all the implications with regard to our home life. In prayer we sought wisdom. Either we needed to put a stop to it altogether, or to decide *what* we could do and *how* we should do it.

Very much on the same wavelength when it came to the use of our home and its resources, we recalled the hopes we'd had when we first saw this property. Since the fire these ideas had taken a back seat in the drive to get back on our feet, provide for our children and establish a new life. But now they all came back to us, full force. While Gordon had embraced several other interests latterly, I had always been confident of my spiritual calling to Africa, though not specifically to the African people. My talents, such as they were, lay in another direction and I'd kept it all locked in my heart as I pondered and prayed.

Even after leaving off teaching agriculture at the mission school, Gordon had stayed involved in ZAGEDA. He joined the Gideons and became active in placing bibles in several local hotels and he also became a regular prison visitor. His continued interest in ZAGEDA brought him into contact with many young V.S.O.s[4] and he enjoyed getting involved with some of Zambia's Agricultural Shows. I, on the other hand, felt as though God was drawing my attention to several other groups that made up Zambia's multiracial population, so many that were outside the reach of the established church and the missions. There were those that travelled unconventionally, often in trouble, ill, robbed or stranded, and refugees, as well as Christian workers in lonely situations who needed a place to rest on occasion.

How would we know which of these to reach out to? How could we judge the truly needy? What about our home-life and children? We were not going to open a guest house as a business to accommodate just anyone. Surely our endeavour should serve a purpose? A ministry such as this would take resources, time, energy and stamina. Without the anointing and enabling of the Holy Spirit, it wouldn't be possible.

The questions kept coming but one by one the answers followed. We became convinced that he would choose the people and the circumstances and, most importantly, he would bring the people to us. It was not for us to judge or choose. For our part, we must trust him in

---

[4] Voluntary Service Overseas

all this, be sensitive and readily accept those who came. Our lifestyle was about to change.

All through the early years in Bulawayo, Kitwe and Lusaka, we had been part of a widespread interdenominational fellowship of mission-aries, and in addition, since coming to Lusaka, had found friends among the various diplomatic missions. As the children grew we realized that we needed a family church so began regular attendance at Lusaka Baptist Church which in turn brought us into contact with the university, its students and teachers. And latterly I'd become a member of a large international Christian ladies' group in the city. We'd made friends in the Salvation Army and in the United Nations High Commission for Refugees. Now all these connections were about to prove very useful in our new endeavour.

For years civil war had raged through Angola to the west, which meant Zambia had lost her rail link with Lobito Bay and in Mozambique to the east, where our connection to the port of Beira was similarly cut. Even these circumstances would have an influence on our ministry and yield a spiritual harvest for the Kingdom of God. Previously, we'd thought ourselves as 'off the beaten track' but now we recognised Lusaka's strategic placement in being such a vital crossroad on the north-south Cape-to-Cairo route across Africa.

A friend came to tea one afternoon, with her mother who was on a visit from South Africa. The mother's name was Queenie and she was a lady of deep faith and a somewhat flamboyant personality. We showed them round the farm and then we all trouped into the house. Our conversation naturally turned to our hopes and the tentative plans for the future. They showed great interest in what we shared and were sympathetic when we recounted our long struggle to build the house. Suddenly Queenie leapt to her feet and, throwing up her hands, she started to pray. Not being used to her ways we were a little startled at first but were immediately riveted by her words.

Gesturing round the room, she prophesied that the day would come, in the not too distant future, when it would be filled with people praising God. Her speech stopped abruptly and there was complete silence in the room. For a few minutes she remained standing, her eyes lifted up as if she saw into another dimension. Then she laughed and clapped her hands. "My dears, believe it and prepare!"

The spell was broken and everyone started talking at once. The air was alive with heightened expectation and encouragement.

True enough, in the next few weeks, more people came to our door and the pattern became clearer. Someone would arrive, seemingly out of the blue, showing unmistakable signs of need. We offered a welcome, good food and a bed, but never money. We accepted them at face value and privately sought discernment regarding their need, especially when it wasn't immediately obvious, and then endeavoured to respond as the Holy Spirit led. When that person left it wasn't long before we were opening our door to another new face.

Another group that came into our orbit was the growing number of volunteers from overseas. Our farm became a 'home-from-home' for several young people who popped in at weekends, Christmas and other public holidays, all eager for Christian fellowship and ready to lend a hand to anything that needed doing. A lot of this was making more room for visitors such as converting some outbuildings and building simple cabins around the main house. Necessity demanded that we utilize all and any odds and ends of building material we could lay our hands on. The result was that each little building was unique. I strongly believed it was essential for our visitors to have their own space although, equally, there was great benefit in coming together for meals.

From the beginning, visitors were no problem to feed. Our farming enterprise gave us great flexibility regarding food. We acquired a few extra cheap iron bed frames while I cleaned and sewed hessian stock-feed sacks and filled them with hay as mattresses. It was a long time before we graduated to three-inch foam! Each bed had one pair of sheets and a pillow, together with one inexpensive, locally made blanket plus a bright cotton cover, and we laid locally made grass mats on the floors. The whole set-up was extremely unpretentious. To ease pressure on the bathroom, sometimes visitors were laughingly waved towards the river.

Family life dictated the framework of our days. Despite the distance, we had chosen to keep our children at home in day school in Lusaka. This meant a twice-daily round trip of twenty-five miles starting at 6.50 am. Later, when the children were split between primary and secondary school, there were four years when this rose to three such trips each day.

Entering into this new style of living, we realized the need for discipline in dealing with our visitors. When they arrived, they were completely unknown to us and we had to take an awful lot on trust – but our trust was in the Lord our God, not them. We had questioned whether we should be attempting to do anything specific, create or promote any particular kind of 'Christian' atmosphere, but decided that we should not. We were not an organisation, a church or a hostel. We were working farmers, a family, operating as a family, who were happy to share whatever we had, including our faith. All we could ever do was to respond to whoever and whatever was presented to us.

A set of house rules was devised. At first this was tacked up on the back of the kitchen door which had become our 'noticeboard.' Later we graduated to a printed card in all the bedrooms.

Anyone was welcome to stay for three days and four nights, free of charge. This gave people the chance to rest, do laundry and attend to any necessary business in the city. After this time, if a guest wanted, or needed, to stay longer, they must come to us and talk it over. This usually meant we would assign work unless the person was sick. They were not allowed to use our telephone or our vehicles. Our vehicles were constantly in and out of town so lifts into the city were easily available, but we insisted we make the arrangements. Visitors were not allowed to involve themselves with our children or require anything from our African staff. We built a laundry facility away from the house for visitors and asked that room keys always be left on the kitchen rack whenever visitors left the farm. Guests were invited to come to church with us or join our devotional and music evenings and we did our best to always be available when someone needed to talk.

CHAPTER NINE

Interlude

School was out and we took a little holiday. We packed our pickup truck and headed west, past the satellite station, that symbol of 20th century progress, and turned our faces towards a taste of the old Africa, at least as much of that as was possible. Even in the remote bush one could see the ubiquitous *Coca-Cola* and *Singer* sewing machine advertising boards outside many a small *duka,* and every now and again the hideous remains of a ghastly accident or the end of someone's dream of European-style riches.

We were looking forward to doing our favourite thing, relaxing in the bush. The road was good and we made excellent time. The two-hundred-mile journey was punctuated with glimpses of the wild and we kept the binoculars handy. Excited, the children giggled to see a family of warthogs running in a line with their tasselled tails held erect like miniature flagpoles. A secretary bird stalked through the tawny winter grass and far away, we saw smoke rising from a bush fire. At one place, there was a small herd of impala antelope not far from the road. A huge truck passed us noisily just as we spotted them and they bounded gracefully away and scattered. We came to a single large tree casting a large patch of shade on the roadside – a good place to stop for lunch, we thought, so we pulled up.

There was no sound except the soft rustle and whisper of grass and trees. A lilac-breasted roller alighted on a nearby branch and then we heard the distant *clank-clank* of a tin-can cowbell and, faintly, the sound of young voices. Turning round, we peered through the long winter-thin grass to watch the ambling group. Traditionally, each boy was carrying a catapult. To amuse themselves, and to eat, they would hunt *kanyoni,* the prolific tiny bush birds. They passed and it was quiet again save for the occasional *thrum* of a passing car.

We packed up our picnic and moved on. The road dropped to the Kafue River where we came to Iteshi-Teshi in the late afternoon. At that time of day, the air was significantly cooler for it was August, and the winter barely over. As soon as we drew up beside our rest-hut, the children scrambled out of the car and then followed us as we clambered up on the huge lakeside rocks. The lake spread out before us, wide, cool and deep. In the far distance, barely discernible, a thin dark line marked the far shore.

Returning to the car, we unloaded our stuff, piled it in the hut and decided to stretch our legs before nightfall. Baboons trooped across the sandy track ahead of us and on the evening breeze we caught the sound of distant African drums. The sun set in an amber blaze and in the brief tropical dusk we made our way back to camp. Deep in the bushes under our window, a Heuglin's robin was singing sweetly. We ate supper sitting on the veranda, watching the stars that seemed particularly close in the clear dry-season sky. At moonrise, the anthracite sheen of the lake was dramatically enhanced by the lunar light-path the moon flung across the water. Somewhere deep in the vastness of the bush, a lion roared into the darkness. We shivered and went inside to bed.

After two days at Iteshi-Teshi, we made our way through the Kafue National Park. Intrigued and enchanted as always and keen to find something exciting around every turn of the road, we came upon one delight after another such as a giraffe slowly straddling his fore feet wide and stretching his long neck to drink at a waterhole, and an elephant sedately ambling along on his own with three egrets perched in a line along his bony spine. We came across several groups of zebra and wildebeest, grazing together. At the sound of our car the zebra trotted off whistling, while the wildebeest, the clowns of the bush, ran off with their typical rocking motion – grunting, snorting and sometimes skipping in an idiotic manner. With their lugubrious bearded faces and somewhat top-heavy look, the wildebeest always raised a smile. Later we caught sight of a group of majestic sable antelope, up to their cream bellies in a *dambo,* idly overlooking a pair of crowned cranes; then, rounding a bend in the track, we suddenly were faced with a stately kudu bull standing stock still in the middle of the road, ears twitching and poised for flight.

One morning, huddled in our jackets against the chill, we left camp very early. It was barely dawn and we drove into the sunrise. The first orange splinters of light were poking through the trees throwing long spindly shadows across the sand road. Narrowly skirting round a bunch of foraging guinea fowl, we drove through a grove of fever trees and I felt Stuart clutch my shoulder. I touched Gordon's arm and he cut the engine, and we silently coasted to a stop. A lion emerged from between the sparse bushes barely ten yards away and crossed the track in front of us. His head, with its great mane, was held low, swaying from side to side slightly in time with his rhythmic padding gait. He took no notice of us but we watched him with bated breath until he disappeared into a dense thicket some hundred yards away.

Remembering to breathe we sat for a while talking in whispers, wondering if there were any more lions about. A hush lay over the bush save for the whisper of a tsetse fly that flew into the car. It settled on my arm and wouldn't go away. Busy trying to swipe it away, I was the last to notice three lionesses that were walking in single file in the same direction. The last lioness had two small cubs at her heels. No doubt she was training them but, taking no notice of us, she led them to a nearby bush and bade them stay. After a couple of tries, they stayed sat down and she went off, following the others to the river.

The cubs were in plain sight. Obediently they sat... for a few minutes. Then they began to fidget and finally gave into the temptation to chase a butterfly. When that proved unsuccessful, they played, all the while tumbling and gambolling their way closer to us. Entranced we watched, wondering just how close they would come, when the lioness returned without the others. We weren't surprised she took no notice of us. Our vehicle was just a shape to her but had we foolishly attempted to get out of the car, it would have been a very different scene. But we stayed quiet and watched her softly call the cubs and sit down with them. The early sun backlit her tawny fur to a luminous golden halo and she was close enough for us to hear her deep throated 'purring' as the cubs climbed all over her, played with her tail and patted her muzzle. Finally, she got up, called her cubs to attention, and they all padded silently away.

Continuing on, we kept to the road for the most part. From time to time we would come across a division in the track where a whitewashed stone pillar would indicate directions and mileage. Very occasionally we'd leave the track to get closer to something that attracted our attention. One such time, it was because we'd spotted a group of giraffe. Quietly, slowly, we edged the car closer. They didn't run but curiously gazed back at us over the top of some small trees they'd been browsing. We stayed a quarter hour watching them, a family group of towering dad, two adult females, a yearling and a baby. They stared back as if the game viewing was the other way round. The sound of our car sent up a flock of hundreds of tiny birds that exploded from a clump of nearby thorn bushes. They rose and swirled, settled and rose again in a fluttering cloud before settling again as we drove away.

The sun-baked savannah stretched before us. From time to time we would startle a group of impala who swiftly dashed away. As we neared the river again we disturbed a big flock of Nyasa lovebirds causing them to rise abruptly from the ground in a pink cloud. Just off the track we saw a lagoon and bumped our way over tussocks of coarse grass and stopped for a picnic. A midday hush lay over the bush. A hoopoe called among the trees behind us and we heard the persistent *knock-knock-knock* of a woodpecker. Mauve water lilies covered much of the water and we caught a glimpse of sunlight glinting off chestnut plumage. With the aid of our binoculars, we discovered a jacana, *a lily trotter,* daintily walking among the lily leaves on precise, thin red legs, all the while stooping and darting in search of prey.

We pushed on and finally left the park by the Kalomo gate. Next day, we took the road to the small town of Livingstone. Seven miles farther south the Victoria Falls, great Mosi-o-tunya ('the smoke that thunders') beckoned. The spray that rose from this huge body of falling water could be seen some miles away and was particularly spectacular in the very early morning when the rising sun tinged this cloud salmon pink, apricot or peach. In the vicinity of this great waterfall, the very ground trembles and you can feel the vibration beneath your feet. On this brilliant sunny morning, the towering cloud of mist was shot through with a double rainbow.

Next morning, we drove back to Livingstone and took the road parallel to the Zambezi upstream as far as Kazungula and the pontoon. There was little traffic and we made good time on the dirt road with the dust cloud kicked up by our wheels streaming behind us to lay yet another coat of red dust on the vegetation lining the road. We passed a couple, walking one behind the other, seemingly miles from anywhere. The man stepped out in front just carrying his stick, the woman several paces behind with her baby tied to her back with a length of *chitenje.* A shallow, wide enamel bowl was perched on her head full of *katundu,* and she was knitting as she walked.

The vegetation was changing. Here and there huge baobab trees stood along the roadside. We could see an eagle soaring skyward carrying a snake in its talons and up ahead a dust devil, a miniature whirlwind, crossed the road swirling twigs and leaves and gravel into the air. At last the road dropped down to the river and we stopped to stretch our legs and watch the pontoon returning from the other side. We took our place in the queue and watched the people disembarking: fishermen, a few villagers with children and bundles, other men carrying their bicycles shoulder high. Then it was our turn and Gordon gently eased the car down the ramp and drove on while we walked and went to lean on the rail.

The ferrymen chanted as they hauled on the lines that linked the pontoon to both sides of the river. Approaching the far side, we passed a group of hippo bobbing in the water up to their pinkish knobby eyes. Occasionally they would yawn, snort or send diamond-bright droplets of water spraying from their flicking ears.

We drove off the pontoon into Botswana. That night at Chobe Camp we sat on a grassy bank watching the sun go down over the mighty river. Somewhere near, there were hippos grunting and fish-eagles throwing their yelping *"kow kow-kow-kow-kow"* across the darkening water. Two fishermen in a dug-out canoe silently paddled downstream, silhouetted by the setting sun, and the evening breeze brought us the distant throb of native drums.

The following morning found us out early exploring the various trails that led out from the camp. At first we didn't see much save for a straight line of interesting pug marks deep and clear on the sand road and a few francolins pottering along. Only the sound of our car engine disturbed the peace. A couple of hours later we found a track that led to the riverbank. All along the edge of the water there were dozens of huge, almost completely round potholes and we realized that what we were seeing were, once again, footprints made deep in the mud by countless elephants in the rains, hardened by the scorching sun. We saw several elephants in a group, leisurely standing amid clumps of papyrus and swamp grass at the water's edge, and stayed a while to watch. In the midday hush the liquid call of a laughing dove and the occasional *boom* of a trumpeter hornbill reached us over the background hum and rustle of somnolent insects and the whisper of gently swaying leaves overhead.

Later in the afternoon we ventured forth again, hoping to see something exciting around every corner. But we hardly saw anything until finally we pulled up in the shade on a straight piece of road with a clear view all round and decided it was safe to step out of the car briefly to stretch and generally rearrange ourselves. I went round to the back of the car and was just about to open the trunk when I looked up and was horrified to see three elephants only forty or fifty yards away. Fortunately, they didn't seem to have taken notice of us yet and only the movement of their slowly flapping ears gave them away. My heart was in my mouth as I sidled round the car and scrambled in, hissing at Gordon to, "Go-go! Please, get going! Please!"

All too soon it was time to go. We came through customs and headed back across the river, back to Livingstone, all agreeing it had been fun and recounting our favourite bits. It had been a grand trip. We headed north and the road rose steadily. When we came to one of the tsetse barriers that guarded the high country from the danger of tsetse-born disease, our car was directed off the road into a large shed and thoroughly sprayed. Then we were free to take the road that followed the line of rail up to Lusaka and home.

CHAPTER TEN

A Well-Watered Garden

S ometime in those early days when we were tentatively exploring the way forward, a friend from Malawi, accompanied by an American evangelist and his wife, arrived to stay overnight. He was driving them to the Copperbelt where a series of special meetings were planned. He was one of the Canadians we had formerly worked with and we'd all had a most pleasant evening together.

The next morning, as soon as breakfast was over, my husband and his friend went out to load the luggage on their vehicle, but the couple and I stayed talking at the table. They told me they particularly wished to pray for me, and getting to their feet, they came to stand behind me and both laid their hands on my shoulders. In their prayer, they quoted from the scriptures, Isaiah 58:10-11, which says:

> "...and if you spend yourselves on behalf of the hungry and satisfy the needs of the oppressed, then your light will rise in the darkness, and your night will become like the noonday. The Lord will guide you always; he will satisfy your needs in a sun-scorched land and will strengthen your frame. You will be like a well-watered garden, like a spring whose waters never fail."

They drew the parallel that if I was faithful in accepting and caring for those who came to our door, and not neglect to show them Christ, the Holy Spirit would give the increase.

It was only after they had gone that I questioned in my mind why they had not prayed for my husband as well. Nevertheless, their prayers for me were extremely encouraging and I pondered their words in my heart. We hadn't told our friends in Malawi or on the Copperbelt about our ideas, nor had we said anything about our burgeoning plans the previous evening. Surely this was confirmation: to accept those who arrived at our door with unsentimental love, as God gave us grace; to offer practical help, a refuge, good food, comfort and friendship with the time and opportunity to consider Christ and allow the Holy Spirit to work.

The first of our group of small, very simple guest houses was built. Many of our visitors who stayed to work had construction skills of one sort or another, or could do a fair job with a paintbrush. Tucked away at the end of a particularly flat section of lawn, formerly a tennis court, we found a small spring in a hollow a little distance from the river. We had looked at this hollow and considered the idea of creating fishponds there to add to our scope of self-sufficiency. Our original idea had been to divide the area into three ponds, with mud wall dividers, designed thus to enable us to harvest and restock in rotation.

Over the following year we deepened the hollow and constructed the walls. The depression readily filled with water in the rains. We managed to get hold of some weeping willow and bottlebrush trees and planted them around the sides. A weir was created to drain into the river and we went to the Government Fisheries and obtained the tilapia bream to stock our ponds. However, because we couldn't afford to line our hollow, though it filled satisfactorily in the rains, it wouldn't hold through the long dry season and one of the interior walls subsided. Reluctantly we relinquished that idea. We planted bulrushes and yellow iris around the perimeter and went looking for lots of water-hyacinth roots which we planted in the mud as the rains began. In time, it did hold water much better as the bottom knitted and settled. We had ourselves a small lake, secluded, peaceful and lovely, that attracted many birds, including migrants.

Originally, we had created a tiny island in the middle of the lake, and thinking it might be nice to see some ducks and geese paddling round, we put one weeping willow and some nesting boxes on it. But that experiment didn't work because they attracted predators. Our poultry was an ongoing target but our stock was penned and the losses were comparatively small. The civet and the genet were among the most common small predators we had to deal with. They are nocturnal and the genet is particularly adept at climbing.

We saved one family of orphaned ducklings and they adopted a visiting hitch-hiker. He'd taken over the job of feeding them and one day, when their pen door was open, they ran after him. Everywhere he went the ducklings would trail in a line at his heels, even down to the lake to swim. He joked, saying he was tempted to take them with him when he left, but couldn't figure out how to train them to fly over the customs post at Chirundu on the Zambezi. I laughed and said it was more a matter of ensuring they knew where to land safely as customs officials probably had big cooking pots.

Beside the small spring that fed the lake was a small shed. We used it as a temporary calf pen and later it was adapted to house a couple of youngsters. A couple of years later, in response to the need of a friend, we extended it again, raised the walls to create a mezzanine floor as a bedroom and re-thatched it. When the children were given a small boat one Christmas, it was habitually moored nearby and the little house was named the 'Boat House'. For fun, we made the two windows in the back wall circular like large portholes to enhance the 'boat' theme.

The downstairs guestroom of the old destroyed house was restored. The walls were the least damaged of all, because of the room built above it. We roofed it, complete with a solar heater. Its French windows opened directly on to the lawn overlooking the garden and although the metal door frames had been slightly warped in the fire, they were still usable. In time, it became known as the Garden Room. Time revealed one indisputable fact: shortage of cash was no hindrance to the Holy Spirit. As the various guestrooms came into being, they were furnished to a standard that I had devised after much prayer and thought on the subject.

No matter what size, shape or location, each room, in addition to the necessary bed, contained a chest-of-drawers-cum-dressing-table, mirror, bedside table, reading lamp, desk and chair, and a towel rail. All rooms had a bookcase half stocked with a bible and Christian books, whereas the other half offered a varied selection of classic secular books. Many of the rooms had a small veranda. Although guests ate supper with the family and sometimes joined us for our devotional/music evenings, I felt it was also essential for them to have some privacy.

As each room was completed, I searched the second-hand furniture mart in town for likely pieces. Sometimes we'd hear of a house sale and go along. Mostly, I renovated and polished, and finished by sewing pretty curtains and bedcovers. When the room was ready, it was dedicated and I would pray there for whomever would come.

In the early days, after a guest had left, the room would be cleaned and I'd only make the bed up after someone arrived. But learning through very late arrivals, emergencies and other unexpected needs, I changed that. As soon as a room was vacated, it was cleaned and the bed made ready again. Then I would go there, taking flowers, to pray. The flowers would be renewed every three days, so they were always fresh whether the room was occupied or empty. The first person to actually thank me for this was a Vietnam War veteran from America who had arrived in a very exhausted and distressed state. He said when he entered the room and saw a posy of sweet-peas and honeysuckle on the bedside table and inhaled its delicate perfume, it was the aroma of peace and rest to him.

Our dining room space was not large, and held a table that would sit twelve, fourteen at a pinch. The kitchen had four stools that fitted under a central table and another four places could be found round the sitting room table. Larger groups would be accommodated on the paved patio, which was furnished with several all-weather garden tables and chairs. Supper, particularly, was always a time of very animated conversation as everyone tucked into our plentiful home-grown produce. The children sat at my end of the long table. On one memorable evening, under the cover of the hubbub, I rather sharply told them to take their elbows off the table. There was a moment of absolute silence as nine other people stopped talking abruptly, and nine other pairs of elbows were guiltily lowered.

Time passed and other rooms were added. 'The Hut', a small thatched and whitewashed converted garden shed beside the rose garden and near a large jacaranda tree, was covered in bougainvillea. 'The Beehive', built utilizing several curved roofing sheets that a friend donated, resembled a wide dome and was surrounded by ferns and frangipani. 'The Cabin' stood beside the path to the dairy and had a veranda flanked with prickly-pear bushes. The old children's nursery with its ivy-covered walls simply became 'The Ivy Room'. Finally, 'The Cottage', with tiny flower beds flanking the front step and the whole half-hidden amid coral creeper and lemon trees, overlooked a field.

Our noticeboard was the back of the inner kitchen door. School routine and farm work shaped our days. On Sundays everyone was invited to join with the family for church and other gatherings on the farm for worship and prayer, but no pressure was put on. In every room there was a copy of our 'welcome / house rules'. Many visitors hadn't lived in a structured Christian home, but this in itself gave rise to many a discussion and opportunity to present the gospel. On a rota, visitors were expected to help with some chores, in our shared space, such as washing the dishes.

The kitchen was the hub of the house. The east window looked out over the drive. From the back door that opened onto the patio we could see all the way down to the river. Countless meals were prepared while getting to know people and many a late-night drink was shared round its central table as serious enquirers delved into the life of faith and grew in understanding.

The kitchen light was the last to go off in the shared part of the house, and the first to go on in the morning when the doorbell rang to signal the night watchmen going off duty. Farm day staff would report and their various keys were handed out. Then, with the distant *clink* and *clatter* from the dairy borne to me on the morning breeze, I would sit on the kitchen step with a mug of tea and feed a piece of bread to my peacock. It was a precious time slot before being overtaken by the bustle of the day.

The peacock, whose unheralded appearance at the farm was the source of great delight to me, had quickly established his own routine. Not everyone appreciated his raucous cries but I rather liked to hear his ringing call punctuating the day. His routine rarely varied. After his meeting with me he walked up the farm lane, had a cursory peck around the stock feed store, strutted around the farm office building and then paraded on the roof. A little later he would disappear into the woodland beyond the dairy. He reappeared in the late afternoon, from the direction of the waterfall, displayed himself up and down the lawn, pecked about under the hibiscus hedge and finally took a potter through the rose garden to complete his day.

Occasionally Mr P., as I called him, would stroll by the turkey pens and try and interest them by a full display of his magnificent plumage, though, I have to say, the turkeys mostly ignored him. Often after rain he'd fly up on a high archway in the garden wall and drape his tail feathers in a resplendent fan against the warm brickwork to dry. It was a mystery where he spent his nights but invariably, at the sound of the kitchen doorbell next morning, he would appear from the garden and take up his position by the kitchen steps.

Although our hearts instinctively went out to anyone who came to us, it was a concern in the early days about how well we would be able to communicate with so many diverse people, from different backgrounds and nationalities. The Lord had confirmed his calling by anointing me with the gift of hospitality and the ability to discern needs before they were spoken. I was able to lovingly accept people just as they were. Scripture tells us that Jesus met people right where they were; they did not change until after their encounter with him. Most people did not take advantage of us in the freedom that was offered, and we had trusted God with the risk of being 'ripped off' from the beginning.

That so many people in so many diverse ways found their way to us never ceased to amaze us. Undreamed of by us, it became evident that there was an invisible network of connections in odd places and in strange circumstances. We attributed this to the hand of God. Situated barely eleven miles west of the city on a country road, we had always thought of ourselves as being 'off the beaten track' but we found out that in many cases the beaten track led straight to our door. We never knew what to expect when we opened the door. Many stories were awesome.

One incident was shared with a teenager staying with us, a lad who came to us through friends. It was just before the house was completed. The builder was finishing our bedroom that week and Gordon and I were sleeping temporarily in the old, hastily repaired kitchen. I woke up after an awful nightmare of being pursued by a ghostly fluffy mauve dog. Every time I tried to catch it, my hand would pass clean through it and the enormous animal would evaporate, only to keep coming back to threaten us. Shakily I got up and went to the door. It was dawn and I stood on the doorstep and looked across the lawn. A strange dog stood facing me, snarling and frothing at the mouth and I guessed it was rabid.

At that moment the door of the main house opened as one of the children let our own dog out. Screaming to the child to get back inside the house and shut the door, I called to my husband urgently. The intruder had turned and slunk into some bushes and our dog followed barking frantically. They fought furiously, terrifyingly, until the rabid animal slunk off. Our young visitor came out and tried to catch our dog, while I was screaming for him to be careful, well aware of the danger that dog had presented. Not long afterwards, the terrible dog was found on a neighbouring plot and our neighbour fortunately had a gun and shot it; when he took the body to the government vet, the dog was confirmed as being rabid. The children were unharmed but when we looked our dog over we realized the danger. He was not injured, but his muzzle, shoulders and throat were covered in the mad dog's saliva. When he was brought into the house again, both the lad and our children had handled and petted him. Between them they had a cut finger, a scratch or two and a couple of grazed knees. We bundled everyone in the car and headed for the doctor in town. He thought it wise to be on the safe side and recommended we all have the rabies vaccination which, at that time, consisted of fourteen daily injections round the navel, and sent us off to the chemist for the serum.

Back at the surgery we all lined up outside the doctor's office. The children were scared and I was doing my best to reassure them. When the call came, our young friend offered to go first – "just to show the kids there's really nothing to be frightened of," he said. Minutes later he reappeared at the door, white as a sheet.

"Nothing to it, kids," he quipped and hit the floor in a dead faint.

It is not that easy to take three small children day after day for injections. They stung like wasp stings and as the course built up, all our tummies itched like mad. But mum and dad routed the group home via the toyshop and the ice cream parlour on alternate days and we got through. On the second Sunday, Gordon and I were both caught standing on the church steps talking to friends, both unconsciously scratching our stomachs.

In the interest of public health and safety, there would be periodic government 'tie-ups' when the public were warned to keep all their dogs kennelled or tied up between certain dates. Then the Government Veterinary Service would patrol the town and suburbs shooting every loose dog without exception.

Our workload increased, with building and the growing farm, and we added to our staff steadily. An amusing side to employing Zambians was their liking for several names; each had a family or tribe name, often a different childhood name, often a nickname, and many chose another name they liked when they grew up. Often these names were of things they particularly liked. Among our staff we had a Thousand, a Tickey (after the Rhodesian name for the old silver three-penny bit), the exceptionally tall Size, a Scissors and a Sixpence, but my favourite was Ikwanira our tractor driver. He was the youngest of a very large family and his mother had named him Ikwanira which means, 'That's enough!'

All this time the farm was growing to include sheep and an expanding dairy. We were specializing in pullet rearing. Brooder houses and growing pens went up and our stock was being shipped all over the country. On the side we had small flocks of layers and table birds, and even experimented with a few coffee bushes. With irrigation we could grow fruit and vegetables all year round. We were well on the way to being self-sufficient food-wise.

CHAPTER ELEVEN

The Open Gate

The steady flow of people continued, each with a story about how they had found us: perhaps by a chance meeting with someone who'd been already; some had heard about us in a letter from a friend; and many acknowledged God's hand had guided them.

It was the era of hippie backpackers who roamed the world in search of adventure, other cultures and faiths, or who had simply 'dropped out'. Many of these travelled through Africa, hoping to find work in South Africa or planning to go on to sample the delights of India. They came singly, in pairs, groups or even as part of an organized expedition. Many ran into problems, being robbed, mugged, falling ill and a host of other tribulations. Among this throng were some consciously or subconsciously on a spiritual pilgrimage. God had his loving hand on so many and it was clear to us that he played a definite part in many of their circumstances.

Some of our visitors expressed surprise that the farm was not quite what they expected, though no one was able to say what that expectation was. Whatever they said on arrival, a hidden need or a deeper purpose would soon become evident. In this quiet backwater, they found the time and opportunity to explore, learn and think, as well as consider the things of God in relation to themselves. There were many stories but it was from those who found God that we heard of the most extraordinary contacts.

One man received directions to us, jotted down and given to him on a boat on the Red Sea. While travelling through Lusaka, a girl became ill and was stranded in the hospital and was given our phone number by a Christian nurse. A university student, after her gap year travels, wrote to her friend in Holland and mentioned her stay at the farm. A year later that Dutch girl came and spent time with us, and found Christ. A motorist, travelling after dark, came across a hitchhiker stranded in the pouring rain and gave him a lift to our gate. Robbed and in pain, another traveller was found beside the road on the outskirts of town and brought to us in a truck. He stayed three months and left a renewed man. One Zambian businesswoman sent a traumatized and exhausted traveller to us in her own chauffeur-driven vehicle after he'd collapsed in her café in the town.

Meeting practical needs, even feeding people, called for ingenuity at times. Very late one night, I nearly came to grief at the hand of our vigilant night-watchman. I'd pulled on an old coat and crept into the kitchen garden in search of some salad stuff to round out the meal I was hastily concocting for a carload of people just arrived. A rapid pounding on our door at bedtime one stormy night presented us with a challenge. A westbound minibus had broken down right near the junction where our lane joined the main road. There were nine mission hospitable nurses on board and they had walked in tired, damp and muddy. Our house was full so while they cleaned up and sat down to soup and sandwiches, a hasty rummage was taking place behind the scenes for as many spare blankets and sleeping bags as we could muster. Finally, I said goodnight to nine cocooned figures packed on my sitting-room carpet, and went to bed.

To start with we knew nothing about LSD and other drugs but as an occasional episode turned up among the guests, as with other new situations presented to us, mainly from our somewhat freewheeling young travellers, we dealt with them with a mixture of tact, discipline, compassion and practical assistance from their fellow travellers. Somehow, we all kept our balance and got through. One of the other ingredients in our household was the presence of other Christians and missionaries from all over the territories, on a short break or staying over before flying overseas or returning, plus the Christians among our staff. It was an interesting mix of many nationalities, Christians and unbelievers, young and old, workers and family. Everyone had something to contribute and a valuable part to play.

The travelling fraternity were not the only ones to come. In addition to the aforesaid missionaries from America, Sweden, Denmark, Canada,

Switzerland and Germany, there were refugees from Angola, South Africa and several other African countries. A sprinkling of local people came into our orbit, Portuguese from Mozambique and people who had settled here after World War 2, from Poland, Greece, Italy, Romania, Yugoslavia and other parts of Africa. Big civil engineering consortiums came in to build our hydroelectric dams, airports, roads and bridges, and their children went to school with ours. Often our work brought us into contact with several diplomatic personnel among whom we also found friends. Through our church we met several foreign teachers from Lusaka's colleges of further education and the university together with members of the Salvation Army. In one year alone we had nine Japanese visitors. And so our sphere of contacts built up.

One very unusual opportunity presented us with the chance to offer aid to a Russian lady and her child, stranded after her Zambian husband had died They stayed with us while waiting for the diplomatic channels to clear the way for their repatriation. In an extraordinary sequence of events, a lovely North Korean girl working as a teacher in Lusaka was brought to us because she was having a housing problem. She was delightful but an Embassy car whisked her away a week later. Perhaps they were afraid of her being influenced by Western Christians. She had so enjoyed those few days with us and we'd loved her; we all wept when she secreted a New Testament in her pocket. Some weeks later, I saw her in the town, though I didn't have a chance to speak to her. She saw me as I approached and gave me a little wave, and I saw her eyes filled with tears as she was hustled away by her companions.

These many glimpses into the lives and problems of other cultures prompted us to begin a collection of foreign language books and bibles. When some of our foreign missionary friends heard of this project, they happily gave us something from their own bookshelves. Most of our visitors had a good command of English but for some it was helpful if they were able to read and study in their own mother tongue.

In addition to the books in the rooms, we turned the old kitchen into a library and bought several tape players and a large selection of cassette tapes by some of the world's leading Christian expositors and teachers, and introduced our guests to them. The Christian Literature Crusade in England generously gave us a grant that we greatly appreciated. It was great to be able to give someone a bible or guidance literature in their own language so readily.

The family and some members of our staff came together each week for a devotional evening and music, usually Grace on her guitar. It was held in the sitting room and all visitors were invited. Sometimes, those who had declined were later discovered sitting on the patio where they could hear everything through the open windows. At one particular time when we had a large group of interested people, a Bible teacher friend came out from our church to hold weekly sessions. If there were any missionary friends staying with us, they could usually be relied upon to contribute.

The arrangement whereby all who came to the farm could stay for only three full days worked very well. We took no cash payment but for those who stayed, work was arranged according to their skills. Quite often a person planning to move on after the three days changed their mind and asked to stay longer. Some stayed a couple of weeks, some for as long as several months. Length of stay was often dictated by their visas but God had a hand in it all. Their work contribution could assist in the house, on the farm or on our campsite project, 'Evangelical Outreach'.

A woman came from New York and confessed she had never actually worked in a garden. So she was placed alongside one of our gardeners and it was lovely to see her enjoying strawberries after she had learned how to weed them. A trawler fisherman from Scotland realized his boyhood ambition to drive a tractor. A man traumatized through illness and loss found peace working in the rose garden my mother had planted for me. An Australian TV producer trying to rebuild her life found a lot of pleasure in helping to arrange a wedding in our garden. Others mended our cars, painted our walls, helped with the driving, tended our stock and mended our fences. Many times I was reminded of the words of Isaiah 61: "Aliens will shepherd your flocks; foreigners will work your fields..."

Everyone enjoyed the fruits of the kitchen, from Danish baking, to Israeli and Greek cooking, to a Swedish girl's artistry in icing a birthday cake. Some learned to churn butter, grow vegetables and sew. Everything needful was accomplished. In addition to the commercial quantities of produce we sold, the farm produced a very high percentage of all the food we needed: pigs, poultry, lamb and sometimes beef; our dairy provided milk, butter, cream and cheese; and we had fruit and vegetables all year round. I made all the preserves, jams, marmalade, pickles and pâté.

Just about everything did well. The exception was my experiment with turkeys. My rosy imagination had me providing economical suppers, holiday feasts and posh dinners, but my ideas soon bit the dust of reality. I had not reckoned on dogs, civets and other feral cats, marauding snakes, hawks and the turkey's own suicidal tendencies.

With some difficulty we tracked down and purchased fifty newly hatched turkey chicks and put them in a chicken brooder house with a batch of layer chicks. It was fascinating to watch their fast growth. After only three weeks they stood above the other chicks as if on stilts. But as the heat was reduced and the time arrived for the flock to go into their growing-on pen, the turkeys objected fiercely. Awkward and fussy, they huddled and fiddled with their food. By the end of the first month, they just stood around in scrawny discontent. Despite our efforts in separating them and putting them into a pleasant, shady, outdoor, covered pen they refused to co-operate and stood sulking in the corner. One by one they gave up until only a handful reached maturity.

Not willing to admit defeat, we decided to keep the survivors and try and breed from them. To my delight eggs were laid and sat on. In due time they hatched but we were not the only watchers. The genets picked off the chicks, then killed the adult birds. The morning came when only ripped wire and bloody scattered feathers remained. The great turkey experiment was over.

When we established our small flock of sheep, there was great excitement. Now there would be baby lambs as well as calves, chicks, ducklings, kittens and puppies for the children to enjoy. Whenever one of the children had a birthday party, entertainment was easy. Mums could enjoy tea on the patio while the children ran off to sample all these delights, go and see the tractor working and maybe get a ride on the trailer, then round to watch the cows being milked. Then they'd all troupe back to the patio where they could take turns with the ice cream paddle.

Size (the tall one) was our shepherd lad. Early one Monday when helping out in a chicken house, he suddenly cried out and fell over, unconscious. His workmates ran to fetch me and I rushed up there, but he appeared to be dead. I tried artificial respiration without success. Gordon was already in town in another vehicle so I snatched blankets from the house and while his mates wrapped and carried him out, I backed up the pickup truck to receive his body, designating one of the men to sit with him as we drove to the hospital.

As I drove, over and above my shock, my mind was scrabbling with a dozen questions. Could he have been electrocuted? We had installed our own electrics but under the supervision of a visitor who was an electrician. Could it have been faulty? He had been checking the automatic water lines. He'd been working barefoot, as did many of our farm staff in the dry season. Even the other poultry-man working in the same building had jumped to the conclusion that "the electric grabbed him" and, with great presence of mind, leapt to shut off the main switch.

At the hospital, Size was officially declared dead and an autopsy was ordered. He was only twenty-one years old. Shaken, I returned home to find his family already waiting, lined up, sitting in the road outside our house, wailing and sobbing. It was awful. When Gordon returned he immediately checked on the wiring in that pen but couldn't find any fault. Two agonizing days later, the coroner's report told us that this gentle boy had died of a blood clot to the brain. Later, his family told us that he had suffered dizzy spells and had fallen over a few times that weekend but nobody had mentioned it or noticed anything amiss when work had begun that morning.

The basic work of the farm was carried out with our regular, paid staff. This was our family's livelihood and its success enabled us to fund other endeavours such as our campsite project for young people. Some of our visitors enjoyed working in the fields or with livestock alongside our Zambian farm hands. One of the traveller girls later became a student at one of England's prestigious agricultural colleges, the director of which was acquainted with Gordon. Consequently, arrangements were made to allow this young lady to come to us for her official practical studies in tropical agriculture. We gave her a piece of land and an assistant to conduct field trials and later Gordon arranged for her to do similar work on a cattle ranch in the north and at the sugar plantations on the Kafue. The result was so excellent that the college sent us other students over the next few years, as did other colleges. All these applications were prayed over and in due time a considerable number found faith in Christ.

The eclectic mix of talents helped things along enormously. Along with the carpenters, builders and mechanics, there were painters, cooks and musicians. Most precious of all, there was always time to talk. A lot of our meals were taken outside on the patio and there were barbecues and film shows of all sorts. On Christmas Eve there would be a carol service on the lawns to which the neighbourhood was invited.

Christmastime was always wonderful. We always managed some sort of a decorated tree. Our traditions, in which our guests participated, started with the workers being off duty except for a skeleton dairy staff. All essential chores were done by family and guests alike. After breakfast and presents, Gordon led a short service in the sitting room, followed by communion for those who wanted it. I cooked dinner followed by an afternoon for games, a football match (staff versus house) if fine, but as it was the rainy season, more often than not our collection of board games came into their own. The following day, dinner was cooked for us by a volunteer and, weather permitting, there was a farm-wide treasure hunt. The holiday was always topped off by a family visit to the theatre in the city.

Three weddings were celebrated, with receptions in the garden, all catered for by our own combined talents. Sometimes Gordon would invite guests to go on fishing trips, or to the game park. He loved going off the main road to where his knowledge of the flora and fauna of the region greatly enhanced the experience.

Many of the old Rhodesian roads were 'strip roads' – narrow twin tar strips where, despite the balancing act required when passing another vehicle, were a great improvement over dirt roads, especially in the rains, as were the single-track roads, nine feet wide. Both these required a driver to keep one set of wheels off the tar when passing another vehicle. Gradually over the years, these old roads were up-graded but however we got there, invariably the fascination of going deep into the bush to see the huge variety of wild animals never diminished.

Overland expedition tours that plied between London and Johannesburg also found their way to the farm. Mostly they were converted Bedford trucks carrying up to twenty people, and self-sufficient. The first driver to find his way to us came with a request. He'd met someone who knew us and who had given him directions. Gordon was busy that morning in the paddocks near the farm main gate and looked up when he heard the Bedford truck drive through and stop. The driver leaned from the cab window and called out.

"I'm looking for Gordon Bland."

"You've found him." Gordon left the paddock and the driver stepped down. He pushed his battered hat back and stepped forward to shake hands. Several faces peered down from under the rolled-up canvas sides of the truck. He spoke for a few moments and Gordon waved towards the farmhouse. The driver climbed aboard and slowly drove down the drive with Gordon following.

I was at the kitchen window when the truck pulled up and Gordon called to me to "put the kettle on". Telling the passengers they could have a swim in the river if they wished, he ushered the driver round to the patio. I took a tea tray out and sat down with them.

"I've had to leave one of my passengers in the hospital," the driver began.

"We're sorry to hear that. Can we help?"

"Well, yes, if you could. It'd take a load off my mind, thanks."

"Right, tell us how," I joined in.

The driver put us in the picture. The passenger had been taken ill shortly after being mugged and robbed in the town. She was expected to be in the hospital for about two weeks. He had to get his passengers to Johannesburg and couldn't afford to wait, though he'd make arrangements for her and be back through Lusaka in a few weeks.

"Look, it's no problem," I spoke up. "I'll pop in and see her. She's welcome to come to us when she leaves hospital and we'll take it from there." I looked across at Gordon for confirmation and he nodded. "Don't worry. Come and see us on your return trip."

"Would it be possible for us to camp here?" the driver asked, looking round. "We've been using that old camp ground just south of town but it's pretty rough."

"Well, yes, I think so," Gordon looked thoughtful. Then more emphatically, "Yes, do that. I'll show you where."

When the truck arrived a month later, the girl was restored to health and in possession of a new passport. Money had arrived from her family and she was eager to be on her way again. But now she was also seriously interested in the gospel of Christ. And so began another phase of our ministry.

Word spread among the drivers of that company and inevitably to other expedition tours also. Soon there was regular traffic of this sort. A simple site was set aside for their use under the shade of some big Cassia trees near the edge of a small plantation of blue gums. Passengers could spread their tents in the woods between the site and the river and were welcome to all we had to offer. They were self-sufficient but enjoyed being able to get fresh milk and produce. There were also plenty of opportunities to mingle with the other residents and they were always invited to whatever was going on. Over the years the interaction with these groups always brought interest, challenges and opportunities to be of service. Not surprisingly, here too was a harvest field in which God moved.

CHAPTER TWELVE

Answers

In all these busy years we had not been back to see our family since 1964. Now, after ten years, I took the opportunity to go to England. I travelled via Switzerland where I visited L'Abri to assist a friend who had been taken ill there. On the way back I stopped over for a few days in Germany with a young friend who had lived with us for the best part of a year. But although I benefited greatly for the break, the worsening pain I'd suffered in my back for years became crippling and I had to take to my bed again.

In 1975, after a particularly difficult bout, Gordon decided we should both go to England, and just before we left, I asked the leaders from the Baptist church in town to come to the farm specifically to pray for my healing. But the problem remained.

By our departure date in October, I was exhausted. Deep down I could not reconcile the prognosis from my doctor, which was that I would be permanently disabled, possibly in a wheelchair within a few years, with the vision I was sure God had given me concerning his work at the farm. Accordingly, I privately resolved to seek out and consult a Christian doctor when I reached England, someone I hoped I could talk to who might understand the spiritual dimension to my situation.

By this time the farm had grown large enough for us to employ a young ex-patriot farm manager, a young man who'd first come to our notice years ago as a VSO teacher. So with the house and farm in good hands, we set off. On arrival we stayed with friends in Purley, London for a few days and on the Sunday we accompanied them to Purley Baptist Church. Before a full church, the pastor got up to pray and, referring to the many people and missions habitually prayed for, said that this day he wanted each person to pray for *one thing for themselves.* And so, in pain and in faith, I silently and simply asked, "Lord, what about my back?"

There was no appreciable difference in my condition except a very slight reduction in pain which I thought was probably due to the fact I was able to rest more now we were on holiday. Three weeks later I found a dedicated Christian doctor in Birmingham, easily accessible from my mother's home, and accordingly made an appointment. Subsequently, an appointment was set up for me to see a specialist in Birmingham General Hospital. When the day came, the specialist was rather abrupt and tersely informed me that there was nothing wrong with my back. His manner suggested I was wasting his time. As I walked down Corporation Street towards the bus station, I felt a little dazed and slowly the realization came to me that my back was healed. To this day, that pain has never returned.

Though quietly thrilled and thanking God, I did not make a big thing of it immediately. Gordon was away visiting some of his family so I decided to wait and give it the test of time. Then something rather extraordinary happened. After a week or so, a letter arrived from the hospital in a brown 'window' envelope. When I opened it, it was in fact the consultant's follow-up letter to my doctor, confirming what he'd said to me even down to a chiding expression of his surprise I'd even been sent to him in the first place.

If ever I was to have doubts, I now had proof positive in my hand. Over the telephone the doctor shared my joy and gave thanks as I explained that the letter had been folded incorrectly so that the patient's name and address, mine, was shown in the envelope's window instead of hers. I promised to send the letter on.

The children were growing up, and the following year, plans were set in motion for Grace to go to Bible College in England. Things were going well on the farm and a friend came to act as housekeeper. My parting instructions to our temporary housekeeper had an amusing sequel. I reminded her not to forget to make the best of the available fruit, especially the plentiful guavas. When I returned I was met with doleful tales of guavas appearing in every guise at breakfast, lunch and supper for weeks, everybody declaring emphatically they never wanted to see a guava ever again!

From the early days of the farm's 'open gate', the wide variety of our visitors had enriched all our lives. We had laughed and cried, believed and prayed together, laboured and supported one another, and many wonderful things had happened. Not all our visitors were young. A lady in her early sixties came to us from Australia. In her working life she had worked in the cutting rooms of an *haute couture* fashion house in London and was a talented seamstress. She was Swiss by birth and had discovered she was a twin, separated at birth. She'd tracked her sister to Germany and, after a wonderful visit there, had, written to us through a contact of ours and asked if she could visit on her way home; she'd always longed to see Africa and meet the people. She was a prayer warrior, an intercessor who was very supportive to me, and she didn't want to go after her ninety-day visa was up. This was at a time when it was almost impossible to get more than ninety days as a visitor, and to get a Work Permit one had to apply from outside Zambia. She went to the consulate and sat praying. When she came home that day, she told us that she'd simply said she had a heart for the African people and wanted to stay and do some Christian voluntary work among them. She got her permission and stayed with us almost three years, learning the rudiments of the local language while teaching some of our African staff and a few local lads English. Some of them she taught to read and then she spiritually mentored them.

Whatever the ups and downs in our family or in the farm business, God's gracious Spirit was quietly at work changing lives and giving new direction to many. Several times our visitors confessed that the farm was an unexpected oasis on their journey. In the early days when we were seeking guidance regarding the ministry, I'd received a vision of Christ standing at our river with arms outstretched. Now we were seeing our beloved *manzi-amoyo* being a source of pleasure and peace to many, and several people were baptized there. Its *bilharzia*-free spring water was safe, revitalizing body and spirit. Nothing more dangerous dwelt there than the tiny fresh water crabs which nibbled the feet and tickled the swimmers.

There were a few people early on in the ministry whose time with us was particularly significant in as much as their friendship and support benefitted us long afterwards. Their witness led to us becoming better known and a few returned to work with us for a while. Many agreed after their visit that when they had been in crisis or totally unable to control their circumstances, God's hand had manifestly been at work to bring them to a spiritual awakening.

Mary came to Zambia first as a Canadian volunteer and returned later to do postgraduate research. We first met her when she was working among the Tonga people and later, when she came up to Lusaka to finish her studies, we met her again. Occasionally she would come out to the farm, and we became friends. Although she had given up her search for God and embraced the free lifestyle of her North American University, it was her testimony that while she was at our farm, God crept up on her, bringing her to new faith and commitment. Later, in her life as a professor of clinical psychology, she played a significant part in intellectual circles.

Now and then it wasn't possible to gauge someone's reaction to what they experienced while with us. All were accepted and loved and sent on their way with our blessing. In England my brother read a long passage in a travel book he'd bought that revealed the author's lasting impression of a stopover he'd made while travelling in Zambia. It was clearly recognisable as being our farm. When my brother told me, I remembered one rainy night the previous year when we'd come across this man several miles outside Lusaka. He was travelling the world on a motorcycle which had broken down. We rescued him and brought him home with us for a couple of days while his bike got mended.

Leaving Mkushi, some two hundred miles north-east of Lusaka, where we had been visiting friends, we gave a lift to a hitch-hiker who waved us down. Close up, he looked in poor condition, and once in the car it was clear he was running a fever, so instead of dropping him off in the town, we brought him home. He was from Chile and although Spanish was his language, his English was very good. Travelling on his own in East Africa, he had been set upon and robbed of all his money, passport and pack. Making his way to Nairobi, he lived rough, sleeping outdoors, while waiting to get his new passport. Once he had it, he aimed to travel south to South Africa to find work. The weeks of poor living and scant food had taken their toll and he'd become ill. Later he told us he'd responded to the gospel when he was young but had drifted since.

When he recovered he stayed on and offered his professional skills to lay the electric power lines across the river and afterwards he completed the wiring to our buildings there. It was a major contribution and saved us a great deal of money. In his spare time our Chilean friend demonstrated great skill at the sewing machine and, having received an anonymous cash gift from someone in the house, he made new clothing, a tent and a knapsack. When he left several weeks later, he was fully kitted out but also with a Spanish bible in his bag.

A group of Christians from Europe who were travelling in Kenya became stranded when their air charter company went broke. With them was an American veteran soldier. The group hitch-hiked south, and when they reached Lusaka, they found their way to the American Embassy where they met a friend of ours and he directed them out to the farm. The American, who had only recently been freed from heroin addition, had planned to get married in Switzerland upon his return from Africa. Now the delays had seriously messed up that plan and his bride-to-be in Switzerland was understandably anxious. He had recently come to faith in Christ but because of this setback he was considerably stressed.

I welcomed them in and offered drinks all round. Among the lively group, I noticed this one tired, thin young man who'd slumped into a chair as if his legs were about to give way. Anxious blue eyes looked at me from a wan, bearded face and the hand that ineffectually pushed back his sweat-soaked hair was trembling. Diffidently he whispered a request for some water, no coffee or tea. Then he sat with hands clasped between his knees as if to still their tremor. As we talked, we realized that we were acquainted with his fiancée's family, who lived about three hundred miles away. Their daughter had been nursing in Switzerland, where the couple had met.

It was easy to get in touch with them and though they couldn't come immediately because of illness, they arranged their daughter's flight to Lusaka and we planned the wedding at the farm. It was our first wedding. In that same group were two girls from Finland who were her bridesmaids, and their dresses were made by our resident Swiss seamstress, Rosina. The girl's parents came to stay and it was a most delightful affair. Several weeks later a much stronger and stable young man took his bride back to America where they made their home.

An English teacher, on contract in Zambia, met a young civil engineer at our church in Lusaka. Both had answered our call for volunteers to help us in our outreach work. Theirs was the second wedding at the farm and we were happy to play host to both sets of parents from England. This young couple remained in Zambia and blessed us for many years with their support and friendship.

At breakfast one morning, one of our guests was expressing his concern over a letter from home with the news that his mother was ill. He'd been travelling for months and now he thought he really must go home. But, he admitted, he didn't have the money. He had been with us for a considerable time and had come to faith in Christ. Across the table a girl leaned forward and quietly said, "I've got enough. Let's go into town and get you an air ticket home." Within forty-eight hours he was on his way.

Our farm manager met his lovely bride who was the nursing sister on the casualty ward in Lusaka's teaching hospital. In time theirs was the third wedding on the farm but by no means the last romance. Once again our lovely Swiss seamstress exhibited her skills. She and I searched the town for suitable material, at one point both of us on our hands and knees in a dusty warehouse trying to match lace. The bride was tall and the result was a stunning dress of pearl grey silk, reminiscent of an 18th century gown, with deep lace ruffles falling from neck and elbows. The back fell in a half-train enhanced by tiny bows from neck to hem.

From France came a young man touring the world with only a folding bicycle, two spare T-shirts and two sets of spare socks and underwear. The bike folded down into a suitcase packed round with a few toiletries and bike spares. With that and a camera, he was travelling the world by flying to various countries and using the bike for local transport. His ingenuity was only matched by his extremely laid-back personality and it seemed we made little impression on him. Staying only three days, he admitted he'd heard of us from a chap in a hostel somewhere and had come out of sheer curiosity. Nevertheless, many months later someone turned up who'd met our intrepid cyclist and in swopping stories our name had come up. But this time our visitor stayed and had a significant spiritual experience.

Two young women from Australia who had cycled vast distances through East Africa came down from Dar-es-Salaam on the train, where they had encountered someone else on their way to us. When they arrived, all the rooms were full except one reserved for an expected guest. A great effort was made to squash them in as they confessed to needing a rest. But after the customary three days, these ladies asked if they could stay another week or two and, if so, could we use them in any way? I very hastily revamped a small shed near the farm office, had it scrubbed and whitewashed, and moved in two beds and an old chest of drawers. I laid grass mats on the floor, and finished it off by making curtains for the mosquito-netted windows and a couple of bright bedcovers of cheap but colourful cotton. The ladies had their own little space and afterwards the little room became our 'emergency spare'. One young woman was a woodworker and the other was a plumber. Together they completely revamped a bathroom, fitting new vanity casing and cupboards.

One rainy evening, just after dark, an overdue expedition vehicle sheered an axle a mile from the farm. It happened so suddenly that the huge Bedford truck lurched into the ditch and the eighteen passengers were thrown about. The co-driver walked in to fetch help. We despatched several cars to ferry passengers and their luggage in. One of the passengers had hit his head so hard when he fell that he was temporarily blinded. The driver stayed with the truck until we could despatch our tractor and men at first light to tow it in. The repairs necessitated waiting for spares to be flown in from England. Meanwhile the driver fell ill with hepatitis and was forced to stay on, and then there was a further delay while they waited for a replacement driver to fly out from London. Fortunately, the man with the head injury recovered and regained his sight and as soon as the replacement driver arrived, the expedition left. But two of those passengers had responded to the gospel during their enforced stopover. The driver stayed until he was completely healed.

At the approaching sound of a motorbike, I peered out of the kitchen window one afternoon, in time to see a huge Triumph braking to a halt. By the time I'd hastened out, the rider had cut the engine and was stepping down. As I took his hand in greeting, I felt the tremor. A lopsided smile did little to hide the feverish glitter in his eyes.

"Hello," he introduced himself in a Kentucky drawl. "Are you Mrs Bland?"

"Well, yes," I replied, "you'd better come in."

"Thanks." The helmet was dragged off to reveal long auburn hair.

"Come right in." I ushered him into the sitting room and waved to an easy chair. His heavy leather boots and dusty apparel didn't bother me. I had long since trusted God with the welfare of my carpet. "You're welcome. Make yourself at home. What will it be, coffee?"

"Great, thanks." He looked around and subsided into the chair with a sigh.

While he drank two cups of coffee in quick succession, I studied his face and decided he was far from well. I knew that most travellers, especially those travelling alone, feared becoming ill on the road, where towns can be hundreds of miles apart. He asked if he could stay overnight, saying someone he'd met on the road had given him our address. Without preamble, I agreed and directed him to the bathroom, then showed him to a bedroom, suggesting a rest until supper. As I laid another place at the table, I asked God to show me his particular need. At supper he didn't eat much but drank a lot and disappeared back to his room.

The next morning it was evident he was seriously ill, running a very high temperature. I bundled him into my car and drove straight to our family doctor in the city. An hour or so later we were on the way back, having stopped only to collect the prescribed medicines from a pharmacy. He lay prostrate on the rear seat, already full of antibiotics, but sweating and shivering. Once home we bedded him down in the small spare room inside the house next to the bathroom, a room often used when we had a guest who was ill.

For three days he ran a very high fever, shivering and being sick. The sound of his vomiting woke me up in the middle of the night and, putting on a dressing gown, I hurried round to his room.

I went in and heard myself say, of all ridiculous things, "Oh dear, are you being sick?"

The irrepressible one from Kentucky gave me a speaking look and drawled, "No, just practising."

We laughed about that for a long time.

Storms were responsible for a number of encounters. A couple of hitch-hikers met up in Tanzania. One of them intended to visit us when he reached Lusaka. They joined up and travelled south together and both came to the farm. Late in the day they got a lift out from town just as a heavy tropical storm hit and they had to walk in from the main road, arriving extremely wet, bedraggled and tired. There was little time that night to learn more than their names in the bustle of offering hot drinks, food, baths and bed.

However, the next morning, while the man who had originally intended to come still slept, his companion walked into my sitting-room and asked if he could talk to me. Prepared to help if I could, I invited him to sit.

"I'm a Jew," he said simply, leaning forward in his chair, "and I've been doing a lot of thinking. Can you tell me about Jesus?" That young man found the Saviour in recognising his Messiah and was one of several Jews that came our way.

About a hundred miles from the farm, sheltering from a downpour in the early hours of the morning, a group of hippie friends were waiting in the little town of Kapiri Mposhi for the train connection to Lusaka. Kapiri is where the railway from East Africa joins the Zambian system. They'd returned to Africa after travelling through India where their spiritual search had proved fruitless. By now they were almost out of money and their intention was to get down to South Africa to find work. They were huddling on the porch of a small general store. The storekeeper lived on the premises and, hearing their voices, invited them to wait inside and offered them all a hot drink.

From their general talk, the storekeeper gleaned some idea of their situation and spoke up. He knew us and before the group left for their train, he wrote our name, telephone number and directions on a slip of paper; he then gave it to one of the men, who stuffed it in his pocket and promptly forgot about it. Later that day, when they found they didn't have enough money for the train they wanted, he remembered the slip of paper and the group decided it was worth a try. They thought at least it might yield some free food and shelter until something else turned up.

It was a Saturday afternoon when the call came through and it took a while before the caller admitted that there were six of them. The farm was fairly full and I already had a whole ham in the oven. *Just as well*, I thought as I rushed round organising the extra beds while someone took the pickup to town to collect them. Next morning some of this new group accepted our invitation to accompany us to church. One of them, enthralled by what he'd heard, asked if he could go with us that evening as well. And that evening he accepted Christ and began a new life. Two of the group were a married couple. After a couple of days, while the husband went down with pneumonia, his wife also came to faith. Before the group split up and left, another man did the same. The two new Christian men spent a long time with us and ultimately both went back to Britain to study for the ministry.

A young farm worker and his wife, disillusioned by poor job prospects, left Britain to travel. Having reached Zambia, they planned to stay with us a couple of nights. They became interested in our farm and wanted to stay on and lend a hand. We gladly accepted their help and during their time with us, they met a Christian cattle rancher friend of ours who offered them a job. Not only did this couple both come to faith, but by taking up this job offer, their prospects greatly improved and they ultimately came to have a farm of their own.

CHAPTER THIRTEEN

The Storm from the South

In keeping pace with the years and expansion of our activities, we were always building. A house for the farm manager was built between the office block and the old dam. This was called 'Bethesda House' and it had a small guest wing and another spare room over the garage. It also had a siren for emergencies. For these jobs, a full-time builder had joined the staff and fairly early on we had taken on a full-time carpenter. The dining room of this house boasted a huge circular table that he had built in situ. The lay of this piece of sloping land and its rocky outcrops enabled us to design a house that stood high above its front lawn with a wide set of steps leading up to the front door, and we used the rocky outcrops to create aloe gardens.

One Sunday morning at our church, we were introduced to a family that had recently arrived in town. They had three children and the husband explained that he had been employed as a builder by a mission station but his contract was up and he had come down to Lusaka looking for work. We had started to build a small house on the north boundary of our property which wasn't very far from the homestead. Work had come to a standstill because we'd had to pull the builder off to work on the farm manager's house as it was needed more urgently. Since he was a builder, Gordon offered him accommodation for his family in exchange for his building skills. They put their children into school in Lusaka and his wife also helped us in the library and the house. This smaller, three-bedroomed house was named 'Sharon Cottage' and after completion they lived in it for a while. Not long after they left, we added a stone chimney and fireplace to the sitting room;

this time the work was done by another traveller whose skills were his contribution for staying.

We sold off our produce by the half-ton daily after taking all we needed. In addition, some was sold on our local milk round and we had a contract with a safari company whose headquarters were just a mile away from our farm. We also had regular outlets, locally and in the town, for our laying birds when they were culled, and were busy establishing a specialist business for raising stock for other farmers nationwide.

My husband's particular pleasure was the flower garden. My mother had established a rose garden for me on her visit in '69, and the jacaranda and flame trees were now fully mature. At one end of the rose garden there was a knoll overlooking the lake; here we planted a Japanese plum tree, a lime tree and a cluster of ginger bushes. On the other side of the bottom lawn, a clump of bamboo trees clung to the riverbank and behind them the rising land was covered in blue gums, a plantation we had painstakingly planted many years earlier.

While I took pleasure in the flower garden, it was the vegetable garden that attracted me more, perhaps because of the connection with the need to feed the family. The only flowers in my care totally were sweet peas which I grew on a field scale for the florists in the city. I brought fresh flowers into the house and guest rooms almost daily, but as the feel of a warm brown egg in the palm of my hand pleased me, so I had pleasure in the rain-shiny gloss on purple aubergines or the crisp snapping sound as the green peppers were picked, and the feel of cool, silky cucumbers.

Chabaila was middle-aged when he came to us from our local rancher friend who sold up and left the country. Originally trained on the copper mines as a cabinet maker, he'd worked on our friend's farm for several years and could turn his hand to anything. Whether it was making furniture, setting roof timbers or stringing wire for a new paddock fence, everything he did was meticulously right first time. He was a tall, quiet bambo. Before coming to us he had lost a finger in a threshing machine accident and his wrinkled face was marred by one eye that had been damaged by a spitting cobra; but he had such natural kindliness and dignity, one was hardly aware of this defect.

Early one morning, I asked Chabaila to make me six seed boxes, asking him to do them as quickly as possible and therefore expected them in an hour or two at the most. When he hadn't brought them by midday, I went to his workshop to enquire. There I found him carefully sanding down the last of his tongue-and-grooved works of art. It seemed almost a shame to put soil in them.

It took me a while to learn about what would grow best, and when, and to get the planting sequence right so that we had a continuous supply of vegetables and fruit all year round. But early efforts with our Zambian gardeners nearly produced my first racial crisis. At this time we only had a couple of workers, who also helped out with the livestock. I collared them one afternoon and attempted to explain what I wanted them to do.

"*Bwerani, bwerani kuno,*" I called to the nearest man. ("Come, come here.") "*Tengani khasu ku khya,*" I instructed as he came to me.

Well, I thought, as he came back from the tool shed with a hoe, *that went well.* Then came the dangerous bit as I tried to explain that I wanted the weeds hoed out and the carrots thinned. He kept nodding so I went back to the house. Just before tea he appeared at the back door indicating he had finished. I followed him to the garden.

The newly turned earth now flanked the rampart weeds and the carrots lay in wilting heaps along the paths. I very nearly screamed at the men, but I managed to control my frustration and suddenly saw the funny side of it all; I weakly leant against a fence post as gales of laughter overcame me. The men stared at me with pained expressions but I couldn't attempt to explain. It was knocking off time so I merely waved them away and mopped my face, thinking, *I'll try again tomorrow. Wow, I do believe I can take Africa on the chin and laugh.* But it would not always be so.

A dark element had entered our lives and its tentacles reached out and touched us all. In the midst of peace and our rejoicing over the spiritual harvest, we were jolted into an awareness that terrible things were happening in the south which was now being revealed in the changed personal attitudes of some local people and the first stirrings of civil unrest closer to home. At first, it was not easy for us to see the incipient threat for what it was: the first rumblings of all-out war. Yet it was to devour us all.

An unknown group from another province booked the use of our facility over the river. There was nothing in their letter-headed inquiry to suggest they were anything other than a genuine Christian group. So they came and camped for five days. Gordon, who had been away from home at the onset, returned and was very unhappy about it. But by then they were halfway through their intended stay and we decided to allow them to finish. However, some of our staff, whose quarters were nearby, were uneasy and reported talk of political meetings, not gospel, and strange rituals instead of evening campfire singsongs. In anger, Gordon said he'd go over after our evening meal and see for himself. Taking a good torch, he went off at about 7.30pm.

Time passed and the children went to bed. I took hot drinks into the group round the log fire in the sitting room. More time went by and he still hadn't returned when everyone but me had gone to bed. Feeling anxious, I unaccountably recalled my husband telling me years ago that when he had been in government service in Nyasaland many years previously, he had gone to see an African tribal initiation ceremony forbidden to white people. Surely this could not be something along those lines?

When he came back he was grey-faced and uncommunicative. He pushed my questions aside and tersely told me to go to bed. As I lay awake I could hear him gasping and gagging in the bathroom. I never did learn just what he'd seen; he admitted later that he'd watched hidden behind a tree. By morning the group had gone and the incident slipped behind us as more pressing concerns held our attention.

Among our staff at the time we had two brothers; one worked in the dairy and the other in the garden. One Saturday evening, after drinking rather too much homemade *chibuka,* the brothers had fallen into a fierce argument and a fight broke out. Naturally anything that happened in off-duty hours did not concern us and we knew nothing about this until, shortly after dawn on Sunday, our off-duty dairyman arrived at the kitchen door. He was badly hung over, with a hideous wound across his face. Part of his nose had been bitten off and he pathetically offered me the shrivelled piece in a brown paper bag, still covered in dirt and blood. Could I take him to the hospital? His brother reported for work on Monday with half his cheek torn away. It was far too late to restore the nose, and the other's cheek puckered as the crater healed. Though both continued to work for us, it was evident they weren't so close anymore and we never found out just what element in their fight had sparked such ferocious anger. But constantly seeing their mutilated faces around the place was a disturbing reminder of the latent savagery around us.

The "winds of change" referred to by the British parliamentary leader Harold Macmillan, way back in 1960, were beginning to be seriously felt. It had been acknowledged long since in the South African parliament that the African National Congress was awakening everywhere. The wind of change was blowing through the whole continent and the growth of this consciousness was already a political fact. The 'lion of revolution' had stirred and stretched and was beginning to roar. Forces were set in motion that could not be quelled and a more complex future faced us all.

After Southern Rhodesia's unilateral declaration of independence, the unrest there had steadily gathered momentum and its effects were becoming more visible. By the mid '70s it was no longer safe to travel through that country and the overland expedition companies, who were booked well ahead, had to adapt a policy of driving south as far as Lusaka and flying their passengers over, where they were met in South Africa to complete their trip. Those joining expeditions in Johannesburg to travel north were flown to Lusaka in like manner. If the trucks meeting groups in Lusaka were not on schedule, we collected groups at the airport and accommodated them in the meanwhile. And at this time it was deemed unwise to pitch tents that could be taken for military from the air, so the passengers came into the guestrooms.

This situation also meant that temporary workshop facilities were set up on the farm so the drivers could service the vehicles before their turnaround. Again, there were more opportunities to assist or aid the drivers. If a driver became ill or had an accident, we were there to help if we could. Friendships were formed and in due course a spiritual harvest was reaped. As the civil war raged in S. Rhodesia, it radically changed conditions in Zambia.

By 1977 the ripples of conflict in S. Rhodesia were spreading farther and farther. Military roadblocks and guards on all our bridges were a constant irritant to residents and visitors alike. Most of the travellers that reached us reported problems. By early 1978, the difficulties of travelling around our part of Africa became more pronounced and trekking all but ceased. The unrest was spreading to residents in Zambia and no one was unaffected by the struggle across her border.

Food shortages were becoming more pronounced and people grew wary of any stranger.

In the overspill of the civil war that was escalating in Southern Rhodesia, Zambia was also suffering, playing host to thousands of Joshua Nkomo's freedom fighters. Several of these camps were bombed and the pressure on Zambia's residents became intense. With her borders closed and access cut off from all ports and rail links, food shortages became severe. Tension had gripped the nation and everyone was on edge. Suspicion and fear ruled.

On the farm, those of us in leadership positions frequently met together for prayer, and I could be glad that Grace was safe in England. However, both boys were still at home. One particular afternoon our farm manager stopped work and called those of us who were Christians up to his house. A few weeks earlier news of the massacre of the Elim missionaries at Umtali had reached us and this had sent a tremor of foreboding through us all, for although the incident had been in eastern Rhodesia, a long way off, we were very aware that the whole territory was poised for the mayhem to spread. Our farm manager's wife was very fearful, but she hid it well.

That afternoon, we sat around taking turns to pray. It was apparent that the Swiss lady's spirit was heavily burdened. She had always displayed great insight into problems and now she voiced her increasing disquiet about the present situation. Previously she had hinted to me about "looming problems" she sensed among us, but without being more specific. I had responded by just asking her to cover us all in prayer and thanking her again for all her support. Later, the Holy Spirit chided me for ducking the responsibility of insisting she tell me exactly what was on her mind. She'd told me she had not shared this concern with my husband. Now in this gathering, she became very vocal in the Spirit and uttered a grave warning. She warned of a great threat coming against us and called on each one of us to examine our hearts as we faced the coming darkness. She concluded by saying that those of us who kept our eyes fixed on the Lord through the storm would rejoice in the light that would follow.

Afterwards, I pondered long on her choice of words. Talking it over later, I realized many had very real fears, while I, thinking only vaguely about the possible threat from the south, had latched firmly on to the "light" that was to come.

Weeks passed and the builder and his family went to England for a holiday. He was no longer working for us as he had found another job, but they were still living in our cottage. In June my husband announced his intention to go overseas and take our daughter on a trip to Europe in her summer vacation. He didn't return until the middle of November. Late in July our Swiss lady finally left.

Military roadblocks increased and paramilitary personnel were highly visible. Reports kept coming through of more atrocities south of the border. We had a camp of several thousand freedom fighters only four kilometres up the road. The district began to be plagued by small incidents and the farm workers were anxious about the safety of their women; they sent them back to their tribal villages deep in the bush. Christians among the staff met with me daily for prayer as a new menace rained from the sky. Up to this point many of our workers had only looked up in excitement if a low-flying aircraft had come directly over the farm. But now when they heard a plane, the cry went up, *"Ndeke! Ndeke!"* as a warning.

As the low-flying planes of the Rhodesian Air Force screamed in at speeds that gave us practically no warning, buckets and hoes went flying as our workers hurled themselves into the nearest ditch while I, a child of the Second World War, hit the floor in the house. Empty 30mm canon shells bounced across our lawn and the noise was deafening as the planes commenced their run up to their target. The first time it happened, Stuart got so excited he climbed on the roof to watch, which horrified me. But there was no mistaking the seriousness of these events. Next door two men were killed in such a raid. We could see plumes of smoke rising above the trees. A property less than half a mile away had been purchased by the freedom fighters and they used it to conceal a fuel dump. The day that it was bombed it caused a major conflagration that shook the whole district. Often at night we could hear the muffled explosions of bombs going off in the city as Rhodesian forces tried to root out the rebels hiding there.

Early one morning a helicopter landed on the road in a residential area just as people were leaving their driveways to take their children to school. A policeman held up the traffic and once the soldiers had jumped out and the helicopter had lifted off, he calmly waved the traffic on.

Still my husband didn't return but wrote instead saying he'd decided to stay on and return in time for Christmas, and would bring Grace, who would have finished her studies by then. The builder's family returned to live in Sharon Cottage.

In the midst of all this, an Australian arrived. Hearing the dogs barking, I put down my rolling pin and opened the back door to find a somewhat dejected figure below the step. His thin shoulders supported a tattered backpack that appeared to be near empty. His bony knees showed through torn jeans and he wore broken shoes and no socks.

"Mrs Bland?"

"Yes. Hello. Come in." I held the door wide open and invited him to enter. He let his pack fall by the door and slowly walked into my kitchen. "Would you like a cup of coffee?"

He nodded silently and slid on to a stool I pulled forward. I pushed a mug of coffee and the sugar toward him and watched his gaunt face as he picked up the mug with both grubby hands and gulped it down. Silently, he accepted a refill. Then, with him still silent, I turned to the refrigerator and quickly assembled a sandwich, put it down in front of him and quietly went back to making my pie.

"Thanks," he said in an Australian accent and tried a tremulous smile. "Thanks a lot."

After a bath with the loan of a razor and another good meal, I gave him the keys and showed him to The Cabin, where he slept the clock round. The next day, he told us of his extraordinary trek.

As a hitch-hiker, before the Rhodesian civil war took over, he'd decided to remain in Rhodesia and found work as a teacher. He married a Rhodesian policewoman. Later he'd done something rather foolish and got thrown out of the country with 'PPI' (Prohibited Political Immigrant) stamped on his passport. Unable to get back to his by now pregnant wife, or find a job in South Africa, he hitch-hiked through Botswana and entered Zambia that way. Somewhere along the way he'd been given a lift by someone who gave him our name and directions on a slip of paper. Weeks were going by, and by now, extremely anxious about the welfare of his wife, he'd used up his dwindling resources to reach Lusaka.

In Lusaka he was picked up on the street by the police, thrown into jail as a political suspect, only to find he'd lost the paper with our details on it. Two days later he was released and told to quit Zambia immediately. So he found a lift to the Malawi border, some four hundred miles to the east. There he wandered around for a while, sleeping rough and selling off his few possessions for food. He was getting more worn and extremely anxious as he'd lost touch with his wife. Fortunately, at this stage he didn't know she'd had a miscarriage. Finally, he came across some people who knew us and they suggested, if he could reach us, we were the people most likely to be able to help.

And so he hitched all the way back and finally collapsed in a Lusaka street. Someone helped him and drove him out to our gate where, worn to the bone, he just about managed to walk down the drive. He had been driven by fears for his wife and his determination not to leave Africa without her.

CHAPTER FOURTEEN

Black Wednesday

An air of palpable tension gripped the nation. Rumours abound-
ed. Tales of raids by the Rhodesian forces upon pockets of
freedom fighters were given credence by the echoes of
explosions and gunfire. Travel after dark was fraught with danger. In
the daytime we would be often confronted by the sudden appearance of
soldiers and turned aside without explanation. Military roadblocks
seemed to multiply and we had to go through two at least just to reach
town.

In the countryside, travel was becoming more hazardous and the
roadblocks even more aggressive. Very often we were not just stopped,
but ordered out of the car, while the car was rigorously searched even
to the point of having the seats removed. It was tedious and nerve-
wracking and, moreover, it wasn't even our war. The fiancé of one of
our guests, on a sales trip for his company, didn't take them seriously
and was shot dead at a bridge checkpoint.

The air raids by the Rhodesian Air Force on the nearby camps were
almost daily. As soon as we turned on to the main road going to town,
we would see the crowds of freedom fighters who had come out of the
local camp for fear of being bombed; rows and rows of them sitting on
the grass verges. Whenever we were in town, we'd see long convoys of
assorted vehicles laden with the wounded from various camps, wending
their way to the hospital which was under military control. Towards
the end of 1978, the tide of war washed right up to our doorstep.

The flow of visitors virtually came to a stop. At the farm at that
time, in addition to me and our two teenage sons, there was the

Australian, the builder's family and our British farm manager, his wife and our secretary. Two American boys were also there, young sons of a missionary couple living two hundred miles away, because the school hostel in town was full.

On Tuesday, November 7th, Lusaka's main street erupted into violence and the police were rounding up unfamiliar Europeans without ceremony. Our secretary, the daughter of Swedish missionary friends, was on the street shopping that day and was narrowly saved from a nasty experience by a gentleman who hastily bundled her inside a building.

In recent years, when a property changed hands it had become harder and harder to be certain of who one's new neighbours really were. The bombing of the fuel dump had shaken us, and a neighbouring farmer was killed in broad daylight as he was walking on his own land with his wife and child. It became dangerous for us to cross our river and we discovered a placement of anti-aircraft guns on the hill overlooking the river on our north-east boundary.

In part, the escalating war was being fought over our heads. That Tuesday evening everyone gathered at the farmhouse for prayer. The farm manager's wife was the only exception because she had broken her leg two days before and was up at their house in bed. We shared Psalm 91.

On Wednesday morning, November 8th, I took Stuart and the American lads to school in the farm manager's personal car. My car had been giving a little trouble and our Australian guest said he would take a look at it. The farm manager had already taken the pickup off on farm business. The builder's wife had gone up to his house to assist his wife. John, our youngest boy, had pleaded he didn't feel well and I'd allowed him to stay at home. Because I had planned to do some shopping, I said I'd be staying in town until it was time to bring the youngest boys home for lunch.

It was not long after I'd left that a large group of freedom fighters, heavily armed with AK47 assault weapons, moved on to our farm. They roughed up several farm workers and caught the farm manager on his return as he parked the pickup outside the farm office. They manhandled him into one of their vehicles and drove off the farm. The ladies at his house knew nothing and at the first hint of trouble, his house servant took off without saying a word. Shortly afterwards, as the builder's wife left his house, she was caught and bundled into another vehicle and driven away. And then the Australian was captured and taken off in my car.

Our secretary was in the study at the farmhouse talking to John. Suddenly they became aware that the house was surrounded by heavily armed men and some had walked into the house. The men forced the two youngsters out at bayonet point. Told to bring the household keys, they were then pushed round all the rooms and outbuildings. Any door for which they couldn't produce a key was ruthlessly bashed open. The children's dog went berserk but fearing it would get shot, John managed to get it under control. He'd only just had his fifteenth birthday and our secretary was very slightly built and wearing jeans and a little check shirt. Although she was over twenty, she looked like a teenager. Perhaps the men took them both for kids and therefore didn't harm her, something for which we were all profoundly thankful later. It was very frightening but both young people kept their heads and were not hurt.

When the group reached the farm manager's house, it was the first inkling his wife had that something was wrong. Apart from wondering why her house servant hadn't answered her calls, she was unperturbed as she was used to her husband being busy on the farm for long periods of the day. The freedom fighter prodded the youngsters through the house right into her bedroom, then seeing her in bed he stopped short and said, "Oh, Madam, you are sick." He then inexplicably backed out leaving the bewildered trio. They heard men shouting outside about coming back, there was the sound of vehicles leaving, and then silence.

In the bedroom the two youngsters explained what they knew. Although very relieved to be together, they were nevertheless quite shaken. However, the farm manager's wife was mature and spiritually strong. She held them together and prayed, bearing in mind that I was due back soon.

About one o'clock I drove in and, having a message for the manager, I stopped at their house first. I left the two American boys in the car where one of them had fallen asleep, and ran up the front steps expecting to find them at lunch. Instead my son ran to meet me looking very upset. When I heard what had happened, I went into the bedroom and we discussed what we should do. The car was far too small for me to evacuate them all, especially with her broken leg that was in plaster from ankle to thigh, and she was helpless without them. I had driven in without incident but none of us knew what was really happening. We decided I should go for help while they prayed I'd get out safely. Meanwhile the youngsters would help her get dressed, ready to leave.

I dashed to the car and told the boys to lie down on the floor of the vehicle and to stay down. I told them not to be frightened but warned them that there were some robbers around and if they jumped out at us from the bush, I was not going to stop. Brave words, but my heart was already thumping with alarm and I was feeling very scared.

Spinning the little car round and putting my foot down hard, I wondered if we could make it out to the main road safely. Were those men waiting in the bushes? Why had it happened? Who were they after? With a huge sigh of relief, I rocketed out on to the main road without incident and sped towards town. About a mile down the road was the headquarters of a safari company. They bought our produce for their camps and knew us. Thinking of them as men with available guns, I turned into their gateway with the notion of asking for their help. No help was available though, so with adrenaline pumping I careered out of there and headed for town.

My mind was racing. What did I need to do? And in what order should I do it? Very much aware that the two boys were badly frightened, I strove for control and talked to them quietly. It was the height of the hot season and perspiration was pouring off me. I prayed and asked God to calm my agitation and give me a clear head so I could think clearly about the best way of dealing with this crisis. And although my heart was still thumping at an alarming rate, my mind cleared and became calm.

By the time I reached the outskirts of the city, I knew exactly what I was going to do. First, I was going to drive through town and take the boys to our pastor's home. I explained this to them and reassured them they would be safe there. After the initial shock of our arrival in the midst of their lunch, the pastor and his wife readily took care of the boys and I asked if they'd contact the nearby headquarters of the Africa Evangelical Mission and ask that a message be sent to their parents via the mission radio and also a message to our secretary's family at Mpongwe. Figuring what to do about the trio left on the farm was a bit more difficult. My suggestion that maybe there might be someone in the church with a suitable vehicle, willing to go out to the farm, seemed best. But I had to leave that in the pastor's hands and, as I learned later, in this he was successful. As I left the house, he was already alerting the whole church to pray.

I went to the police to report the incident, thinking naively it wouldn't take long, but in that I was very much mistaken. I reported at the front desk and was immediately hustled upstairs into a large room where several high-ranking officers questioned me. Other officers and some paramilitary were summoned and after that it became somewhat of an ordeal. Though I didn't know it then, we were not the only people attacked that day, though our incident was the only one involving kidnapping. An hour later they said I could go but my relief was short-lived. Outside in the corridor I was pushed into another room with a policewoman guard and told to wait.

Silence reigned, save for the frantic buzzing of a trapped bluebottle on the dusty windowsill. The Zambian policewomen sat stoically, arms outstretched on the desk, looking at her hands. I sat on the only other chair, watching the clock on the wall. Dying for a drink and desperate to get out of there, I sat in post-shock dishevelment and reaction, trying hard not to think about what might be happening at the farm and wishing the hands on the clock would move.

I tried to talk to the policewoman, to ask her if she knew what was happening now. But she only shuffled her feet, and stabbing a forefinger in my direction, she said, "You don't talk. You stay." Desperate to escape, to get to my Embassy, I fixed my attention by clenching my hands in my lap and silently praying. After a long forty-five minutes, an officer came to the door and said I could go.

About that time a couple of brave young Zambians from our church were on their way to the farm in a borrowed station wagon. They carried the farm manger's wife out and laid her on a mattress on the vehicle floor, then drove her safely to her friend's house in town and delivered the other girl to the manse. Meanwhile John found the spare keys to the pickup, which was still standing outside the farm office, and drove it off the farm behind them. Later we learned that the freedom fighters did return and take possession of the farm before nightfall.

I left the police station and went straight to the British Embassy where the supportive diplomatic machinery was set in motion. They also acted on behalf of our Australian guest since the nearest Australian Consul was in Dar-es-Salaam, Tanzania, and after giving a full report I was offered a phone call to Canberra on his behalf. I also tried to telephone Gordon in England but it transpired that he was travelling and I had to leave a message with his brother in Croydon, who promised he would find out where he was and see that he got my message.

It was after five o'clock before I reached Stuart's school to collect him. Earlier I hadn't been too worried because I knew he'd be playing sports until about 4.30 but now I knew he'd be very anxious, wondering why I was so late. After putting him in the picture, we drove back to the manse. By this time there were several supportive church members there. The builder had fetched his boys from school and had made his own arrangements for them to stay in town. The radio messages had brought the Americans in to collect their boys and the Swedish family were on their way from Mpongwe to collect their daughter.

It was too soon to know what we were up against. I accepted accommodation for my two boys in the home of one of their school friends, and I arranged to stay with a friend who was a doctor, conscious that perhaps I might need her professionally as I faced the total responsibility in this horrific situation.

It was very late before I got to bed, totally exhausted. With only the clothes I was wearing with me, I washed them in the bathroom knowing they'd dry before morning. My last waking thoughts were a prayer for our three people who'd been so cruelly snatched away.

Unknown to me that night, heroic efforts were being made by a Christian friend of our farm manager who'd discovered, by accident, that his neighbour was a high-ranking freedom fighter. Making the most of his opportunity, he went to him and pleaded for our people, putting himself at considerable risk. Before daylight, two Zambian police cars were despatched to the area a few kilometres from our farm and the missing trio were somehow 'found'. All the details of that night were shrouded in secrecy in the highly sensitive political circumstances. But it was enough for me to know that God had answered my prayer.

In the grace of God, the builder's wife was put in one car and the two men in the other. Her face bore a mass of contusions, two ribs were broken and she had been raped. Totally exhausted, she vomited in the back seat of the car and the policeman asked her where they should take her. They delivered her to the manse, where she was safe, but for the men it was very different.

The message from Lusaka Central police station to the doctor's house, to say the two men were being detained, reached me about 6 am and I hurried there immediately. I had to plead repeatedly and insistently before I was allowed to see them. They were being watched over by a couple of indifferent guards and I was shocked to find them lying on the floor, where obviously they'd been dumped. It took a few minutes for the truth to sink in. Our men were being treated as suspects.

They had received no aid and nothing to drink. Both were filthy, covered in blood and sand, and in shock. The Australian was barefoot, his feet slashed to ribbons, and he'd suffered a blow across his throat from a rifle butt. He couldn't speak and could hardly swallow. His wrists were in bad shape where he'd been strung up in a tree with baling wire.

I found out later that while this torture was going on, a snapshot of his native Rhodesian wife Siboniso, taken from his room at the farm, was waved in front of him and threats against her were made. His tormentors said they saw this photo as damning evidence that he was involved in the southern conflict and that was part of their reason for the attack. Our farm manager was not too bad off but he'd been interrogated, handled very roughly and knocked about.

Horrified, I pleaded for some aid for them but was told we'd have to wait until the day shift came on at 8 am. Telling the men I'd be back as quickly as possible, I drove back to where I was staying and put washcloths, a towel and a bottle of water in a basket with some antiseptic and a Thermos of hot, sweet coffee. Armed with this I drove to where my boys were staying and collected Stuart. I felt I needed someone with me and this turned out to be a wise decision.

Back at the police station I told Stuart to wait in the car for me. At the front desk I was very insistent, demanding that I be allowed to see our men again and eventually they let me in. I did what little I could for the men and waited with them, hoping that when the day staff came on duty, we could sort something out, but it was a forlorn hope.

The day shift came on and all my pleas for some medical help fell on deaf ears. The realization of just how bad this situation really was, was finally sinking in. Once again, I found myself shunted into a room where several men waited round a table. I was told to sit down and took the only vacant chair with my back to the door. The men facing me wore no insignia and as they proceeded to interrogate me, I began to comprehend the depth of suspicion and animosity surrounding us. I pleaded again that our men might be allowed some medical assistance and again it was refused. They also re-emphasized that the police had no intention of releasing them.

Nearly two hours went by. I was trying hard not to show how frightened I was but I was struggling. Increasingly anxious about my son left in the car park, anxious about our men, I was wondering how on earth this misery was going to end. A couple of men in police uniform and one in paramilitary gear had joined the crowded room and I was feeling increasingly claustrophobic and threatened. I couldn't really understand their attitude towards me. I was doing my best to answer the constant barrage of questions but all my efforts to keep a semblance of control in the situation were fading.

The door opened behind me and to my surprise and relief, the Director of the Churches Medical Association in Zambia walked in. He had stopped at the police station on an errand and had seen a very worried Stuart hovering near the front desk. He was a friend and had heard about our incident, so he went up and spoke to him. Stuart was desperately glad to see him and poured out his anxiety for me. The Director offered to help.

The Director stood beside my chair and put a reassuring hand on my shoulder with a slight pressure as if to say, "Leave this to me." He had a quiet but commanding presence and as soon as he got involved, things began to move.

It was agreed that our two men could be taken to hospital provided they were under armed guard and we used our own transport. It took some time for a policeman to be detailed to accompany us and for him to be issued with a weapon. Finally, we all trooped down to the cells and our men were assisted into the Director's car as it was bigger than mine. Stuart and I followed.

Once we were on the way, I began to feel better, but we were still embroiled in a massively difficult situation. On our arrival at the casualty department there was another delay. At first, the nurses were uncertain about admitting the armed guard who was sticking to the men like glue, and for our Australian guest it was the last straw and he panicked. But in the grace of God, the first senior nurse to reach his stretcher was a Christian, someone he'd already met at our farm. Finally they were admitted – with the armed guard beside them, sitting with his rifle across his lap.

Next I needed a permit to visit since the hospital was full of Rhodesian injured freedom fighters and under full military control. Since I was not actually a relative of either man, this proved difficult and the authorities were adamant. I rushed out and was just in time to catch the Director as he was leaving the building and asked if he could help me. Immediately he came back inside and accompanied me to the appropriate office.

There he quietly but firmly reacted to the repeated refusal by reminding the administrative officer that, not so long ago, his Christian Medical Association had helped the hospital by providing much needed drugs when they were struggling with their supply lines and now, please, he would like this one favour in return. We waited for a long minute while the administrator stared at him. Then, without another word, he picked up his rubber stamp and thumped it on a paper; and I had my permit to come and go whenever I wished. There were no formal visiting hours.

This then became my daily round. The police had asked me to check in every morning and I did this first. Then I went to the hospital to check on the men's progress and see if there was anything they needed. I learned that our nursing friend had alerted all the other members of the Nurses Christian Fellowship in the hospital and a group of them had encircled the Australian's bed, held hands and prayed just before he was taken down for surgery. The Australian Consulate in Dar-e-Salaam had allowed me to telephone Canberra to ask for assistance for our guest. At the same time, I asked for permission for his wife to enter Australia if it were possible to get her out of Rhodesia. Subsequently, the Vice Consul flew down to Lusaka to expedite his release and return to Australia.

At the hospital the whole incident, with the care and attention and witness of the Christian nurses, had generated a significant interest among the rest of the hospital staff. When I told some friends about this, they gave me a full box of Gideon New Testaments and in the two weeks immediately afterwards, almost fifty of these were distributed in response to individual requests.

Throughout the emergency I had a very strong inner peace. Despite the nerve-wracking circumstances that took a heavy toll on emotions and energy, the deep-seated sense of having my Lord close, almost tangible at times, never left. Isaiah's words came to mind several times: "You will keep in perfect peace those whose minds are steadfast, because they trust in you."[5]

---

[5] Isaiah 26:3

Chapter Fifteen

Echoes of Conflict

Although my inner peace sustained my spirit, the daily pressures were all too real. Gordon had not returned and there was no message for me. By the weekend I was too exhausted to go to church and once my round of police and hospital was done, I had to rest. For these reasons, I was not in church that Sunday to hear the builder's wife give her testimony, and not until after the event did I hear about her interview with the British Broadcasting Corporation's reporter in Lusaka that week.

A couple of days later, I went to the manse to see the builder's wife. While I was talking to her in the bedroom, the phone rang in the hall and it was for her. To my astonishment, I heard her use my husband Gordon's name, so I ran out to ask her to let me speak to him, and had to be quite insistent before she relinquished the telephone. He made only a brief, somewhat perfunctory inquiry after my wellbeing and did not even ask after our boys.

Surprisingly, he told me he was taking the time to travel round England visiting the families of the two kidnapped Brits, and then asked me to put the builder's wife back on the line. How had he known where she was? Why hadn't he contacted me? Didn't he care about his family? Bewildered, disappointed and very let down, I knew the news of our situation would have reached him through his brother to whom I'd sent the message from the Embassy, but I didn't even know where he was and had no contact number. The whole scenario smacked of betrayal but I was too tired to engage in a confrontation with the builder's wife just then; I judged it better to wait for Gordon's return.

The pressure of our situation pushed these thoughts aside. I had to concentrate on the job in hand. A message reached me, brought to town by one of our workers, that the freedom fighters had left the farm, albeit they were still camped just up the road. The farm was out of stock feed. In the first place, I had an awful job to persuade the Milling Company to send out ten tons immediately and, as usual, they demanded payment in advance. Because our normal business of sales and payments had been interrupted in the emergency, I was dismayed to find our bank reluctant to release the money for this, further evidence of how badly the raid on our farm had coloured their thinking. I had a hard job persuading them.

Once I could pay for it, the load was promised for the following day, provided their truck didn't enter our property. So a compromise was reached and accordingly I sent the messenger back with instructions. The feed company would deliver to a point about a mile short of the farm and unload on the roadside. Some of our farm workers had to be there to meet it with the tractor and trailer, and ferry it back in smaller loads according to the capacity of the trailer. Two men were to stay with the remainder at the roadside to guard it until the last load was safe

In between hospital visits, reporting daily to the police and keeping in touch with the Embassy as requested, I was kept busy with the needs of my sons. It was difficult dealing with our bank because before they gave me their full co-operation, they wanted to know more about our position than I could calculate, and it was a major headache in the circumstances with no money coming in and no sales being made. The farm manager was released from hospital and gladly joined his wife and they made immediate plans to return to England. Our Australian friend was recovering from the operation to repair his damaged feet but the armed guard was still beside his bed.

For days I'd been wearing the same clothes, washing them every night and ironing them first thing every morning. Friends helped the boys out and a few days later a gift of second-hand clothes arrived for me and I could temporarily outfit myself. Our bank was giving me a hard time and so I dared not use money for anything except absolute essentials: food, petrol and the most basic of the farm's needs.

A few days after the raid, I reported at the police station as usual and found that the atmosphere had abruptly changed. Suddenly my reception felt hostile again. I was more closely questioned, separated apart with guards and later hurried down the steps of the police station between two silent policewomen holding my arms. No one would answer my questions and tell me where we were going. In desperation, when I saw an acquaintance approaching, I shouted out to him to inform the British Embassy in case I didn't report there within three hours. That he understood was all I could hope for as I was bundled into the back of an unmarked car with the policewomen still glued to my sides. Both the driver and his companion were in plain clothes and neither spoke to me or answered my questions. We took the road west and it was not until the car turned into our farm drive that I admitted to myself how frightened I'd been, afraid I was being taken somewhere more sinister.

The state of things at the farm was awful. Our workers were lined up on one side of the lawn flanked by armed police and paramilitary. Spent ammunition lay scattered about with a lot of other rubbish. My two particular guards stayed very close to me and even accompanied me to the toilet after searching my handbag. A heavily armed paramilitary officer took charge and questioned me at length over a table where a couple of handguns, aerial maps of the farm, our farm manager's walkie-talkie radio – used to save him endless walking all over the property – all lay amid a welter of loose ammunition and farm papers. Even the old binoculars that Gordon used for bird watching looked anything but innocent in the middle of this jumble.

I tried to explain about the aerial photos, that many farmers had these. They said they believed that all this stuff had been used for ground-to-air communications despite my vehement dismissal of this charge and my denial that any of the weapons were ours. Nothing appeared to register with them at all. I could only keep repeating that no one on our farm kept a gun but because of their unresponsive attitude, I'd no idea if I was believed or not. After a while they took me on a tour of the whole place and the devastation the attackers had wrought sent more shock waves through me.

The main house was a mess: broken ornaments and rubbish all over the sitting room. All small loose items had vanished, linen, tape-players, a radio and all manner of kitchen equipment. Mirrors and clocks had been ripped off the walls and some curtains were missing, some torn and still drunkenly hanging off broken rails. I'd seen some ripped bedroom curtains scattered in the garden. One single mattress and its pillows and linen had been slashed, probably by bayonets, and lay strewn half-way through a window and on the grass outside. In another room one whole single bed and mattress had disappeared and the remaining bedstead lay drunkenly upended against the wall. In our room, the safe door hung on one broken hinge, empty. One of our family's passports was found ripped up in a flower bed. Another was reported found in the neighbouring bush days later. Other important papers were never found.

Everywhere, drawers were pulled out and the contents scattered; some drawers were missing altogether. The pantry, refrigerator and the freezers had been stripped of their contents and bleach had been thrown all over the floors of the bathroom, hallway and kitchen, taking the colour off and leaving large, ugly white patches. In our home office-cum-study, papers and files from the filing cabinet were dumped on the floor and empty boxes of family photos were scattered everywhere. The whole mess had been covered in flour and the squeezed contents of several tubes of duplicating ink. Evidently the raiders had then walked over it all for there were imprints of their heavy boots over the papers and all the way down the hallway.

With the guards still close about me, we then went round all the other buildings. Where no key had been available, the doors had been smashed in. The heavy steel door to the laundry bore the imprint of a particularly ferocious attack around the broken lock.

In the guestrooms that were unoccupied, similar damage was found, but the Australian's room had been thoroughly, savagely ripped apart. However, Sharon Cottage and Bethesda House were hardly touched. It confirmed my growing suspicion that they had particularly targeted my family – but I still didn't understand why.

I had not been allowed to talk to any of our farm workers and was unsure what was happening to them. With none of my questions answered, I couldn't even guess how this was going to turn out. I was taken back to the car and driven back to town. In the police station car park I was simply told I could go. Still a bit shaken but greatly relieved, I drove to the Embassy to find they had received my message. I was reassured that had I not reported in, they would have instigated inquiries.

Meanwhile, the farm manager and his wife prepared to return to England and I was offered the use of a house that belonged to friends who were away overseas.

During the week after the raid, I had many opportunities to thank God for our workers' faithfulness, although I only gleaned some of their stories weeks later. After the initial confrontation with the attackers, the farm workers had fled and shut themselves in their houses. One or two intrepid souls crept forth the next day and very cautiously came to see if they could reach the stock unmolested. They were not harmed so they came to pump water, feed the stock and milk the cows, and generally do the most important jobs. The resident freedom fighters allowed them to move about freely and in the course of the next few days they achieved some remarkable things. One of them found the keys to Stuart's abandoned motorbike and surreptitiously walked it through the bush to town where he enquired until he found out where the boys were staying. This relieved pressure on transport because Stuart, in his senior years, could take his brother to school independently.

Another worker found John's dog and brought it to him. Some of the others took empty stock-feed bags and stealthily packed all the books from our library, which they carried across the river and hid in their own houses. Someone reached my bedroom, grabbed a bag and stuffed it with a few remaining odds and ends, and that too reached me.

When Gordon finally arrived a week later, he left Grace in England. He was irritated by what he deemed the unnecessary untidiness in our quarters, which I thought was unreasonable in the circumstances. Surely he could understand how difficult it had been trying to find a place in someone else's house for the piles of donated clothes and miscellaneous flotsam of bags of rescued bits and pieces. True, I had stuff on the floor of the spare room and part of the hall, but I was ragged with tiredness and strain. He was impatient with my attempts to share some of the truly good things that had happened, aspects in which I felt God had really governed. He cut me off with a curt, "You've handled it all wrong. Now leave everything to me."

Within the hour he was off again. He'd been out of touch during that traumatic week and had not even enquired about our welfare, and even when he sent a message to say he was returning, he'd not asked if there was anything I or the boys needed.

The police advised him not to try and get back on the farm to live until he was told it was safe. However, he took to going out for a short visit each day in an effort to get things together and keep the farm going. The invaders had killed and made off with some livestock and raided the garden. Also with the farm manager having left for England before his return, he had a lot to sort out regarding customers, orders and so on.

One day, in my absence from the house we were living in, he sent the farm tractor and trailer with an assortment of stuff from the farm – odd clothes, kitchen odds and ends, papers, office stuff and books, much of which was damp and dirty from being outside on the ground. This hotchpotch of miscellaneous broken and torn things was stuffed into several old 44-gallon oil drums and although they had no trace of oil left in them, they'd stood outdoors for years and were rusty and dirty, especially around the bottom. The workmen brought them straight into the house and left them on our friend's sitting room carpet. Why our benefactor's house servant had not told them to put the drums outside on the covered veranda, I'll never know.

It so happened that before I got back to the house, the father of our benefactor's wife had called in to see how we were getting on, and seeing this mess, he was appalled. I arrived shortly afterwards and found him very distressed and angry. He was a dear friend, an elderly saintly man. I was horrified. In vain I tried to explain to him, to apologise, to assure him such blatant disregard and carelessness of his daughter's home was not of my doing. But he was too upset to listen. My distress over this incident was a catalyst. Suddenly all the shocks, uncertainty and the exhaustion hit me like an avalanche and left me sick and shaking, unable to do any more.

The next day, a Zambian police car drove up to the house. The house servant was off duty and I was alone and feeling nervous. When Gordon went out, I'd made sure the back and front door were locked. Through the front windows, I watched the policemen approach but I couldn't bring myself to open the door. Without realizing it, I'd backed up the hall while they pounded on the front door, and I kept retreating until I was up against the far wall of the bedroom. Mercifully they finally gave up and went away but I was left feeling shaky and very aware of how vulnerable and shattered I'd become. Gordon came back and apparently he'd been in to see the police because he said they'd asked him to return with me.

It was obvious that the police had been making extensive enquiries about me and, thankfully, had found plenty of people to corroborate my story. The reason for the attack on us had become clear. A malcontent, formerly dismissed from our employ, and sympathetic to the southern cause, had gone to the freedom fighters' camp near us and informed them that I was harbouring a spy from the white regime in Rhodesia, our Australian.

So when we arrived at the central police station that day, the atmosphere was dramatically different, almost cordial. The group that formerly interrogated me now shook my hand and explained that the result of their investigation was that I was completely exonerated. They hoped I would not be discouraged from continuing my "Christian social service".

The police reiterated that it was unwise to attempt to go back to live at the farm as there were still pockets of unrest in the area and we should wait until things were more stabilized. Gordon decided the boys and I should go to England and wasted no time in getting our tickets. Safe in my mother's house a few days later, and reunited with Grace, I busied myself with outfitting the boys. Then I had to switch my attention because Siboniso was due to arrive.

On the day before I left Lusaka, I went to say goodbye to our Australian friend. The armed guard had disappeared and he was recovering well. He also had some wonderful news to share. When an Australian newspaper had picked up the story of our raid, his father had read it and managed to get a telephone call right through to his hospital bedside. Apparently, he had left the family when his son was a small boy and this had been the first contact he'd made. He had asked for his son's forgiveness and received it. This, together with all his experiences over the preceding few months, together with this reconciliation, left an indelible spiritual impression; our guest had a whole new lease on life and his prospects were changed dramatically. Only one thing remained for his cup to be full: Siboniso.

Getting Siboniso out of Salisbury at such a time was a miracle of God's love and provision. At the time of the Australian Vice Consul's personal visit to Lusaka to look into his situation and put into motion arrangements for his repatriation, the question of Siboniso had also been discussed, but her situation was much more difficult. Since Southern Rhodesia's unilateral declaration of independence and seven years of civil war, it had been a diplomatic 'black hole' and so nothing direct could be attempted. Despite the fact that she had no passport, I believed there had to be a way. I knew my Lord to be faithful, so after prayer, asking the Holy Spirit to give me guidance, I sat and thought about our Christian network of friends and contacts.

I managed to get a call through to some missionary friends in Malawi, asking them to get a message to Siboniso, through a contact of theirs in Salisbury. In it she was informed of the plan to get her out and asked to get ready. This contact, a Christian pastor, also helped her get a travel document to exit Rhodesia and drove her over the border to the home of friends of his, an Afrikaans pastor and his wife in Pretoria. They welcomed her to stay while she waited and saw to it that I was kept informed and had their contact details.

Meanwhile in London, I was able to arrange an air-ticket for her, from Pretoria to Johannesburg and on to Melbourne via London where I would meet her. I'd had to plead with the UK immigration authorities to allow her to fly via London and then had to apply to the Heathrow port authority for permission for her to land. Wonderfully, the Lord cleared the way and all this was accomplished within a week, even to the provision of the money so I could pay for the complete trip and have her ticket issued, ready for her collection at Pretoria Airport.

I met Siboniso for the first and last time at Heathrow Airport, where she was released into my custody. She had several hours to wait for her onward flight to Melbourne so I took a room at the nearest airport hotel where we rested and talked. It was evident that the way things had worked out so wonderfully had given her much food for thought. I could only hope that it would not end there, that in the fullness of time both of them would come to full, mature faith. Just beforehand, friends had sent me a gift of money "for whatever needs may crop up" and this enabled me to give her a jacket, for she had no coat, a little Australian currency for incidentals and a bible. We'd received a message that her in-laws would meet her as she would arrive in Melbourne a few days before her husband. I waved her off and returned to my mother's house to address my own needs.

My boys still needed some things and, with Grace who had joined us, we went shopping in Birmingham. We were walking along New

Street near the railway station when a near panic hit me and instantly I grabbed the children and vehemently insisted we find a photographer first. They couldn't understand why it had to be *now* and I tried hard to get them to understand the thought that had arrested me: if any bad thing happened to any one of them, right then I didn't even have so much as a snapshot of any of them. Their bewilderment gave way to shrugs of acceptance and we trouped into the huge railway station and found a photographer's booth on the shopping concourse.

The children and I were separated for Christmas. There was not room for us all at Solihull so I sent them to their cousins in Sussex to have as normal a Christmas as possible with them while I remained in my family home and succumbed to a bad chill. It was a particularly cold winter and thick snow lay for weeks. The house was beautifully warm but outside I huddled in a collection of my mother's clothes and her second pair of fur boots. The family lovingly met all my needs and suggested that I shouldn't go back. But I was not ready for that decision yet. Gordon hardly ever wrote and when he did, it was a very short aerogramme with very little personal content.

Stuart flew back in January 1979 as he had nearly finished school. He was eighteen and had his own motorbike for transport so it was arranged he'd stay in town with the family of a school friend. Bearing in mind his experience with the freedom fighters, we thought it best for John to remain with his cousins and go to school there. And as things worked out, he remained in England for several years.

While all this was going on, news of our situation had reached many of our extended spiritual family overseas. Many gifts of money reached me, one of them specifically designated to replace our kitchen equipment. These gifts and their accompanying expressions of love and prayer support helped me believe we would soon have a restored home. The January sales were on and I made good use of the money, but then wondered how I was going to get the stuff out to Zambia. Then the representative of a missionary medical supply organisation contacted me and kindly offered their assistance. Subsequently they shipped out several tea chests for us, free of charge, to a mission station within easy reach, a service and gift that we deeply appreciated.

In Zambia it was two weeks after my departure before Gordon could return to live on the farm. Just before Christmas I'd had a letter in which he'd said that although the situation was still unsettled, he felt our living was in jeopardy and he needed to be there. He was feeling the loss of the farm manager keenly and it was taking a long time to get the ransacked office back into some sort of order and to look after our customers. Trying to fill orders was chaotic because of the heavy stock losses. He wrote he was virtually camping out in the house and would leave things as they were until my return. What he did not tell me was that the builder and family had returned to Lusaka. They had since split up because the husband was having an affair, but the wife had moved back to the farm.

Chapter Sixteen

No Turning Back

Northern Rhodesia was prosperous when we first lived there. The copper prices were good and the country had excellent transport connections with the south. Most businesses had their head office in Salisbury and business flowed effortlessly. Lusaka was a smart town with many beautiful flower beds, and Cairo Road, its mile-long main street, was a double carriageway with a grassed centre reservation, shaded by magnificent flamboyant and nande flame trees. Most of its side streets were shaded by huge jacaranda trees, the blossom of which drifted the pavements to create a deep mauve carpet in October and November. Colourful umbrellas shaded small tables on the lawn outside the Dairy Produce Board and one could lunch or take tea on restaurant balconies or in the pavement café on one prominent corner. Smart shops catered for the expatriates and the Africans got shunted round the back.

Decimalisation came in 1968; the kwacha replaced the pound and its value was pegged at ten shillings, so K2 = £1. The ngwee was the name given to the cents. Both names represent dawn and freedom. For several months both currencies were usable until the old pounds, shillings and pence were withdrawn. For some it was slow work and a great many rusty old cocoa tin 'safes' were dug up at the last moment. I suspect our farm workers were typical of many: for nearly a year, on payday, we had to first explain the equivalent entitlement in 'old money' before they were comfortable accepting the cash.

For the first time, *anyone* could open a bank account with just a small amount and be issued with a cheque book. Unfortunately, that led

161

to a few hopeful souls not understanding that one had to put money *in* the bank before you could take it out. In a bank queue one day, I waited several minutes while a somewhat harassed teller tried to explain that to the man in front of me. In possession of a cheque book for the first time in his life, he had thought that independence and freedom meant he could get money whenever he wanted it. If only that were so!

More than twenty years later, in post independent Zambia, Lusaka was showing signs of an encroaching dilapidation, along with many other towns. Some of it was due to the wear and tear of someone else's war and some of it bore unmistakable signs of neglect and reduced resources. True, the small red brick hospital where our sons had been born was now flanked by the huge University Teaching Hospital, and the University of Zambia stood proudly above the Great East Road on the way to the New International Airport. But on Cairo Road the pavement stones were broken and the flowers beds were bare. Zambia's own people queued for staples such as sugar, cooking oil, salt, soap and maize meal. The pavement café had become a small supermarket but there was no flour and very little tinned stuff on the shelves, and bread was unofficially rationed. The outdoor market between two of the main street's parallel roads had grown considerably and the overspill of vendors often encroached along the shabby side streets. The population had swelled as the people flocked to the line-of-rail towns and shanty townships sprawled for miles around the city without the benefit of proper roads, electricity, sanitation or an adequate water supply.

Since the unilateral declaration of independence, the struggle against the white majority rule in S. Rhodesia had steadily escalated. The dogs of war were unleashed and the country was engulfed in a most bitter civil war as the Shona and Matebele people of the region stepped up their fight against the white government.

When Zambia closed its borders, residents outside the country were allowed back in but all other traffic was suspended. I was on a brief holiday in Salisbury at the time and hurriedly drove home. There was a tangible atmosphere at the border post when I came through; it was like hearing a prison door slam behind me.

Zambia had always traded with, and indeed was dependent on, the south, so the closed borders initiated an escalating cost of living, more shortages and real hardship. Zambia was landlocked, cut off from the port of Beira to the east by the war in Mozambique, and had already lost access to the western sea port of Lobito Bay by a similar situation in Angola. At this time there was no rail link to the ports in East Africa and only a dirt road to the port of Dar-es-Salaam. This road became the notorious "Hell Run" as enterprising private road transporters attempted to haul in everything Zambia needed. It was bad enough in the dry season, but in the rains it was fifteen hundred miles of mud hell. Petrol became rationed and for a period of several months, petrol was air-lifted from Elisabethville in the Congo. The supply of new vehicles and spare parts had long since dried up and we were forced to use our vehicle tyres down to the canvas, and then patch the canvas.

For us the most difficult problems were shortage of animal feed, agricultural and car spares, and fuel. Even paraffin was hard to come by. After some time, the government brought the Chinese in to build a railway from Dar-es-Salaam to Kapiri Mposhi, a small town about a hundred miles north of Lusaka, where it met the Zambian rail system. However, it was of a narrower gauge and so didn't quite connect and all the goods had to be transferred. Nevertheless, it was a most welcome life-saver and slowly the situation eased.

Thousands of Chinese workmen came to build this railroad and they were housed in large camps along the route. Many Christians longed for the opportunity to reach these people with the gospel but the camps were guarded and the men never allowed in our towns except in supervised groups. Zambia paid for the railway by a trade agreement that flooded our shops with Chinese goods. Happily for us, they were cheap and of fair quality. The tinned foods were particularly good and life brightened up a little.

The road to East Africa was finally tarred and things eased a bit more. Then came the overspill of Rhodesia's fight for national independence and while the Shona leader Mugabe fought from behind the Mozambique border, Joshua Nkomo's freedom fighters camped and trained inside our borders. Zambia's sympathetic President Kaunda allowed them first call on staple foodstuffs so matters did not improve for the ordinary Zambians in this respect.

Eventually matters came to a climax and strenuous efforts were made by all concerned which would ultimately allow the 1979 Commonwealth Conference to be held in July in Lusaka, albeit contingency plans were made in Nairobi, Kenya just in case Lusaka proved not to be safe enough when the time came. Early that year things began to calm down, and at the end of February 1979, I made preparation to return to the farm.

Gordon had warned me that he'd been concentrating on the farm business and had hardly done anything to the house, but I was not prepared for the shock that awaited me. Anxious to get home, I was disconcerted to see the builder's wife with him at the airport. We had no privacy to talk and there was a further delay in that he said he needed to go to the pastor's house first, though when we got there, nothing really important was said. We just sat around and talked generally for an hour and it began to feel like a delaying tactic. I was tired after my flight and wanted to see Stuart, but most of all I wanted to get home.

When we finally arrived at the farm, it still bore all the outward marks of devastation; worse still, no effort had been made to put the house even basically ready for my homecoming. My bedroom was unprepared and there was evidence of the builder's wife's occupancy everywhere, despite the fact that Gordon had known I was coming for the past two weeks.

Instead of the calm, thankful return I had looked forward to through those dark winter days, I was swept into a maelstrom of emotion and shock. Someone I had befriended and helped had become my husband's mistress. Before leaving, I had had suspicions but not actual proof, and when challenged he had not admitted anything. Later, when he'd told me in a letter that the builder's family had gone back to England, implying they had gone for good, I'd thankfully assumed that the threat was over.

Nothing could banish the chill of that homecoming, although she tried to win me over with fake tears and pleas for forgiveness, while Gordon offered awkward, blustering excuses. I sat in the study rigid with pain, relieved only that Stuart was still living with friends in town.

Gordon took her back to town. Her children were in boarding school and her husband working away, their divorce proceedings already started. I gave orders for my room to be thoroughly cleaned before my domestic staff were to turn their attention to the rest of the house. Evening came and I was left wondering how on earth could we go on from this?

Before sunrise I arose and walked in the freshness of a new day. It was the "time of the horns", as our old Matebele herdsman had once told me, that first glimmer of light when the herdsman could just make out the shape of the horns in the cattle kraal against the pre-dawn sky. Dew-wet grass soaked my sandals and the hem of my dress as I walked by the river, a place I often sought for solitary prayer. Terribly tired and emotionally exhausted, I was overwhelmed and quite unable to formulate specific prayers. I just wanted to lean on the Lord and feel his arms around me until the pain subsided.

Turning from the waterfall, I walked up the sloping lawns towards the lane. The sun was rising in a dazzling display to awaken the morning glories on the fence and give the tips of plumed grass in the near paddock a rosy haze. Looking around, I thought of our early struggles, of what we'd shared and seen of God's grace. I was very conscious of my own limitations. I was the product of a sheltered upbringing, schooled in a very conventional church. I did not see divorce as an option. It was against everything I believed in regarding Christian marriage. It was all very well for some to say it was acceptable in cases of adultery but for me, in reality, there were no such pat answers. That was the way to certain destruction, of our personal lives, our family, our work and our witness. Surely we had not lost all faith, all mercy, commitment, honour and integrity? No, I would not hurry down that path. Instead, I would pray and believe that one day my husband would have the desire to get right with God.

The sun cleared the horizon and from where I stood, the line of paw-paw trees at the edge of the vegetable garden was in silhouette. Above them a skein of egrets, white against the clear sky, flew from the reed beds beyond the farm manager's house. I had made my decision to come back, to follow through on my commitment to my calling. Besides, I'd believed the builder's family had gone and the crates of new household items, given in good faith and Christian love to replenish our home, were due to arrive. I couldn't just run away – and anyway, where would I go? What would I do? I didn't have the money to go back to England. I turned and went back to the house.

Forcing my attention on what was immediately before me, I began by restoring some order. However awful our personal situation was, I was not willing to live in a mess. It was a huge task and having something to focus on helped me ride out the aftershocks. Nevertheless, swift grief would occasionally wash over me and I'd sit with my arms clasped about my body, rocking and silently weeping for lost dreams and impossible hopes. Yet the inner peace of God and his very evident constancy inevitably prevailed and once again brought me round to a renewed resolve to persevere.

I took stock of the task that confronted me. Piled up high in one shed was a miscellaneous collection of household goods as well as stuff from the various guest rooms, broken furniture, torn curtains and broken fittings, dirty mattresses, pillows and cushions, bedding and clothes; all dirty with even a rat's nest or two. Much of it was wet from where the shed roof leaked. The whole sorry mess put me in a militant mood that fortunately generated the energy I needed. This awful stinking pile was a stark symbol of my life and anger fuelled my resolve. This was something I could get to grips with; this was something tangible I could control and remedy.

It was an enormous job. I gave instructions to a couple of workmen to haul the sorry mess out of the shed and dump it where I could see everything and sort it. For a while tears threatened as I came across some of my favourite pictures amid broken glass that still clung to the damaged frames, one of a pair of vases, a few remnants of our music collection, the tapes pulled out and tangled, a handful of 35mm slides of the children hopelessly ruined. Gradually, three piles emerged: curtains, bedding and linens that could be laundered and used again; furniture that could be mended; and the rest for burning. And there was enough of that to keep a bonfire going for two days.

It was nearly a month before an appreciable difference was made to the house. I was determined that we would be clean and comfortable again despite our personal problems. There was nothing to be done about the damage to the floors, but some mending, scrubbing, polish and a load of white paint made a big difference to the interior. The carpenter, Chabaila, worked wonders in repairs. Even when he made a new drawer for my desk to replace a missing one, he carved the front to match the rest.

Our boxes arrived and I took a lot of pleasure in refitting my kitchen. I spent days at the sewing machine I'd brought from England, a gift from my family in Solihull. Some rooms, such as the sitting room, needed new curtains, but some of the old ones, once laundered, were cut down and used for smaller windows. The sitting and dining room furniture was mended and the gouges and scratches smoothed out, then re-stained and polished. Slowly but surely, the house came back to life.

Amazingly, the sitting room carpet had survived. We hauled it out on to the lawn, scrubbed and re-laid it. Most of the house bore some reminders of vandalism but this sort of damage was easy to deal with. It was the abrasions of the heart that were difficult.

Time moved along and things began to feel more normal. Business picked up and that eased our situation. Gordon found a young Zambian graduate from the agricultural college to replace our farm manager, to assist under his direction. The authorities had advised us not to go on our land across the river. Nevertheless, a huge mopping up operation was under way. The Zambian parliamentary forces were moving round the area, searching through each property. They were all very well controlled and thorough, causing no damage, but their presence was unsettling. We had our first visitor, a friend, staying with us for a couple of nights. Knowing nothing of their presence on our land, we went to town leaving her alone for a couple of hours.

When she saw the armed soldiers come up to the house, she was so frightened that she shut herself inside a walk-in stationery cupboard. Terrified, she heard the sound of heavy boots striding across the stone floor. The cupboard door opened and, near fainting, she heard a courteous voice say, "Good morning, Madam. Why are you hiding in the cupboard?"

"I was frightened when I saw the soldiers," she whispered.

"No need to fear us, lady," the officer replied, probably aware that she had every reason. He turned and went out, leaving her limp and rooted to the spot. Shortly afterwards he came back to the house to tell her politely that they were satisfied there were no ex-combatants lurking about and, accordingly, they were about to leave.

After the farmhouse, I turned my attention to the guestrooms. Even if there were to be no more visitors, it was unbearable to see them in such a deplorable state. One by one I put them back in good order. Doors were re-hung and windows were mended. From the remnants of the damaged furniture, enough was repaired to fix up a few of the rooms for which we had bed frames. I managed to find enough reconditioned things to refurnish them with linen, mattresses, drapes, lamps, mirrors and books. The remaining rooms were just repaired, scrubbed and painted and left empty for the meantime. By faith I worked and prayed, dedicating each room again for the Lord's use, should it be needed, before moving on to the next. It was the first week in May when I finished the last one. Indeed, it still required a final touch up on the paintwork when I returned to the house one afternoon to find seven people had arrived.

Their coming was a vindication of my hopeful labour, yet, knowing the future was bound to be affected by our personal situation, I feared the mainspring was damaged. The outcome was not yet evident. Some would say that we had no business attempting to serve the Lord when we had such problems, but people still found their way to us, and in God's grace still found him and were helped. Should we have turned them away?

Gordon was spending more time with his other outside interests. But since my Lord had not dismissed me from his service, and since my calling held firm, I chose to trust in my Lord's ability to protect and help me. However faulty my judgment was at the time, however imperfectly we functioned, God's grace to those who came was very evident and it was clear that he had not abandoned us. Even while Gordon and I tried to salvage our relationship and get our lives on a new footing, a steady trickle of people came and went, and those that God touched seemed unaware of the tensions within the family.

But I was only too aware of the chasm in our marriage. I longed to see true repentance that might pave the way for reconciliation and renewal. Could we rebuild in faith and love for each other, let alone others? Could we find a secure footing on a level path to the future, a straight way? But alas, I could detect no change in him, no unbending. I struggled to suppress my doubts, although I hoped. Was it to be an entirely false hope?

From now on I could only answer for myself. I had chosen to return. There was no turning back. In England I had bravely answered the misgivings of my concerned family. In the security of prosperous, peaceful England, they had expressed grave doubts as to the wisdom of my decision but only in relation to the conditions in Zambia. If they had any other doubts or suspicions, they were not voiced.

Several weeks later, our friends in Katanga told us just what had happened there at the time of our raid and we we marvelled again at God's protection. One of their Christian brethren, a native of the Congo, had been cycling along a bush track and was compelled to stop, whereupon he received a clear vision of our farm with the clear knowledge of the danger we were in. He went straight to the mission station and told them what he'd seen. So detailed was his description of the vision, that two of the missionaries, friends who had been to the farm, recognised it as being our farm and called their colleagues to intercede for us.

How could I explain the 'rightness' of what I felt? Much as they loved me, my family in England did not fully understand my commitment. Now I found myself re-evaluating that commitment; but in that, I'd come full circle. I had made my choices a long time ago but was only too aware now of a new vulnerability; yet my spirit was buoyed up by my recent experiences of God's grace.

CHAPTER SEVENTEEN

Brown Grass

Zambia in 1980 was a mixture of relief that the Rhodesian conflict was over and a tussle to sort out the problems left in its wake. It was a huge exercise to repatriate the freedom fighters, round up the weaponry and repair the damage. In a situation where a gun could change hands for a few cigarettes, it was inevitable that many arms filtered into the hands of local civilians. For most of the expatriate population it was just a matter of picking up and carrying on. But for many, things were never going to be as before.

In Lusaka plans were going ahead for the Commonwealth Conference that would ultimately lead to the Lancaster House, London talks on the future of Rhodesia/Zimbabwe. Just before the Commonwealth Conference, when all Lusaka was gearing up to welcome Queen Elizabeth II and the British prime minister, Margaret Thatcher, we received page 2 of a letter from the British High Commission.

When Gordon showed it to me, it appeared to suggest that there was an event to which we were invited. But we couldn't tell what it was. This page informed us about "hats and gloves optional" and "lounge suits for men" and was obviously the tail end of a letter setting out the dress code for some function. Should the letter have come to us at all? Or was it a mistake?

He went off to the British High Commission to make enquiries and came home with the proper invitation in full. We were invited to a private reception to be held by the Queen at the British High Commissioner's residence. It was to be held on the Sunday morning before the conference began and was for those British people in Zambia who had suffered during the hostilities.

Along with many others, we lined the path round the lawn while the Zambia Police Band played on the tennis court. The Queen, accompanied by the High Commissioner, walked slowly round clockwise, stopping every few paces for a brief greeting. Prince Phillip was escorted round counter-clockwise. The Queen, briefed with our names and a sentence encapsulating our experience, spoke to us personally. When we were introduced, she said she'd understood even our telephone was out of order that day and "that must have been very difficult for you to get help". The smile was genuine and as I looked at this small woman in a simple summer frock, her kind eyes and exquisitely beautiful complexion, and took her hand, I was surprised by the palpable sense of majesty she exuded. In that moment, I was very conscious of all she represented and felt honoured.

For a short time after this we enjoyed a slightly more mellow time in our personal lives. One memorable evening, we walked after supper, as we had often strolled before. At a time like this it was easy to remember how it had been in the early years. For a little time we could forget the differences that were pulling us apart and briefly enjoy the beauty of the night. As we'd done countless times in the past, we followed the circular lane that linked our houses. The great blue gums rustled gently above us and from the stock sheds we passed there came small sleepy sounds and stirrings in the straw. Nothing marred the peace and because there were no city lights or industrial pollution in the air, the high dome of heaven shone far above us in all its starry glory.

The warm evening air brought the sweet scent of citrus blossom drifting from the orchard. A bushbaby's plaintive cry came from the wild fig tree beyond the dairy and we flashed our torch and caught its saucer eyes reflected brightly for a moment. As we walked on, our dog padded up and snuffled through the fence at the bullocks dozing under the cassia trees. Rounding the corner towards the house, the sweet smell of *datura,* the moonflower, wafted around us from where its large creamy bells hung against the library wall. Down by the river, the trees looked dark and mysterious. Only the waterfall and the soft, distant *hoo-hu, hoo-hu, hoo-hu* call of an owl broke the silence.

The boys were home briefly and Grace had also come back with the intention of staying in Zambia so we took a family holiday in the bush.

We piled our gear on the back of the pickup and headed out. Our first stop was Chipata, approximately four hundred kilometres east of Lusaka and an overnight stop with friends. Then we headed north to the South Luangwa National Park.

Military roadblocks were still in place and this made the long journey tedious. Although we had been forced to learn to live with these for years, I was never at ease and disliked them intensely. Fluent in the language, however, Gordon was never at a loss. The soldiers understandably got bored, stuck out on the road miles from anywhere as they were, and were often a bit edgy. Like many other travellers we took magazines, sweets, booklets and tracts to ease the way. Cigarettes were a favoured gift but we didn't carry any. However, what we did offer was usually received well.

All the minor irritations were forgotten once we arrived. The camp was made up of several thatched huts with an ablution block and an open thatched veranda overlooking the river where we ate and could watch the wildlife. On arrival, we'd handed over our groceries to the camp cook who would prepare all our meals, and our days quickly assumed a pattern.

Shortly after dawn, with the sun scarcely above the horizon, we would leave the river and drive into the bush. As the dry season progresses the tall grass thins out and the waterholes diminish. It was August and the game was slowly concentrating toward the river. When we returned to camp some two or three hours later, the smell of newly baked bread greeted us and we fell on our breakfast with great satisfaction. Lazing through the heat of the day, we would sally forth late in the afternoon as the bush stirred to life, to return at dusk replete with pleasure to recount our day over a hearty dinner while we watched the moon rise over the river.

All the old magic was there. One night under a full moon we were woken by the sound of munching and looked out through our wired door to see a rhino crunching fallen seed pods in the area between our huts. We could breakfast as we watched elephant families come to drink, or pick out the flash of a diving kingfisher or the submarine glide of a darter as we lazily lunched, binoculars always at hand. We watched Carmine bee-eaters in the sand cliffs along the river and felt a deep delight as a flock of Nyasa lovebirds suddenly took off in a cloud of colour. We laughed to see rafts of hippo frolicking in a lagoon and later had a real fright when an elephant we were following suddenly turned round and came towards us in a threatening manner. Gordon swiftly reversed, straight into an anthill, and we experienced an electrifying few moments before, pale-faced and sweating, we crashed out over some tree roots and small bushes to get back on the road and away.

All too soon the holidays were over; the boys returned to England to college and Grace decided to stay and study to train as a legal secretary. Life on the farm settled into its usual routine. Nevertheless, overall it had been a difficult year. The upsets and setbacks of the preceding months had left a painful legacy and the economic and climatic conditions in the country only compounded the struggle.

The rains were late and the ground was hard like stone. I left the farm and turned onto the main road. The slate grey ribbon of road unfolded before me in the early morning sunlight. The air was still fresh but it wouldn't last. My passenger, the anxious wife of one of our workers, was cradling a sick child and my first stop was to drop them off at the hospital. The vehicle was laden with produce to be delivered, and a shopping list and details of a spare part needed for the tractor were on the dashboard.

Nearly two hours later I was stuck in traffic. Gordon had said not to be late and here I was crawling up Leopard's Hill Road feeling cross with myself for not avoiding this route. It wasn't easy to forget that maybe there'd be holdups on the road, and knowing my husband needed the car back as quickly as possible, I'd made an unfortunate choice. I banged my hand on the steering wheel in frustration and then felt guilty knowing I'd do better to thank God it was not *my* family trailing to the cemetery. AIDS had tightened its hold on the land. It was becoming commonplace to see ordinary vans and trucks driving with their headlights full on, carrying a coffin and loaded with mourners. Zambian custom demanded that oncoming traffic should stop and pull over while the sad cavalcade passed. I had already done this twice on my way into town that morning. Whenever I heard the mourners' dirge, it never failed to trigger tremors of compassion for their plight. It was such a stark contrast to the sleek, silent limousines and funereal clothes of more wealthy citizens.

Finally, I was past the cemetery gates and able to put my foot down. My errands completed, I thankfully left the overheated city and took the road home. A column of white smoke rose high to the south where a bush fire raged outside the city limits. Twice I passed small fires where the dry grass verge was burning. Where previous fires had passed, I saw long vistas of utterly dry blackened ground. Even the road was rough, with un-mended potholes and patches resembling cracked dusty concrete where the tarmac had eroded altogether.

With a sigh of relief, I drove through our farm gate and found Gordon standing in the shade of a towering blue gum. He flagged me down and turned from the worker he'd been talking to.

"I've been waiting. You're late, Anne," he said, without the preamble of a greeting. His words sounded like an accusation.

"Sorry, I got delayed."

He brushed aside my attempt at an explanation. "Just give me the keys. Did you get the part?"

"Yes, do you want it now?" I reached into the car, grabbed my bag and called the worker over to unload and carry the shopping down to the house.

"No, drop it off at the workshop on your way down. I'll see you later." With that he slammed the car into reverse on the grass verge, spun the wheel and dashed off.

Perhaps I was being unreasonable, but knowing he was worried and rushed did not help. Ever since my fateful homecoming after our brush with the war some eighteen months previously, the strain between us was all too perilously near the surface, the veneer transparent in times of stress. The strain was constant and we no longer shared spiritual fellowship because he always shied off when I attempted to confront him, managing to avoid facing every issue, totally refusing to be in any way accountable.

Our pickup had been stolen from a car-park in town and we couldn't replace it because there were none in the country. Every day presented us with new logistical problems. I refused to succumb to the idea that problems were worse in Africa; it just seemed that way, especially when they crowded in day after day in bunches.

Walking down the lane to the house, I gave myself up to the simple pleasure of admiring the towering poinsettias. Their magnificent dinner-plate-sized heads of scarlet bracts reared up against the cloudless blue sky with such intensity that the feast of colour was almost too much for one's eyes to bear.

The lawns showed brown patches among the dun seeded grass. Formerly there had always been enough water to irrigate them but now this precious commodity was reserved for only truly essential needs such as the houses, marketable crops and the livestock. Since we were at the head of the river, we had a legal duty to see that water was kept flowing to our neighbours downstream. This meant that at the extreme end of the dry season, we had to build several sandbag bunds across the river at intervals, creating a series of small dams. After taking the minimum we needed each day, these small dams were then left to fill up and the water thus kept trickling down. Thankfully, the spring-fed river never entirely dried up.

But somehow this dry season had seemed twice as long, more than twice as tiring. Our practical problems appeared larger and the solutions seemed more elusive. Gordon said little apart from making conventional conversation relating to work. Except when he was absent, I had little to do with the running of the farm now. My stamina and willpower were finite. At that time it took all my energy to fight the doubts that crowded in.

Was I a fool to go on hoping and praying for renewal? How much of the present deadlock was my fault? Should I be doing things differently? I knew that if ever my doubts and fears gained the upper hand, the solutions would recede farther and what little resources I still had would dissolve. Resolutely, I pushed counterproductive thoughts aside and concentrated on the tasks in hand.

Across the road a mulberry hedge bordered the top field. Its deep green luxuriant leaves stood out fresh in the dusty atmosphere. A long stretch of it had been layered to form a thick impenetrable barrier against the livestock. The rest of it, together with a shorter hedge near the house, was growing free, reaching some eight to ten feet high. With the pastures dry and stock feed in such short supply, we'd been forced to harvest this bounty, cutting it fresh daily and feeding it to the milking herd together with chopped up banana leaves and a quantity of straw from the deep litter poultry houses. This litter was valuable for the amount of poultry meal it contained, dropped from the feeders, and the milk yield kept up reasonably well.

The work of God was still going on, though slowly. A church had become established over the river and we had found a young Zambian man to take care of it. There were very few visitors apart from the occasional overland expedition groups. Military mopping up activities were still ongoing in various areas and occasional curfews still reminded us of the war. There was a spate of armed robberies and the mother of a child at the boys' old school was shot dead in the car park when there was an attempt to steal her car at gunpoint.

Food shortages of all sorts were now the norm. Prices rocketed as inflation soared. Good housekeeping meant learning to keep one's ear to the ground to detect spasmodic supplies arriving at various points round the town, furious telephoning round to alert one's friends, and queues. I became adept at gathering supplies from afar, even as far away as South Africa and England. Hardly anyone travelled without a list of what to look for or track down. Among farmers, barter became fashionable again. What tiny amount of flour was available in the country went direct to bakers to keep them in business but bread was in very short supply. I rationed bread to one meal per day, usually breakfast, and hoarded a little flour for the rare treat of an occasional birthday cake. This treasure was kept in the freezer to keep it free of weevils. I experimented with homemade cereals using sun dried fruit, oats brought in from South Africa and local ground nuts.

It was November and the rains were late. For days we'd seen the sky to the north light up with flashes of forked lightning and heard a few distant rumbles of thunder, but nothing came our way. The limit on our water had been reached and we were forced to stop pumping once our tanks were full. It was taking almost twenty hours for the weir pools to fill and very little was flowing downstream. It had never been as bad as this before.

The previous two seasons had been drier than usual, acerbated by the growth of the city, the official limits of which now came within a few miles of the farm. Over the whole area, the water table had dropped ten feet below what it had been when we had come to the property. It was looking very serious and owing to the setbacks in our business during and since the war, there was no spare money to sink a borehole. A great deal was riding on our hopes for good rains.

Storm clouds continued to pile up to the north – great grey towers that promised so much but as yet had not delivered their bounty. Perspiration trickled down my back as I pushed straggling damp hair off my face and sighed. The faint sound of muted thunder reached me but it was miles away. Everything was wilting under the brassy noon sky. I went to the open kitchen door and, holding my hand across my face against the relentless sun, stared out. It seemed as if the whole arid land was groaning and panting. Only the constant sound of the cicadas in the trees lacerated the stagnant heat haze.

Down in the garden I saw our old gardener unhurriedly going through the motions though there was almost nothing to be done. I smiled to see him working his way towards the place where he'd surreptitiously planted a dagga plant or two. Did he think we had not noticed? He glanced at the sky and, evidently deciding it was lunch time, wandered off and flopped down in the shade of the jacaranda tree. I watched him rummage in a tattered pocket for his habitual bit of snuff. He rolled it with gnarled fingers in the palm of his hand, then took a pinch with finger and thumb, lifted it to his nostrils and luxuriously inhaled. I watched him lay back on the grass contentedly and for a moment I quite envied him. If only our problems would yield to such a simple remedy. He was a faithful old man long due for retirement but we had no desire to deny him the dignity of a job while he could still manage the flower garden.

All morning echoes of past struggles and doubts had drifted un-bidden through my mind. They were less prevalent now that some of the bad memories from the previous two years were cloaked with time. Nevertheless, from time to time I did remember the massacre of the Elim missionaries a few months before our raid and the deaths in our own neighbourhood. No doubt, many of these people had prayed for protection. Why had we been spared? I was everlastingly thankful that we *had* been but there was no room for complacency. I was not particularly brave, no more than the next woman, but in God's grace those fears had subsided as I remembered the Holy Spirit's enabling power to meet my needs, whatever they were.

Two days later the rains broke. A new breath of life flowed over the land. I stood under the eaves as the rain water sluiced off the roof like a waterfall, washing over the patio paving and running down the sloping path. Throughout the garden, leaves gleamed as the dust was rinsed away. Next day, there was no trace left as the hungry earth had absorbed every drop, but the air bore a hundred new fragrances and we knew there would be more rain before nightfall. Momentarily my problems faded into the background in the face of such blessing.

CHAPTER EIGHTEEN

The Camp

With the onset of the rains we all felt revived. Business picked up and supplies eased a little. During the preceding dry season we had not been able to get on to all our land across the river and a priority was to assess the damage to the buildings there. These buildings were all grouped directly across the river to the homestead and all belonged to what we called "the campsite" (officially, Evangelical Outreach).

Originally set aside for a young people's facility, it had been used on two occasions as temporary housing for missionary families who had to flee from their homes in Katanga Province, Zaire, at a time of political unrest and danger. As soon as we could after our raid, we went over the river to assess the damage and found that most of the equipment and simple furniture had been stolen, so we left the remaining doors locked and decided the whole complex would have to remain closed until such time as we could begin repairs and start again. A pile of timber roof frames, purchased for the new dining hall and delivered just before we were forced to abandon the land, were now useless, half hidden in the weeds where they'd been destroyed, eaten by white ants.

When we first came to live there, we'd decided that the land immediately across the river should be set aside for the possible future development of our mission work. For several years we'd not known exactly what form that would take, so we waited. Even after the difficult years following our fire, we clung to the hope that the day would come when the door would open for something specific. We had no money to invest ourselves but believed the land would lend itself very well for some sort of Christian venture. Like the land on which we'd built our homestead and farm buildings, it sloped down to the river in a series of natural terraces with many fine trees and grassy slopes, and it had a dirt track leading to the main road a half-mile or so beyond our farm turnoff.

Early in 1970 it had come to our notice that an interdenominational group of people in Lusaka were actively seeking a site on which to hold camps for young people, seminars, conferences and the like. The first indication we had of this was when we heard the need mentioned among the notices given one Sunday in church. So we spoke up and invited the group to come and look at our site. It so happened that another piece of land not very far from us was also offered about the same time.

In due course, the interested group arranged to view both sites Afterwards it was always encouraging to reflect that they had this choice because when they accepted our site, we felt it was confirmation of our hopes for such a project.

The downside was that this selection committee was not in a position to finance any development themselves; they were first and foremost concerned that there should be such a place near the capital in Zambia's Central Province. There was only one other such facility and that was in North-West Province, several hundred miles away. But their acceptance was the 'open door' that we'd waited for so long. Very soon talks began in earnest and produced ideas as to how exactly this site could be utilized.

It was decided that in the main the site should be used for organisations such as Scripture Union which was strong in many secondary schools, Nurses Christian Fellowship and the Evangelical Fellowship of Zambia and that other church groups and missions might well use it for training sessions. Indeed, so many opportunities now seemed possible. In time, we came to see many of these things happen and the camp became a valuable asset to much Christian endeavour.

Within a month we received the first donation and although it was small, it kept up the momentum of interest in this new project. The narrow dirt track that led to the main road was cleared and made good to take vehicles. The project was well publicized among the churches in the area and practical offers of help soon came in, particularly from our own church, Lusaka Baptist, where there was a large student body from various colleges and the university.

It was at a gathering of young people from the Brethren Church, who had spent an afternoon at the farm, that the meeting took place between a young German volunteer who was teaching at the Trades Training Institute, and a shy, clever young British accountant. The German young man came forward very early on. He was a civil engineer and he started off by surveying the site and searching our land for any useful natural resources we might use such as stone, sand and gravel. Coming out to us after work, this enterprising young man rigged up an extension light so he could work late in the evenings. He made experimental building blocks, designed the first houses and made models to interest other people in the project.

After a while he asked us if he could live at the farm, which would make it easier for him to give more time to the project, and this proved to be a very happy arrangement. He and the accountant talked a long time at that first meeting and it was obvious that the accountant was very interested. Neither said anything to us that day and the first intimation we had that they had formed a working partnership came later that week. The accountant, very correct in his business suit, arrived late one afternoon complete with briefcase. He walked straight into the house without a word and headed up the hall to our German friend's bedroom. The duo appeared a little later on with the accountant dressed in old shorts, a battered hat and clutching a shovel. As I watched the animated pair head toward the river crossing, I smiled to myself over our engineer's habit of keeping his tools under his bed, though I must say he always brought them back clean.

Both young men enjoyed the partnership and together they achieved a lot. When our young engineering friend returned to Germany at the end of his contract, the accountant took over his room and became a part of our family. He quietly created great enthusiasm and before long another young civil engineer got involved and the work went on apace. Both these young men met their future wives among the Christians in Lusaka during this period and we hosted one of their weddings.

In the dry season, working parties became a regular event. From time to time, such an event was advertised amongst Lusaka's university student body and our farm truck would collect willing workers from the campus on a Saturday morning. Once on site, everyone pitched in,

180

dug, shovelled, pushed wheelbarrows, carried water or manned the concrete mixer that our local civil engineer had gifted to us. Of course, our children loved these occasions too. The sound of this happy activity floated across the river and often attracted some of our visitors to join in.

Late in the afternoon, work would cease and it was time for hungry, tired youngsters to slough off the dust and sweat by a swim in the river before flopping on the lawns to enjoy homemade hamburgers and cool drinks. Usually there'd be someone with a guitar to start a singsong as darkness fell. Then everyone would clamber aboard the truck for the trip back to town.

The project was named 'Evangelical Outreach'. Cash was slow to come in but progress was steady. Sometimes the farm contributed some skilled labour and, of course, all the transport needed, and our farm carpenter supervised the fitting of door and window frames. There proved to be very little useful building material on our land with the exception of a small amount of slate and stone which was used for low ornamental walls and the steps in front of each house.

The first houses were of three rooms each with a veranda. We added a separate kitchen unit, two ablution blocks, two large buildings to serve as dormitories and another building for meetings that also housed a library. This complex gave the camp considerable flexibility and we planned to add a dining hall and chapel later.

It was planned that the camp should be used in the dry season only, from Easter until late November. It wasn't just a question of shelter from the rains, but also consideration for the grounds. Whatever wear and tear took place, the five-month rest in the rains allowed for replenishment and the site kept its fresh, natural look. Meals were taken outside under the shade of the trees on a grassy slope near the kitchen, the site also of the campfire. The iron rim of a car wheel hung in a tree and, struck with an iron bar, made a simple and effective gong that announced both meals and meetings.

The whole site sloped down to the river and all the buildings were built on the contour, no one overlooking the other. They all faced the river and most had front steps, according to the lie of the land, which were popular gathering places. We'd taken care to preserve the indigenous trees. All access to the river was below where we pumped our water and there was one lovely reach where baptisms took place.

The Baptist minister's wife, who taught hotel management skills, offered her expertise; she worked out some simple recipes and made a chart of food quantities needed for various-sized groups. This was made available to all group caterers and cooks, as they were all self-catering. The lockable kitchen was furnished with an industrial size bottled gas stove and heavy steel table but until the time when we could have a permanent manager living on site, all other equipment was kept in store on the farm. I looked after this and issued it at the start of each camp: cutlery, tin mugs and plates, washing up bowls, water containers and jugs, cooking pots, mattresses, chairs, benches and tables, brooms and a cylinder of gas. And because we had electric lights throughout the camp and had put in the appropriate fitting in the kitchen, we had a large tea urn that went as well. Fresh milk from our dairy and some produce was available at cost.

Designed as it was, the cost to campers was very low so that the whole facility was within the reach of as many people as possible, particularly students. As the years went by and the costs inevitably rose, we kept to this policy even when it became necessary to personally subsidize the project.

The first phase of the campsite could sleep a hundred youngsters, sleeping dormitory-fashion on mattresses on the floor. We could hear their singing from the homestead. The traffic between farmstead and camp was constant. In the second year, a large area that was fairly flat, next to our boundary, was cleared to establish a sports field. *"Tiyende ku caya bala,"* the cry would ring out. ("Let's play football.")

Often the campers would erect tents to house family parties and occasionally a large marquee was added for a particularly large group. On one memorable occasion three hundred people built grass-walled 'stockades', each with a central fireplace, and slept under the stars.

Throughout the years of unrest, we'd struggled to keep our telephone working; not always easy when newly repairs lines were purloined for the value of the copper wire. We invested in a new telephone system. The thirty-foot radio mast had only just been put up and the service initiated when a call came through on a day when Gordon was away. It was the United Nations High Commission for Refugees (UNCR) office in Lusaka. We were well acquainted with their personnel, having been involved in several instances. The caller needed our help.

Apparently, a refugee camp only a few miles south of the city had been bombed that morning and it was necessary to evacuate more than eighty of the un-injured Angolan refugees without delay. Cluster bombs had been dropped and the place was in a shambles. UNCR would provide blankets and food, together with some supervisors.

"My husband isn't here," was my first reaction.

"It is really urgent, Mrs Bland. The Salvation Army people haven't the space – and anyway, we think your place is more suitable." The line went quiet.

I thought for a moment, wishing Gordon were around to take the responsibility, agree or refuse. Our camp, unofficial and farther away from the city, was more easily isolated and more suitable as the situation was politically sensitive. I snapped back to attention as the voice came again.

"Mrs Bland? What do you say?" The voice now had a slight edge. Time was obviously at a premium. Then the clincher: "Two thirds of them are women and children."

"How soon do you want to come?" I asked.

"ETA is about an hour and a half. Thanks," and he rang off.

I put the phone down with a whispered prayer. I had a sick feeling in my stomach and thought Gordon would probably not approve because of the political angle. I swiftly took the campsite keys from their hook, grabbed a bag of sugar and a packet of tea from the kitchen, and ran to the equipment store, shouting across the field to summons the nearest farm workers. My tone brought them on the run.

There was no vehicle handy except for the tractor so I summoned the driver and bade him to couple up the trailer and, unlocking the store shed, issued instructions to the gathered men. Thankfully there was a new, full gas cylinder and as I urged the men, I ticked off my mental list of what they'd need. Time was of the essence. It was better not to be there when the refugees arrived and I wanted to get the stuff delivered as quickly as possible. Once the tractor was headed for the cattle drift over the river, I followed on foot, calling at the dairy on the way to arrange for a gallon of milk to be sent over immediately. While the men unloaded the tractor-load on to the veranda, I opened up the kitchen and laid the keys to the other buildings on the table, flanked by the tea, sugar and milk churn. Quickly despatching a man to the water pump to ensure all the tanks were full, I told all the others to go back to the farm with the tractor.

As I filled the tea urn, I prayed for the refugees in their trauma. I so wanted to bid them welcome but I knew I shouldn't stay; it wasn't necessary or wise. Turning the urn to low, I left the camp. As I crossed the drift and turned along the river path towards the house, I heard the refugees' trucks pull in.

CHAPTER NINETEEN

The Hidden Snare

Life in Zambia was slowly restored to normal but it would never be the same as before. Inevitably, there were many weapons left behind or cheaply traded. This ushered a period characterized by an upsurge of armed robberies. Out of town, farmers and plot holders beefed up the number of watchmen they employed and patrolled their boundaries, while we put some money behind the building of a new police post a mile or so away on the main road and the acquisition of a vehicle that patrolled the district. That vehicle's driver had radio contact with all the local residents and we got used to having a receiver crackling away on the mantelpiece in the sitting room or in the bedroom, depending on the hour. In town, private home owners built security walls around their properties and employed night guards and deployed dogs. These walls were usually built of concrete blocks, some six to eight feet high, topped with broken glass. This meant employing a night watchman who was also on hand to open up when the resident returned home. But these precautions then became a danger as people were sometimes held up and robbed as they waited in their vehicles for their watchmen to open the gates. Gradually or speedily, we all adapted to the new conditions and life went on.

Grace trained as a legal secretary. On completion, she got a job and founded a youth group that met in the Salvation Army Hall. She'd always had a particular interest in reaching the young people in the city, many of whom she'd known at school. They were an interesting, varied group from a dozen different cultural backgrounds. Later, those who had responded to the gospel became integrated into the local churches.

Zambia and Rhodesia/Zimbabwe were still sorting out a few problems left over from the war, not least of which was the rehabilitation of thousands of freedom fighters. A large portion of these had been forcibly bussed from their villages as children and had grown up in the camps, only taught political propaganda, how to use weapons and how to kill. Once our area had been cleared, we were not affected by these activities. But in October 1980 a curfew was imposed, very hurriedly with little warning to residents.

We had planned an evening barbecue to celebrate Grace's twenty-first birthday and we had to cancel at less than twenty-four hours' notice because our guests couldn't travel after dark. Our telephone was out of order at the time so we couldn't even contact most of them. But everyone figured it out and our friends started arriving from lunchtime, so the party happened impromptu and ran all afternoon. And when everyone had gone home, just the family and farm residents were left to enjoy a barbecue under the stars.

The large farm manager's house was not needed for Gordon's new assistant. Instead he was housed in the flat above the garage and the house was rented out to some friends, a professional couple with children.

When Gordon decided we should have a holiday in England, in the spring of '81, I was delighted. But because he didn't want to leave his somewhat inexperienced new assistant in charge for too long, he decided I should go first for a few weeks, then he would join me for a day or two, and then I would return before him. I accepted this arrangement because I wanted to see my family and our boys.

After the holiday, Gordon said he'd check on my flight departure time and without checking it myself, I accepted his estimate of when we should set out for the airport. But by the time we arrived, I'd missed the flight by nearly two hours. There wasn't another flight for forty-eight hours so I had to return and change my ticket for two days later.

Eventually, however, I was on my way, and as I breakfasted on the aircraft, the African sunrise streaked the sky orange, gold and lemon. My, but it felt good to be coming home. I loved the overnight flight, that little space between two worlds. Saying goodbye to my family as the sun set on scenes of my former life was always a bit sad. But waking up in a new dawn while speeding towards the land of my adoption and the work I loved, I was always filled with contentment and felt a small frisson of excitement.

Our descent began and as the undercarriage clunked down, I looked out of the window watching for the first sight of that vast expanse of brown grass far below. As the first glimpses appeared below the thin drifting cloud, I felt again the familiar warmth of affection for this land. The earth rushed up and I felt the ground effect cushion our impact, then the touchdown 'squeak' of the tyres meeting the runway followed by the long drawn out vibration as we rumbled to a halt. Breathing a brief thanksgiving, I unbuckled my seatbelt.

My luggage cart sped away in the charge of our driver and I followed him to the car park. At the pedestrian crossing on the forecourt, I lifted my face to the ever-constant breeze and was greeted with the familiar *ping-ping* wind snap of the flag halyards against the poles lining the airport approach. Driving down the Great East Road towards the city, I reflected on the past week. It had been such a let down to find I'd missed my plane.

My overlapping days with Gordon had been a strain. These unexpected two extra days with him had exhausted me. I tried to talk to him but he was evasive and easily found reasons to be elsewhere. I was anxious to get back. I was heartsick over the rumors that had reached me regarding my husband's behavior while I'd been away. He wouldn't be drawn on the subject. All my old misgivings rose up to haunt me. I didn't want to go back; I didn't want to stay. Only necessity pushed me forward.

We skirted the city and took the road out to Lusaka West. Thumping down off the ramp on to the last half-mile of dirt road before our signpost, we sped down the sand lane and in through the gate. There were cattle grazing serenely beneath the blue gums in the top paddock and as we slowed down for the last corner at the end of the drive, I caught a glimpse of the waterfall glinting in the sun, a picture framed in fronds of golden shower creeper. The driver tooted and stopped the car in front of the house. The dogs rushed out to circle the car in noisy welcome. I was home.

Within the hour I was facing a barrage of difficulties in the office as our secretary had walked out the previous day in dubious circumstances. She'd left a cryptic message to say that she'd originally planned to stay until my return but when informed of the delay, she'd decided to go and not wait. She was the daughter of Christian friends and had played a part in the ministry, so I was both puzzled and deeply concerned. She'd offered no other information or explanation, and I couldn't understand why she'd not waited until my arrival.

Hard on the heels of this setback, there was even more unsettling news. Our young farm assistant had been drunk on several occasions and had beaten his wife and put her in the hospital. I began to think things were seriously falling apart. But worse was to come. Our tenant from Bethesda House came down to see me. In a painful interview, he told me about my husband's determined and improper visits to his wife. There was no mistake; there were witnesses. I could only share his distress and reluctantly accept that our ten years of friendship were over and that they were leaving.

By the end of the week it seemed as if I'd never been away, except now I was two valued friends short. They had left the farm immediately and a few weeks later left for America. My saddened spirit sank to a new low. When I confronted Gordon on his return, he rationalized his behaviour and became very angry. In no way would he be accountable.

Sometime before these events, he had moved from the church in town and with the help of two young Zambian brethren had commenced services in one of the suburbs in order to plant a church there under the umbrella of the established Baptist church. He made it clear he expected me to go with him and so began another very difficult period for me. He was spending a lot of unaccountable time away from home. About that time, I discovered a quantity of pornographic material hidden in the office and confronted him. He retaliated angrily and physically, knocking me across the room with enough force to break my glasses. This was very frightening and I began to dread his abrupt mood changes.

Previously, I had gone to the church leadership about his infidelity, but he was a deacon of some years' standing and they had difficulty in believing me against his smooth denials. His apparent sincerity and personal charisma carried the day; he was a master at dissembling. The pastor did not take any action and ostensibly Gordon carried on. However, I later learned that the pastor had been uneasy and continued to be suspicious.

Only recently recovered from a bout of amoebic dysentery, another health issue began to plague me. My deepening anxieties were having a debilitating effect. The accidental discovery of the pornographic material amongst my husband's things had sent me on a hunt throughout the homestead. One day, in his absence, I made a bonfire of what I'd found. I knew I could not clean up someone else's mess but my revulsion demanded I take some action. He never asked me about the disappearance of this material and when I challenged him, he denied its existence to my face.

I embarked on spiritual warfare, combat that lasted for years. I would not tolerate such an invasion of my life and home. As I discovered later, he merely moved such material to outside hiding places. I did not fully understand then that all this was but a symptom of a far deeper disorder.

My health demanded a short stay in hospital. It seemed as if I was being attacked on all sides. The day after I came out of hospital, my laundry worker brought the day's basket of clean laundry to me in the kitchen. As I picked up a pile ready to stow away in the linen cupboard, I leapt back in terror. A puff adder was coiled between the folded sheets.

Confrontation with Gordon proved futile. He rationalized his behaviour, angrily accusing me of being domineering and prudish. On the day I found irrefutable evidence of his continuing relationship with the builder's wife, my anger, frustration and anxiety reached an explosive level. I felt I would fly into a thousand pieces. I didn't want to start anything in the house because of the presence of other people and managed to hang on until I saw him walk down to the river. I followed him.

"Gordon, wait. I must talk to you," I began as I caught up to him.

"What about? Can't it wait?"

"No, it can't," I replied, striving for control.

He was still walking. "Be quick then. I'm going to the cattle dip." Then he stopped and faced me with a closed expression.

"I know you continue to visit her," I said, naming her. "Why do you persist in appearing one way publicly and yet act so differently in private? Why have you broken every promise you've ever made to me?" Despite my efforts to keep calm, I was conscious of my voice rising.

"What are you talking about?" he demanded furiously.

"Don't deny it. You've been seen with her."

"So what?" he snapped back.

I gasped at his obduracy. His eyes were cold and his whole demeanour frightened me but I tried again. "When are you going to face up to what you're doing? Are you not ashamed?"

"So, what's it got to do with you? I'm my own master. I will not be dictated to!" His face contorted in anger and he took a half step towards me threateningly.

"What's it got to do with me? You carry on living in this double standard manner, showing one face to the church and one face to those who look up to you. You're nice to other people and so different to your family." In my helpless rage I spluttered to a stop.

"You're hysterical. Stop this stupid shouting." His implacable coldness was like hitting a stone wall.

I began to cry, wringing my hands in distress.

"For goodness sake," he went on, "pull yourself together."

But I was past caring. "You're a real sheep in wolf's clothing. You've got me over a barrel. You know I'm not well, but you don't care, do you?" I was pacing back and forth in my agitation. "You just go on doing exactly whatever you want. Why do you always want to look so big in front of other people and ignore the love and respect your family would give you if only you'd stop acting this way? Why don't you practise what you preach?" I ran out of steam and stood gasping, tears pouring down my face.

"Stop this puritanical tirade. I'm your husband. I'll do what I want and how I want. Don't let me hear any more of this dramatic nonsense. I'm responsible before God, so shut up! And stop blubbering," he finished irritably and strode off.

He really does think it's okay, I thought in frightened astonishment. *So be it...*

Dispirited, I trailed back up the house, deeply thankful that we had been out of earshot. It was becoming more and more difficult to be round other people, conscious as I was of our deepening animosity. How was it all going to end? I was fast becoming conditioned to expect more difficulties and the one I feared most was the state of our marriage. I felt so helpless without resources of my own.

My mind was in constant turmoil and in desperation I talked to my doctor, who prescribed Lorexepam, trade name 'Ativan'. It was the ultimate snare that would bring me down. Designed to allow a person to cope in a time of crisis, Ativan pills were small, blue and oblong. I learned later that the assumption by the medical profession was that once the period of crisis was over, the patient would not need them. My prescription was one in the morning and one at night and I never took more than this. They did help me at first but my doctor kept me on them continually, even when I began to report odd side effects. Having no other recourse than to accept what he advised, I was to take them for four years.

Almost no one came to visit now, which was not surprising, with the exception of missionary friends from time to time. A mixed-marriage refugee couple from South Africa came to us while waiting for the UNHCR[6] to arrange their passage to Brazil, and after them an Australian lady and her three children after the sudden death of her husband.

On the day, I had to go into hospital again briefly, there were still some remnants of tension in the country. Medicines and medical equipment were in very short supply and there was still a military presence at the hospital. Having been advised to report at 6 am, ready in night clothes, we arrived to find the hospital gates closed and guarded by soldiers, who were turning private vehicles away. So I had to walk in from the road in my dressing gown. Just as well it wasn't raining!

That afternoon, as I sleepily recovered, I looked around the ward. A 'pinky', the ward maid who wore a pink uniform overall, was sweeping the floor in a desultory fashion. She ended up with a small pyramid of sandy dust in the middle of the room. I watched as she looked around for something to use to pick it up in lieu of a dustpan. She moved towards my bed, took the clipboard from the end of the bed, brushed up the dirt and threw it out of the nearest window. Casually giving the board a swipe against her pink rump to clean it off, she solemnly returned it to the end of my bed and sauntered out. I smiled. Somehow, for a moment, that humorous little tableau lightened my heart.

Once fully recovered, I began to think of leaving but the way was fraught with difficulties. I had no money and no alternate place to go. Grace was working and temporarily house-sitting in town with a friend. In England, even if I could get there, the boys were in lodgings and my brother and his wife were sharing my mother's house and caring for

---

[6] United Nations High Commission for Refugees

her. It wasn't possible for me to set up alternate accommodation locally in Zambia and, in any case, that wouldn't work. It was a time of great emotional confusion as I struggled to find a way out of my dilemma.

Deep down, I knew I had to make a change, for God is not the author of confusion. I did not believe it was his will that my life was being reduced to nought in this manner, nor was it pleasing to him that our family and all we'd worked for and believed in should disintegrate. However, God's word also warns his people saying, "Depart, depart, go out from there! Touch no unclean thing! Come out from it and be pure..."[7] It goes on to give a promise of his provision and care in such a situation. But before I could make plans, the opportunity was lost.

---

[7] Isaiah 52:11

CHAPTER TWENTY

A Portentous Letter

Gordon announced he was going away and in a matter of days was off to England. This had become an increasing defence pattern. Unwilling to be accountable, he would go off somewhere at short notice – to the bush, on a trip with friends, to England "on business" – leaving me with the responsibility of the farm. Not that I was unable to handle this, indeed I was very capable, but it completely tied my hands. Despite a certain relief his absence gave me, the respite from personal strife, I was still committed to the belief that it was possible for our marriage to be healed if only he would face the problem, be accountable and confess the sin and ask God to help him. Whatever my outward demeanour communicated to those around me, I began a deep personal pilgrimage, deeply convinced that in the power and grace of God, it would be possible to rebuild.

Before he left, we shared a rare, precious moment when he took me aside and confessed he believed he'd had two demons with him since childhood. In tears, he begged me to pray for him, which I willingly did then and there. I had long known that he'd had many difficulties in his childhood but I had no knowledge or experience to understand the possible ramifications. It was totally outside my experience. After we talked, I laid hands on him and commanded the spirits to leave in Jesus' name. He gagged and retched and keeled over. I opened all the windows and sat beside him praying quietly.

After a while he recovered and I suggested, since we had been on our own, that we drive into town and share all this with the pastor. Gordon agreed. I wasn't sure how much experience the pastor had in these matters though. Afterwards I continued to be deeply concerned and could only pray that this would prove to be a turning point.

This exceptional interlude refuelled my desire to leave no stone unturned in seeking a lasting solution. Shortly after Gordon's departure, I sought an opportunity to consult the only person I knew of with the right experience. He was on a mission station some seven hundred miles away, two days' journey. There was a degree of difficulty in this because I didn't want to divulge my real motive for the trip to anyone else and I didn't think it wise to attempt to travel so far by road on my own in case of a breakdown. I waited on the Lord for an opening and put out a few feelers.

Within a few days, a large mission headquarters in the city contacted me. They needed to get a consignment of X-ray plates to their hospital way up in the north which was within striking distance of where I wanted to go.

Fortunately, at the time we had a mature couple staying at the farm, long term friends of ours, who were very helpful. The husband agreed to go with me and share the driving while his wife agreed to take care of my houschold. So off we went with our precious cargo well packed and crated. We broke our journey on the Copperbelt overnight and pushed on the following day. The badly corrugated dirt road was rough and he did the lion's share of the driving that day so that we reached our destination just before nightfall.

The next morning, I sent him on with the X-ray plates to the hospital, knowing he'd be gone all day, and I spent the day alone with my host and his wife who'd received me very graciously. It was agreed that they would invite Gordon and me to a missionary gathering to be held later that year at their home. For my part, I was to do everything I could to persuade my husband to take me there.

Encouraged and hopeful, I returned home. The trip had been tiring: hundreds of miles on 'wash-board' road often with tree roots exposed, alternating with patches of soft sand. I knew I'd not have managed on my own and was deeply grateful to our friend who had shared this journey with me.

When my husband came home, we talked it over and he agreed we should go. Accordingly, in September we made the trip. Things between us had eased a little since his return and I had high hopes that the visit would prove spiritually beneficial. We were warmly welcomed and the general fellowship greatly blessed us. True to his word, our host took care to spend some time privately with Gordon and he, in turn, opened up to a remarkable degree. Then our host specifically instructed him in what to do when he returned home, referring to what is taught in Luke 11:20-26. For example, he should clean out any remaining pornography, with repentance and in obedience, and walk the farm with witnesses, claiming back any area given over to the enemy; he should do everything necessary to ensure that Satan had no further foothold there. We journeyed home in harmony.

Yet after our return, I was dismayed to find there was no immediate sign of him doing any of this. Knowing he had to do it himself, I sought the Lord in prayer but put no pressure on him. I could only promise to stay by his side and support him. But as the weeks went by, my heart sank as I saw no sign in him that he intended to follow through on the good advice our friend had urged him with. I wondered what the future would hold if he disobeyed.

During October and November, we were plagued by several thefts. By Christmas there had been a dozen or so incidents, stock theft large and small, break-ins to house and guest rooms, and another of our vehicles was taken. On Christmas Eve, I drove the farm van to town, taking cream and eggs to a friend. Shortly after turning on to the main thoroughfare into the city, where the road curved, I felt something akin to a push between my shoulder blades that caused me to swerve. The van crossed two traffic lanes without colliding with another vehicle and hit the concrete base of a street light at about forty miles per hour. At no time did I black out and I actually got myself out of the van, only to fall on my knees on the grass verge. Our almost new van was a total write-off. I suffered damaged ribs, a sprained thumb and a nasty bang on my forehead where it had connected with the rear-view mirror. My left knee was deeply slashed with a sliver of metal and my nose was bleeding profusely.

A passer-by stopped and came to my aid and that's when I discovered that the impact had caused the eggs and cream to ricochet from their place in the back and they'd hit the back of my head and dress. The gentleman who had come to my aid took me to my doctor and said he'd go out to the farm and inform my husband. The doctor stitched up the slash on my knee and administered an anti-tetanus shot, but she was concerned about the injury to the ribs and insisted I go to the hospital for X-rays. Gordon caught up with me in the hospital but I really didn't want to be in hospital for Christmas, so he persuaded them to let me go.

By the time I got home five hours later, the broken eggs and cream together with the blood had caked hard on my pale grey dress and in my hair. I was stiff with bruises, reaction and pain and hardly able to walk. I must have looked a sight but was so glad to be home. Afterwards it wasn't possible to work out why the accident had happened. To my knowledge, my husband never had the van examined for a possible fault, and it remained a mystery.

Two days later, while I was in bed, a thief came through the low open window and snatched my handbag from the dressing table. He was so quick and I couldn't move to stop him because of my injuries. It was a considerable time before my cries were heard at the other end of the house, and he was long gone.

Directly after Christmas, Grace went to Salisbury, soon to be named Harare, to make the arrangements for a further study course. While she was there she had her passport stolen but managed to get back by special travel document. The real shock came when the British High Commission in Lusaka who had issued it refused to replace it. Born in Bulawayo when Southern Rhodesia was a Crown Colony, she was registered British at birth and had held a British passport since age twelve. Now in the changing political climate, neither her British registered birth certificate nor her British parentage could help. It didn't make sense and we found it profoundly shocking but the authorities were adamant and all our appeals fell on deaf ears.

Since she had been resident in Zambia since three weeks old, we commenced proceedings to apply for Zambian citizenship and provided a complete dossier to verify this. But it also proved futile. She was stateless.

If there was real trouble, the British High Commission would act for us but would not for her and I couldn't bear to think of her left alone in a time of national emergency. Gordon merely commented with a shrug, "Whatever..." Insidiously, the pressure on me was building and my feeling of hopelessness and fear increased.

There was a sequel to the church leaders' disquiet regarding my husband's questionable behaviour. Having told my husband that he wanted to talk to both of us, our pastor, who still harboured grave doubts about him, came out to the farm. My husband told me the pastor was coming on urgent, confidential church business and that I should leave them uninterrupted. On the day, he met the pastor's car in the drive and conducted him directly down to a seat beside the river. From the kitchen I could see the two men sitting and talking. After an hour or so, Gordon walked the pastor back up the far side of the lawn to where he'd parked his car out of my sight. I heard the car leaving and later my husband entered the house but didn't say anything about the visit.

Years later in Cape Town, on a visit to that same pastor, I learned that my husband had actually told him that I was away from home, so sure was he that I would do exactly as he instructed and not show myself. When I heard this, I realized just how much I'd been manipulated. The pastor admitted to me that he'd come to challenge Gordon and although he had been expecting to see me, was more or less convinced by my husband's assurances but went away still feeling vaguely uneasy.

We had a friend who'd completed his tour of duty with a large mission station to the south of us, yet still had some time left on his work permit. He offered to use the time helping us if we could house his family as his three children were in school in Lusaka. Since we had hopes of the Evangelical Outreach work resuming on our campsite, Gordon agreed to let them live rent-free in the then farm manager's house, which was vacant at the time. They came and I welcomed them, sure they would prove an asset.

Shortly after this, in January, Stuart took some friends out in my car and was involved in an accident, though fortunately he was not hurt badly. But I was still not fully recovered from my own accident and went down to Salisbury for a convalescent short break with friends. A couple of weeks later I came back feeling very much better but I was increasingly concerned because Gordon had still not followed through on the advice he was given on our trip north months earlier. When I asked him when he intended taking the actions our friend had suggested, he made excuses and rationalized his inaction, and then became angry. I tried to encourage him but that seemed to fuel his anger more. I recognised that the demonic spirit that had not yet been dealt with was reacting to the presence of the Holy Spirit in me.

Months were going by and there was no progress in the matter of Grace's citizenship. Meanwhile, the farm was experiencing financial problems. Stuart, who was marking time before going to college in America, worked on the farm that season. His one desire was to fly and after much effort he won a place at LeTourneau College in Texas that specialized in Engineering and Flight. In April he was welding security bars on the windows of one of our houses when thoughtlessly he forgot to snap down his visor and injured his eyes badly. I rushed him into town for treatment and he was blind for two weeks but thankfully no lasting damage was done. Weeks later he had a bad motorbike accident. The year was becoming a nightmare. The hospital had no plaster in which to set his leg, so he lay immobilized by sandbags while we sent a request by radio to the nearest mission hospital; they kindly spared us some and we arranged its transport up to Lusaka. Gordon returned but my health was deteriorating. As I grew weaker in body, Stuart made a good recovery and finally left for America.

That same week, I was so weak one day that I slid down the wall on which I was leaning and was unable to stand up again. I crawled to my bedroom. A subsequent consultation with my doctor led to an arrangement for me to go down to South Africa for surgery.

In late September, Gordon drove me to Durban in Natal where we stayed with a friend about sixty miles down the coast in the little seaside town of Margate. Such was the state of Zambia's economy at the time that we were officially not allowed to take any money out of the country whatsoever. We were glad that our car had been originally registered in South Africa before it was imported, otherwise we would have been required to deposit its worth at both the Zambian and Zimbabwe borders. Unofficially we had a tiny amount of U.S. and South African cash from friends to help us.

There were two weeks to wait before I could have the surgery and Gordon waited with me until we returned to Durban. Then, while I was in hospital, he met a stripper and actually brought her with him one day to visit me. I had no idea what she did then, and surprisingly she came again on her own to see me. She was a pleasant woman and I'd accepted his explanation that she was someone he'd met at the guest house. We talked easily and even touched on the things of God. When she left that day, she promised to pop in again before I was expected to leave hospital so I obtained a bible through a local church visitor and she readily accepted it. Years later, I met her unexpectedly. She had long since left that job, married and professed Christ.

Gordon returned to Zambia before I left hospital, saying it was important that he should get back. Fortunately, during this time we had also met up with former colleagues from the Canadian mission days who had retired to that area. Their daughter came to visit and it was arranged she would drive me back to Margate and my friend's home when I was released from the hospital. So despite his defection, I was well looked after.

But after a few days I began to feel extremely ill again and a visit to my friend's doctor put it into perspective. When I went in for the surgery, the medics there had withdrawn the Ativan in favour of their own medication and I had not resumed taking it. I was experiencing withdrawal symptoms. This doctor asked me where I was from and when I told him, he said he'd become used to European women coming from the north, fraying at the edges. He gave me a prescription for Ativan again, dismissing me with a fatherly smile and wishing me well.

Thankfully, I felt much better and healed well, but it was almost Christmas before I was strong enough to make the journey home. Through a friend in England I was able to get enough money for an air ticket and give my friend a cash gift to cover my stay. The flight back to Lusaka was nerve-wracking. For some reason, our plane was diverted to Mozambique to refuel. We were not allowed to disembark and had to remain in the aircraft for two sweltering hours, with only a large number of soldiers and a dilapidated collection of army-type huts to watch. It didn't appear to be a regular civilian airfield.

Eventually we arrived safely in Lusaka in the early hours of the morning. Apparently, there had been no communication regarding our ETA and the airport authorities had advised the waiting people to go home and phone later for news. I was exhausted and this was the last straw. I didn't have the taxi-fare for the twenty-five-mile journey to the farm but managed to get a phone call through and a somewhat disgruntled Gordon came back having done the fifty-mile round trip twice.

There had been several disquieting indications of a growing discord between the children and their father. How much was due to teenage angst I couldn't guess, nor did I understand the flashes of real animosity in our youngest. It distressed me greatly when this hostility surfaced since neither child took me into their confidence and my perception as to the probable cause was way off. The knowledge that they had become aware of his infidelity with at least one Zambian woman at this time came to me much later. However, the full truth proved to be far beyond my imagination.

Grace was still living and working in the city and there was no progress on her citizenship application. I wanted to go to England to see my family and extend my convalescent period, but Gordon kept telling me I shouldn't go in the winter but rather wait. It was late March before he relented and bought me the ticket. During the flight, I felt feverish and generally unwell but put it down to tiredness. Then, no sooner had I arrived at my brother-in-law's house in Croydon than I collapsed with an extremely high temperature. I was taken by ambulance to hospital and isolated. I had acute malaria.

Two weeks later, still shaky and feeling weak, I arrived in Solihull and was so run down that I developed a sinus abscess. Before this had cleared, my mother fell and broke her hip. This gave us all grave concern because she had to wait several days for a hospital bed. By the time I returned in May, I was neither rested nor prepared for another crisis.

During my time in England, I'd received a few brief letters from my husband but these only containing general news of the farm, nothing personal or specific. But a lot had been going on. Apparently in my absence, his inappropriate behaviour had been noticed by several other people and when one well-meaning friend had confronted him, he was shocked to be angrily rebuffed.

At much the same time, a missionary in Zimbabwe, who was aware of our work but did not know us personally, had a dream one night. Convinced it was from God, he was impelled to travel nearly three hundred miles to our farm to bring God's warning to Gordon. He located the farm and made contact with our friend who was living in the farm manager's house. The two men gathered a group of four other godly, highly respected Christian men from Lusaka and together they faced Gordon with this warning and pleaded with him at length.

This confrontation took place immediately after my arrival. No one explained to me what was happening; Gordon just said some people were coming to see him and they'd use one of the empty guest houses for privacy and it didn't concern me. I gave it no more thought, busy as

I was with adjusting to being back, unpacking and so on, and none of these gentlemen spoke to me at all.

When they emerged several hours later, I was sitting on the patio. Gordon brushed straight by me and entered the house, and the others, with the exception of our friend, went straight to their cars. I asked my friend for an explanation but he didn't stop to talk either, only brusquely said over his shoulder as he walked away, "You'd better ask your husband that!" I went into the house to talk to him.

Clearly, whatever had taken place had left him very angry. Stubbornly, he refused to talk and I was left puzzled and perturbed. Later, I went up to Bethesda House and insisted I be told whatever was going on. It was then that I learned about the dream and the messenger's journey from Zimbabwe, and the warning: that if my husband did not truly repent and be accountable, he was going to lose everything he held dear.

About a week later, I received a letter from Zimbabwe in which the messenger informed me that at the conclusion of their confrontation, the group were not convinced of my husband's true repentance, though they had pleaded with him with much prayer. Therefore, the writer continued, they had ended by warning him further. Convinced that his initial show of remorse had not led to true repentance, his attitude had gravely concerned them all. Accordingly, they had concluded by invoking the disciplinary scriptures found in 1 Corinthians 5 regarding sexual immorality. Verses 4 and 5 say, "When you are assembled in the name of our Lord Jesus, and the power of our Lord is present, hand this man over to Satan, so that the sinful nature may be destroyed and his spirit saved on the day of the Lord." The writer went on to warn me that now anything was possible. I could expect anything to happen, anything at all, even my husband's death. He then suggested I could show this letter to my husband if I so wished.

The letter gave me a considerable jolt and at first I didn't know what to do. But later that day I took it up to our friend in Bethesda House. He said he'd come with me if I wanted to show it to my husband and that's what we did. We sat with Gordon in the study and I asked him to read it. His reaction dismayed me even more because after reading it, he tossed it contemptuously aside, his face set and eyes glittering with anger. Badly upset, I grabbed the car keys, and leaving the house, I drove blindly into town and ended up in a friend's front drive in a flood of tears. I took the word of God seriously, and the enormity of the warning and my husband's contemptuous dismissal of it alarmed and horrified me.

I don't suppose I made any sort of sense to her or her husband but they were kind and ushered me into the house and waited patiently until the storm of tears abated. Hours later, they escorted me back as far as the farm gate. My husband didn't even ask where I'd been all that time, and by then, I just wanted to get away.

A few days later a friend mentioned that she was driving down to Kariba and I begged a lift, saying I had friends I wanted to see just over the border. That much was true, so far as it went. Quite unable to plan ahead, and in a frenzy to get away, I took my passport, a small case and what little money I could find. My friend was visiting on the Zambian side so she dropped me at the border post and I hitched a lift across. It was true, I did know the Christian couple who ran a hotel just a mile or so over the border. They had spent time with us at the farm the previous year and I thought they might help me so I took a room there, hoping to talk to them immediately. They were busy so there was no opportunity that evening. That night, in great distress, I wrote letters to family and a couple of friends trying to explain my predicament and posted them before breakfast. Immediately after breakfast, I approached the couple again and asked if I could talk to them privately but they said they were very busy, hopefully there'd be time later that afternoon.

While I was at lunch in the dining room, Gordon suddenly showed up, and with his usual outward show of urbane charm, he gripped my arm cruelly and impelled me out of the door. He silently stood over me while I packed, then hustled me to his car. His whole manner was intimidating and he drove the hundred miles or so back to the farm in grim silence. I had neither the physical nor emotional strength to resist. The Psalmist's words echoed in my head: "Listen to my cry, for I am in desperate need; rescue me from those who pursue me, for they are too strong for me..."[8]

Shortly after that, in a painful formal meeting, my husband was disciplined and put out of the very church he'd helped to establish. The woman involved was also severely censured.

---

[8] Psalm 142:6

CHAPTER TWENTY-ONE

The Siege of Honour

My attempted defection had only made matters worse. I was nervous and jumpy, waiting for some sort of axe to fall, not knowing from what direction the next calamity would come. It was almost impossible to act normally round other people, especially the new farm manager.

She was a sophisticated young redhead of acid wit and patronizing disposition. Where he'd found her and what governed his choice was anyone's guess. He did not discuss this decision with me and her youth and manner were an unwelcome surprise. Not very long after her installation, Gordon fell severely ill with hepatitis and lay like a yellow skeleton, totally unable to function. Still refusing to act on the advice of our experienced friend up north, he didn't appear to connect his illness with his disobedience. Our friend from Bethesda House came often to spend time and pray with him and I, engulfed in a wave of compassion, attempted to talk to him, assuring him of my full support if he would try and face up to things – but he was adamant, he would not. His illness forced me to deal with the new farm manager at times because I was the farm bookkeeper. But sure of his support, she ignored any request or suggestion I made and became a constant thorn in my flesh.

It was weeks before Gordon could get around the farm again. His attitude to our friend at Bethesda House had become hostile but strangely he didn't tell him to leave. His attitude to me was distant. On one occasion when our friend and his wife rendered me a service, his anger was loosed again with real fury and he made threats against them. The threats may only have been verbal but I felt torn apart and at the end of my tether. He was operating on a very short fuse and I was physically afraid of him.

Gordon suddenly decided to go to England for a spell and I felt relieved. But the farm was in an increasingly bad financial position and one day I went up to Bethesda House to talk to our friends and ask them to pray with me. They invited me to sit down but then came the bombshell. They said they wouldn't pray with me and proceeded to take me to task for being passive. This was a shock and especially difficult for me to take on board as I'd been fighting so long and welcomed their presence, feeling positive about their contribution.

If only our friend or one of the other ministers had fully briefed me about their meeting with Gordon that day, warned me what was afoot and kept me in the picture... How much anguish that would have saved me! I did believe, however, that they were doing their best in a very difficult situation, but I was nonetheless left guessing what was going on and bereft of support.

Seemingly, I'd done all the right things: married for love to a Christian who gave every indication of being the genuine article and who persisted in claiming that in public, even to holding office in the church, a man who had appeared to share my calling and ministry. Accordingly, I felt I had every right to expect him to adhere to those principles upon which we had based our mutual life. Surely then, clinging to that same standard and desiring above all things his true repentance and the healing of our marriage was reasonable? But I was in the dark as to the true perverseness of his nature and, among the people round me, the last to learn the true extent of his perfidy.

Whenever he went away, Gordon rarely set a date for his return. Because I didn't know when to expect him, I often had to take the responsibility of making decisions if matters could not wait. If any of those decisions did not please him, his annoyance would rankle a long time.

My main reason for staying now was Grace, trapped in Zambia without a passport. It was two-and-a-half years now and we still had received no answer to her application for Zambian citizenship. Gordon went to the appropriate authorities but met with no success. The farm's financial struggles deepened. A continuous plague of robberies and stock theft hit us and then, for the first time, disease fell on some of our crops.

Periodically I returned to my doctor in an effort to get help. Despite my pleas and in the face of continuing very odd symptoms, he offered no other help except to repeat my prescription for Ativan. Swamped by feelings of anxiety, palpitations and trembling, pin-pricks of pain all over, the panic attacks and disturbed vision became continuous. Back I would go to my doctor, asking whether these symptoms might be linked to the medication, but he seemed oblivious to my increasing desperation. He didn't suggest stopping the medication, nor did he offer any alternative, and by this time I didn't think I could manage without it.

Then a young man who had come to Christ on a former visit came back. He stayed at Bethesda House and having somehow acquired knowledge of something very shameful that happened, he came down to the farmhouse to confront me. Later, I learned that at the end of his first visit he'd become so troubled that he had withdrawn to fast and pray. He'd returned to confront Gordon with a message he'd received while in the Spirit. It was a warning to the effect that if he did not repent, God would bring upon him the thing he feared most: the loss of everything he held dear. This young brother in Christ sat at my table over tea and without preamble expressed his outrage that my husband had sexually abused our daughter.

"What I don't understand," he blazed in anger, "is how you can just sit there. What are you doing?"

The force of his rage totally overwhelmed me. I recoiled, stunned and stumbled to my feet, backing away from him in shock.

Then the tone of his voice changed. "My God, you didn't know, did you?"

He reached out to me but I was gone, out of the door, across the lawn, only to stop hard against the calf-paddock fence. I stood there a long time, my hand absently brushing the protruding nail heads in the rough wood fence posts. My mind grappled with this new horror as I tried to bring my sense of panic under control.

The truly awful thing was that I didn't doubt what I had just been told. Once the words were said, they rang with fatal finality. I felt as if I were outside my body watching myself and was only surprised by the fact that I wasn't surprised. Shocked, angry, disgusted and heartbroken, but not surprised. It was as if the last piece of a jigsaw had slipped into place and I could see at last the whole picture with its central flaw. This then was the rotten foundation stone that lay, unsuspected by me, beneath everything we had endeavoured to build. The lid was off the can of worms.

Overwhelmed with guilt that I had not known of this betrayal, I was dazed. How had I not known? How was it possible? Yet even while I shuddered in my soul, I knew it to be the truth for it explained so much that had eluded me. And why, dear God, *why* had no one told me? Was this what people around me thought I had condoned? Did they think I could possibly have been party to this betrayal of my children, this travesty of fatherhood?

Later, when I learned just who had known, people I'd worked with and those I called my friends, my anger, humiliation and despair were compounded. And when I learned who else had been involved, my sense of devastation was total.

In private, I tried to find some gesture to express my deep anger, repugnance and grief, and wrenched my wedding ring off and threw it in the waste bin. Then I collapsed on the floor in a paroxysm of weeping that left me sick for days. The screws were being tightened down on the coffin of my marriage. This knowledge was to change my life. It was the finishing stroke.

Whatever this young man had said when he faced my husband and delivered his warning, neither spoke of it to me. He left the farm immediately afterwards and went back to South Africa.

Gordon suddenly announced he was going to America to visit Stuart and would return via England. In a few days he was gone, after instructing that our friend, the tenant at Bethesda House who had joined the other ministers when they had challenged Gordon, had to take his family and leave before Gordon's return, though, once again, he didn't say when that would be.

They didn't need to be told. His work permit was almost expired and they prepared to leave. They didn't have enough money to ship their heavy goods so he came to me to ask for help. I believed there was no problem about eventual repayment so was happy to do so but following Gordon's withdrawals for his trip expenses, it was a strain on the farm's finances.

All through the weeks my husband was away, I was still dealing with the after-shock and would sit shivering, my arms wrapped round my body, hugging myself as I wept for my children who were now grown up and away from home. I wanted to talk to my daughter but she was living in town and when I went into her office one day in an effort to contact her, I sat for over an hour in the reception area but she didn't come.

Unable to form words to pray, I could only manage low, keening noises of anguish. Panic attacks became more frequent to add to my list of physical miseries, and in desperation I decided to go to England to consult my mother's doctor who was a Christian, though I couldn't leave before Gordon's return. The farm couldn't support another big expense so in an agony of apprehension and tension, I sought a trusted friend and borrowed the money.

When Gordon returned, I explained to him about the loan and was so relieved that the repayment cheque had arrived the day before. But he was furious about it and tossed it back in the drawer, refusing to pay it into the bank. I paid it in myself the next day, yet he continued to be stroppy, nursing his anger. I found it hard to be near him and he knew it. For a long time I'd been increasingly fearful of contracting AIDS or some other dreaded disease as a result of his selfish immoral living.

I planned to visit England after a few days. Those days were difficult, handing the farm business over to Gordon again, bringing him up to date, explaining the decisions I'd made in his absence. We existed in an atmosphere of chilly necessity. He didn't like it that I was now going for a break and it bothered him that somehow I'd found the money to do so. I didn't explain. I was through trying to get him to understand and accept his part in the situation. In the end, he wouldn't take me to the airport but it didn't matter; the farm driver took me.

The long weeks I spent in England in the autumn of 1984 were a see-saw of emotion. My family were puzzled and distressed to see me in such a state but I was unable to divulge that final horror. My mother's doctor was kind but unable to help. He prescribed two other alternatives to Ativan but they made me very ill with disturbing symptoms. I thought later that was probably due to what was already in my system, but the end result was negative. I was still only taking the original dose and now tried halving it, but a near collapse in a public place frightened me and, reluctantly, I had to carry on with it.

However, the association with this doctor bore unexpected fruit. Although he couldn't help me immediately with the Ativan problem, his family did welcome me to fellowship with them and later they invited me to go with them for a weekend of special meetings in Ely, Cambridgeshire. There the Lord met me in a wonderful way and it was the highlight of my entire trip. Although I had not solved my immediate problem and was far from stable physically and emotionally, I did receive the first powerful ministry into my overall need. As I listened to God's word and later received specific personal ministry and prophecy, I gained new insight and strength.

I decided to go back. I didn't really want to but with my experience of African emergencies and political instability, there was no way I would permanently leave Zambia while Grace was stuck there without a passport. She was living in town and the rift between her and her father was complete.

However, right on the heels of my return, she found a window of opportunity and successfully applied for a one-off travel document to go to Zimbabwe. I went with her and in two days she obtained a Zimbabwe birth certificate, identity card and immediately applied for a passport. Thirty days later she was advised her passport was ready and I flew down to collect it. We had gone through too much to risk it in the post. She had been stateless for two years and ten months. Once in possession of her new passport, she set about raising her airfare to England which she did through her art. She was determined to leave Africa, the land of her birth, for good.

Through the months following my return, an uneasy truce prevailed in our home. I had given up confronting Gordon and we existed in a kind of polite remoteness with me concentrating on keeping myself going and praying for a solution for Grace. John had returned, having given up the idea of going to agricultural college and wanting instead to get married. He was running a small-holding north of the city, but he did come over for Christmas day.

Our daughter left early in February and soon after that Gordon decided he would visit our former pastor who was living in Cape Town. He said he accepted that he needed counsel and help. I wanted to believe him and hoped he would indeed receive the help he needed. Within a couple of days, he had gone, but once again did not set a return date.

Almost immediately I was faced with a crisis in Stuart's affairs. For a long time, Zambia had been in such economic straits that no foreign exchange was allowed, save only for further education – and now that had been cancelled too. He was halfway through his studies and faced with the possibility that he'd have to give up on his chosen profession. The farm business was sliding further into decline and again I was reminded of God's warning to Gordon. Now Stuart was suffering and I was helpless in the face of his acute disappointment. After an agonizing interval and consultation with his tutors, he chose to switch to business studies which were approximately half the cost of training for a career in flight. To this end he worked a forty-hour week in the city's ambulance service to pay his way thereafter.

During this spell of Gordon's absence, I was really not fit to carry on alone. The responsibility of the farm was a heavy burden. Though I was thankful Grace had got out, I had no idea when I would see her again and I missed her. I was moving in a cloud of despondency, for which, as I later discovered, the Ativan was largely responsible. Every day was a struggle and felt increasingly hopeless. Because my doctor seemed incapable of understanding or offering an alternate solution, I moved on a treadmill of misery.

There was no one around except the Zambian staff and a former friend of our boys, working for us as a driver. Gordon sent no letters and I had no idea what he was doing or when he might return.

In March I had a visitor. We had a mutual friend in England and this lady had written asking if, on her way to Zimbabwe, she could stop over in Lusaka and meet me. I'd agreed and she duly arrived. Her company for a few days was welcome. By the time she arrived, I was feeling ill all the time. Sharing my fears with this lady led us to make it a particular matter for prayer together and I became convinced that if I was ever to get free of this cursed medication, I must help myself.

My visitor left and I was alone. Salu, my house servant, was there in the daytime but from 5 pm to 7 am the next day, there was no one except the night watchmen patrolling the farm. Salu had come to work for us almost twenty years ago, first as a gardener. After observing him over time, we offered him a better job and I brought him into the house and taught him to clean and launder. He was a very quiet African with a gentle, ready smile, whose personality suited me, and over the years we had established a bond. We had sat together on my backdoor step sharing our grief when his twin daughters had died and now he hovered and brought me a tea tray from time to time as I lay ill and frightened.

I'd come to the end of the road. There was no help but that which I could muster for myself with the help of God. I'd become convinced that my life was effectively over unless I could gain control. One evening I decided I wouldn't take another Ativan, and I did not. I shut myself in my daughter's room and lay down in total reliance upon God. All I could think of was Esther's prayer: "If I perish, I perish."[9] I lay all night with my head and heart pounding.

---

[9] Esther 4:16

CHAPTER TWENTY-TWO

Green Apple Soap

Feeling extremely ill and very frightened at being alone on the farm, I telephoned a friend in town the next morning, hoping she could let me use her guest room for a few days. I wanted to be with other people and nearer medical help. But she already had guests so I asked the farm driver to take me to someone else who might help me, a family that we had helped in their own crisis some time before.

The family had a town house now and agreed I could stay but warned me that they had weekend plans and were going to be away until Saturday evening. It was now Thursday. Despite my explanation, that I had stopped taking Ativan and was experiencing withdrawal effects, they didn't seem concerned. I later wondered why they didn't summon medical help or take me to the hospital.

Alone in their spare room, occasionally hearing their house man come into the kitchen to feed or let the dogs out, I struggled with a truly vicious headache. By the end of that day, I was hypersensitive to light and sound. Unable to stand properly, I became delirious. The walls alternately leaned over me or receded, changing into distorted shapes. At times I knew I was talking but knew I wasn't making any sense, the babble of words echoing in the empty house.

The family came home on Saturday evening and, apart from looking in, made no effort to assist me other than to bring me a drink. Surely, they must have noticed the state I was in? I struggled through another night and in my few lucid moments I repeated God's promise that he would get me through this terrible time.

Strangely, I awoke next morning feeling slightly better and with a clearer head. It was Sunday and I felt even better after a bath and shampoo. Afterwards, as I made my way down the hall, my host met me and asked if I would like to go to church. Striving for some semblance of normality, I thanked him and said yes. Again, neither he nor his partner appeared to notice anything odd in my manner, nor did they say anything about my state over the preceding forty-eight hours.

By the time we were due to leave the house, I was feeling very odd again. I'd only taken a little breakfast after eating almost nothing the whole time I'd been there and now I was stumbling, not able to walk properly and felt quite disorientated with my vision blurring. As I approached their car, it changed shape and I had difficulty in opening the door. Once in, their voices seemed to come from far away and I couldn't understand what was said. The fact that they didn't comment, help me or seem to notice vaguely puzzled me although I was concentrating on trying to act normal. Yet all the time I knew I wasn't and they didn't seem to notice, which seemed strange.

We arrived at the church and I got out of the car, expecting them to do the same, but to my astonishment they drove off. Up to that point I'd assumed they were coming to morning service as well. In a daze, I walked across to the church porch, went up the steps and saw someone I knew. I greeted her, reached out my hand and remarked on her child's very pretty dress. She grabbed the child in a defensive move and backed away from me.

The church was full and yet I felt as if in a cocoon. The faces round me began to distort and dissolve and the fellowship chatter of greetings echoed and boomed, surging around me in waves, until I couldn't distinguish what was real and what was not. Kind people came forward and helped me out into a side room and later I was taken to their home where I lay for the rest of the day. There were lucid gaps and I kept a fair reckoning of time. Just before sunrise I got up and found my handbag on the dressing table. Beside it lay my bible and in it I wrote a note and dated it; then I had a short but precious time of prayer before everything round me got cloudy again.

Later that morning they got me to a doctor and although my memory of that visit is extremely patchy, I realized someone had called my son John and that his sweetheart had been in the ambulance with me – an act of kindness I will always remember.

I awoke to see my hand stretched out against a roughly painted wall. Above my head was a frieze of bright flowers. As I turned over, I became aware that I was just lying on top of an iron bedstead. I gazed silently at the faces that swam around me above carelessly arranged cotton wraps or shifts. No one spoke. My fellow patients, all African women, were staring at me curiously. I was in a locked ward at Chainama, Lusaka's mental hospital.

The room held six beds. The wall opposite had holes in it and a protruding pipe where a washbasin had been taken down and not replaced. Necessity helped me push off the bed and investigate the toilet in the corner. There was urine on the floor and the cracked bowl held an unsavoury residue because it didn't flush properly. There was no paper and no door.

I kept telling the nurse – and the doctor, when he came – about having stopped the Ativan suddenly. It was impossible to know if they believed me; no one commented on this or talked *to* me about it and I found this very disconcerting. After the doctor's visit, I was taken for a shower in a communal shower room. It was while I was standing in line and naked, waiting to be handed a coarse cotton overall, that the builder's wife came up to me. She worked in the hospital.

At a time when she was endeavouring to get her life together, before I knew the full extent of her relationship with my husband, I had bought her professional uniforms in England as a gift. I remembered that she didn't work in this department but I wasn't up to wondering how she'd got there. For a moment now, our meeting was surreal. There she stood so crisp and confident and expressing surprise. But although she appeared sincere, I didn't trust her. I was only conscious of my total humiliation.

At least I felt clean now – but the day wasn't over. My mind was clear and I was lying on top of my bed trying to make sense of what was happening, when Gordon walked in with a couple of hospital staff and the doctor. Not one of them spoke to me but talked over my head. He may have been shocked to return home and find me hospitalized but to me he wasn't real. It was as if a pane of glass separated us. They all went away again without addressing me directly.

The next day, I was moved into a small open ward, and although it had two beds, I was on my own. But I had no toiletries and no underwear. The wife of an American missionary friend came to see me and upon returning home sent me some sets of new underwear; and a dear friend, who was married at the farm, also came and she brought me some Green Apple soap. On subsequent visits she also brought me some English food and books. Another friend sent exquisite flowers.

The clean, cool smell of that soap became my focus. Its evocative fragrance reminded me of all that was good and clean, pure and unsullied. I held it to my face every time I prayed and thanked God for it every time I washed.

Staggering a bit on 'jelly' legs and feeling a little disorientated for a day or two, I found I was in the rehabilitation ward. In the communal ablution block, out of eight toilets, only one had a door and it was always available when I needed a little privacy.

Then Gordon turned up again. He sat and talked to me and even showed me photographs of his trip to South Africa. In a meeting with my doctor, he was still unreal to me, though I heard him distinctly tell the doctor that he had no knowledge I had been on this drug, as if it were something secret. Four years on a prescription drug that had openly stood on my bedside table! Was he trying to destroy my credibility? I wasn't well enough then to be forceful about it but I did protest and my mind registered his disloyalty. I found it difficult that the doctor still didn't talk *to* me or question me directly. Talking round me, over my head as if I was not there, may have been standard procedure but I found it difficult in the extreme. Later in the meeting, when Gordon offered me a glass of cold water from the jug on the table, I wouldn't take it from him, although the day was extremely hot.

Meanwhile I had a room of my own, beauty and privacy and books to read. I walked for hours in the gardens and the field at the back. That was my prayer place where day by day I claimed my life back. Although by now I had some clothes from home and was feeling so much better, in one aspect I was trapped. In my confusion due to the withdrawal from Ativan, I even now clung to the conviction that Gordon was gone for good, probably dead.

When Gordon met a Zambian pastor friend of ours in town one day, and confided in him, that dear man decided to come and see me. This Christian friend came into my room, sat down and simply told me

I'd got it wrong: Gordon was alive and back home. I just stared at him. What reason did I have to disbelieve him? I trusted him. He would not lie to me. In a moment, it all came right side up and I was mortified that I should have thought such a thing. I sent him off to get a message to Gordon to come again as soon as possible, then flew round to the nurses' office to tell them. Less than forty-eight hours later I was home.

No doubt it had been a considerable shock for Gordon to have found me hospitalized. I learned later that on receiving this news on his return, he hadn't wanted to come and see me, but why not? Surely that would have been the natural thing to do? When I heard this I wondered if what had happened to me would have enough impact to bring him to accept a degree of accountability and whether it would help him face up to what he should do. Even those nearest to him found it difficult to tell.

It had been an extraordinary ten days. However, I was not able to rest. Gordon announced his intention of taking me down to South Africa later that same weekend and had informed my doctor of this plan. When I was released, he was given the letter to take with us regarding my medication, which was designed to carry me through the next period of recovery from the Ativan addiction. However, before we could fly, he spent a busy day dealing with farm business and leaving instructions and because of his recent absence, I was coerced into dealing with letters, accounts and other farm business and had to spend several hours in the office.

Strangely, this wasn't difficult at this stage of my recovery. With typical Pharisaic absorption, he made no allowances for what I'd been through; but except for a headache from the intensity of concentration I needed to focus on the task, I managed very well. Then he took me off to Cape Town where we stayed with our former pastor from the Baptist church. It was all ostensibly for my convalescence, but once in Cape Town he revealed plans to stay there. It wasn't easy because one couldn't work without having residential status and one could not become a resident quickly without a job.

When the tablets I'd brought from the hospital in Lusaka were finished, we went to a local doctor, but Gordon didn't seem to have the letter I knew he'd been given in Lusaka about the gradual phasing down of the medication. My Lusaka doctor had told me what was in the letter but had entrusted it to Gordon. Now, in its apparent absence, this doctor simple reissued the original prescription. Gordon brushed aside my protests and questions, insisting I didn't know what I was talking about.

A new symptom plagued me: a lack of concentration to the point where I couldn't read or watch TV. The days dragged. A former friend who now lived in the area kindly lent us a car on two days a week and it was wonderful to be able to go out and about with Gordon, but then it became obvious that he was just using those trips to look for work. My inability to concentrate was agony. I had difficulty in sitting for long and church services were so difficult, as was being in a crowd, but I always went because I was so weary of being left on my own. Some days Gordon walked me round a lot but I began to have an unreal sense of distance and began to fear public places. The space around me became distorted. Far from showing any concern, he then began going out for hours on his own, sometimes for whole days, and then at night. This was quite easy because the guest wing we were in had its own entrance and so his comings and goings were not noticed. Our host was a bachelor with a very busy lifestyle, so there was rarely anyone around for company.

It was on one of the days when Gordon had gone off for the day that the pastor's young assistant and his wife invited me out to lunch. Gratefully grasping at this chance not to be alone, I accepted and they went ahead of me to the front door and down the short flight of steps. But as I put my foot on the top step to follow them, a huge chasm appeared to open up in front of me and I recoiled. They turned at my cry and saw me freeze on the step. Naturally, they saw nothing out of the ordinary but I felt I was teetering on the edge of a precipice and could only retreat. Puzzled, they tried to get me to come out but I could not; I was now the victim of agoraphobia.

Gordon never gave any indication he noticed but, surely, he must have done. I couldn't go out without clinging to him tightly. If he evaded my grasp and walked ahead a bit, I was terrified he would disappear. From some new friends, visitors to the church, he'd accepted an invitation for us to pay them a visit in the small town of George farther up the coast. They were the nicest people but it was so difficult for me. I couldn't sustain a conversation and one day when they took us for a picnic on the beach, every time they walked ahead, they seemed to disappear off the edge of the horizon. I clung to my husband's side, afraid he would disappear too. It was while we were at George that I first noticed that sometimes I drooled and struggled with my co-ordination, finding difficulty in small tasks like doing my hair and writing, which was frightening. Our hosts were kindness itself, but busy, articulate people and I was moving again in a fog of uncertainty, confusion and fear.

On our return to Cape Town, and having the car one day, Gordon took me miles out in the country where he said he was trying to land a job. It was a pig farm set in most beautiful rolling countryside but there was no other farm in sight. The house was dark and dreary and I suddenly had a picture of what my life would be like if ever I got trapped there. He didn't get the job and though I was struggling on so many fronts, I thanked God and resolved to start fighting back.

The next time Gordon went off for the day, I took some money from a drawer in the bedroom and forced myself to go out. In my mind, I clutched the scripture, "I can do [anything] through him who gives me strength."[10] I was really frightened but more scared of the alternative. The household had got used to us being independent, Gordon out a great deal, me resting in my room. So no one took any notice as I crept out. I had to cling to every available thing I could see to get out of the house and down the short drive that led to the street. It was as if I were blindfolded, so hesitant were my steps. I got to the road and stopped. Taking a deep breath, I turned toward the shops, holding on to hedges, garden walls and gates as I went, fighting the sensation of being pulled to the outer edge of the pavement all the way.

At last I reached the little cluster of shops and found the haberdashery I'd seen when we'd first arrived. Getting into the shop was a major effort but I made it and stood trembling just inside the door. Hesitantly I managed to find and buy knitting pins, a pattern and some wool. Still feeling shaky and strange, but greatly heartened, I slowly and painstakingly made my way back the way I'd come, touching walls, gateposts and hedges along the way as before. I was so thankful that this first outing on my own hadn't required me to cross a road. I reached the house again without mishap, exhausted but safe.

We had been away several weeks. I'd gleaned from bits of news from Gordon that John had come to take over the house and farm. He

---

[10] Philippians 4:13

and his sweetheart, who had come from England, had had a civil wedding in Lusaka. It wasn't until after our return that I learned Gordon had led John to believe the farm was now his, so instead of just caretaking, he had understandably made some changes to the house and made decisions on the farm.

Able to read a little now and watch TV for short periods, I sat forcing my shaking hands to produce a garment, which actually was a terrible mess, and with every row I knitted, I prayed to get back home, evoking every promise I could remember. Hebrews Chapter 11 became my litany: "By faith Abel... by faith Noah... by faith Abraham..." *By faith* I was going to get out of this hideous situation. It didn't matter how many mistakes I made in the knitting, I persevered and my fingers improved a little bit. It became a focus for my will to endure.

Our host invited me to join him and two other friends in their weekly game of Scrabble. I played very badly and even simple words were sometimes a struggle, but like my wrestling with the knitting pattern, it did become slightly easier and I was so grateful to be included. His friends lived some distance away and the drive there and back gave us opportunities to talk. It was on one of these outings that I learned the truth about his visit to us years before when he had expected to talk to us both. He spoke of his puzzlement and unease as Gordon had circumvented his opportunity to do so. Now I could share my side of that occasion.

It was to be a long time before I fully realized what a dangerous thing I'd done in taking myself off Ativan so suddenly. A considerable time would pass before I was privy to the information exposed by the media in Britain and the outpouring of information that would then be available on this and other tranquilizers.

I began to nag Gordon about going back to Lusaka. His plans were not working out. I kept up the pressure, talking about going back and questioning his reluctance. Finally, my insistence paid off and he agreed we should go.

CHAPTER TWENTY-THREE

The Shining Night

We came home from Cape Town via Johannesburg. There we stayed a couple of nights with the friends who had lent us their house after the raid. Our friends were lovely and I was genuinely happy to see them again but it was difficult for me.

Since we'd commenced our journey, I'd struggled with the irrational fear that something would prevent me from reaching home. Most worrying of all, I knew I was losing control of some of my facial muscles and the drooling continued at times. I was ill at ease, still slightly off balance and felt clumsy in company – and this knowledge made me very self-conscious.

When we arrived home, it was a jolt to see my home changed and to have to move into one of the guest rooms, but it didn't distract me from my most urgent need, to reach my hospital doctor and get some help. Fortunately, I was given the first appointment after lunch the following day.

As we sat outside the doctor's office awaiting his return from lunch, I saw him approach from down the hall. Even as he came up to me, his eyes were searching my face and I heard his exclamation of dismay. He bade me wait and brusquely ushered Gordon into his office. Did he query what had happened to my medication?

I never found out and Gordon wouldn't tell me just what he'd said. But I had a distinct impression I'd reached him none too soon. He put me on a course of medication to steady things and to my relief it worked. I soon felt better and my slack facial muscles improved. After a few weeks, I was off medication altogether.

Within a few days of our return, new arrangements were made and we were back in the farmhouse. John and his wife had moved into the family size guest house. By the time of our return he was preparing to go down south for an operation on his ear, a legacy of his difficult birth. They went off and were gone some weeks. Our situation was much the same, but not as before. There were changes to the house but I didn't really care. My former drive and initiative were absent and other than look after a few domestic details, I had no role to play. It was a strange time and the farm was obviously diminishing; I found I was reduced to the position of a mere observer.

Outwardly the farm appeared to be functioning but my awareness of God's warning sharpened my perception. Our specialist poultry business was failing as there appeared to be a drop in the market. There was a definite air of dejection among the staff. Workmen walked off, tools went missing. Gordon switched to table poultry but we were not adequately equipped, especially our refrigeration capacity. The plethora of wasted, rotting birds brought a plague of flies. Finally, he gave that up. The market garden produce dwindled away. On the top field, where for years I'd grown a commercial crop of sweet peas for the florists in the city, the cane frames lay discarded in untidy heaps. The steady maintenance of houses and buildings had dropped off and everything was beginning to look very shabby.

Those long service stalwarts, Chabaila and Salu, carried on, as did the cowmen. It was a relief to have Salu's help in the house because although there was a lot less to do, I was still not strong. And because there was little work for Chabaila, an opportunity to make new pews for one of the city churches came our way and he was put to work on those.

Suddenly Gordon decided we should go to Kenya, a little holiday with friends at Rift Valley Academy, he said. To me it didn't make a lot of sense as we had been away so much in recent months. But he was determined. I guessed he was running away from the ambivalent atmosphere at the farm and a fear of not being able to reverse the downward trend, but as usual, he didn't talk about it.

Although I felt as if I was just tagging along, the time away was enjoyable. I hadn't been to Kenya before and the loveliness of Amboseli Game Park and its wildlife and Lake Nyivasha's spectacle of teeming thousands of flamingos delighted me.

Not long after our return from Kenya, John and his wife decided to return to England. They wanted me to go with them, and I was longing to go but I knew in my heart that if I went I would never come back. I debated it in my mind. They were starting out and had no home of their own yet in England, nor were they able to pay my fare. I had no money either in Zambia or England; I knew I would probably have to work but did not feel strong enough for that yet.

I had never had a home of my own in England. My brother and family were generous and loving but were already housing my mother. Staying with them while on holiday for a short time was one thing; living with them long term before I could be independent and forge a new life was quite another. But in the event, Gordon refused to pay my fare, so I remained. I could only pray the words from Psalm 143: "For your name's sake, O Lord, preserve my life; in your righteousness, bring me out of trouble."

The days dragged on and the farm ticked over uneasily. I witnessed the slow but steady breakdown of everything round me. Ever mindful of God's warning, I watched as first one thing and then another fell apart. Once reasonably well-off, we became poor to the point that I had to sell off some personal possessions to buy groceries – something I did without Gordon's knowledge because I was afraid of triggering his anger. We suffered stock theft, break-ins to our houses, more tools and equipment disappearing, and the theft of another vehicle. Then, for the first time ever, disease struck our livestock.

Gordon had a sailboat of which he was inordinately proud. He dismissed the necessity of life jackets, which was distressing to me, especially when he'd take the children out. Once, the boat capsized on the Kafue River when he had a friend on board and we narrowly missed total tragedy. One day he took his boat to Lake Iteshi-Teshi and there it sank at its moorings in a freak storm. When he got it raised and towed home, he couldn't get the materials in Zambia to mend it. So it could not be fixed and lay parked under the bauhinia trees beside the drive, covered by a tarpaulin. For years he'd had a small piece of land at the lakeside where he'd wanted to build a little weekend holiday cottage. Now it would not be finished and remained half-built. It became an eyesore that the neighbouring cottage owners weren't happy about; he would have to sell the land.

Having so little to do was wearisome for me. I could only wait for something to change. I felt detached from the problems around me. Gordon had spells of apathy but did not welcome any input from me. Everyone was going through the motions but the heart had gone out of the place. Now freed from the Ativan addiction, I held on to the promises God had given me and I waited.

With no outside role, I focussed within. It was a period of deep heart-searching and prayer. I dwelt in the Psalms where I could identify with so many of God's people who had striven and agonized, suffered and ultimately triumphed with joy. They expressed so much I could understand and many passages spoke to me very clearly. Above all, I wanted to find my balance in what was unfolding. I did not want to miss the Holy Spirit's leading. I knew full well that my Lord was in control of my situation. Although I was being forced to wait, I knew I must be patient. Throughout those difficult months this assurance deepened and though I had no idea how things were going to turn out, increasingly hope rose high and joy in my Lord quickened my steps.

There were no guests now. The guestrooms only held dust and spiders. To what extent the wider Christian community knew of our private lives, I wasn't sure. No former friend had enquired or visited. However, one day a couple who had been influenced toward Christ in our home called in and in my own sitting room admitted to me, "We thought you must condone your husband's behaviour. You're still here, aren't you?" The hurt went very deep. Associated shame made me silent. I knew my credibility was gone, my witness compromised. In the complexity of the situation I was silent; I had no defence.

Winter came again. There were no crops in the fields and almost no staff. We were alone in a silent house with very little to say to each other. Suddenly Gordon decided we should go to England and my heart leapt in thankfulness. It had been an awful year. Every time a new blow had fallen, I'd gone to the Lord in anguish about my own life going down the drain, and every time, he'd lovingly restored the core of inner peace within me and helped me wait patiently. At last the door was beginning to open.

The cattle were the last liquid asset we had. Foreign exchange now allowed us to take a small amount for travel out of the country. Without the sale of the cattle we couldn't do this or pay for our air tickets. At last the time came when the cattle were sold and our head cowman went with them. Tickets were booked for late in August and I gradually began my farewell to all I'd loved in this place. Only I knew I'd never come back.

I walked in the morning sun beneath the towering eucalyptus trees that lined the farm drive and touched their fragrant leaves, remembering the rainy day when we had planted the six-inch high saplings almost thirty years earlier. Looking up to watch their stately movements against the vivid sky, I thought about my early hopes and their slow demise.

Crossing the fallow fields, I came to the paddock flanked by empty poultry pens. The field was empty now. My boxer dog always had an affinity with the bullocks that grazed there. Their job had been to draw the farm cart and she would play around them or sit beside them for hours. I remembered how her chestnut head would bob up above the long grass and how she'd prance in the sunlight in playful invitation.

The dark, sweeping cassia trees now only shaded the deserted truck camping ground, and at the end of the avenue, Sharon Cottage stood vacant. There was no sound of singing wafted by the breeze from across the river, no sound of a tractor in the fields.

One somnolent afternoon, I sat sorting various papers on my desk for the last time. The wide windows were open and I looked down across the lawns to the silent 'Boat House'. I heard the sharp *clunk* of Salu's axe as he gathered firewood and a wood dove's evocative call from the wild fig tree beyond the dairy.

The river rushed over the waterfall, heedless of the loss of children's laughter. I left the house and walked the path alongside its cool depths and passed by Bethesda House. Crossing the cattle drift, I took the sloping path up to the campsite. I let myself remember the fun and the fellowship of the early days. Now the damaged houses stood silent, showing all too clearly their scars. In the long grass I stumbled over the last termite-riddled remains of the roof timbers intended for the new hall and stood on the veranda steps of the first house we'd built there. Looking down towards the river, I remembered the baptisms in the deep pool below the cattle crossing, and prayed again that something from my endeavour would endure.

On the last evening, I sat on the patio and watched the sun sink behind the trees on the riverbank. From high up in the flame tree, a goshawk took wing and skimmed the lawns in the brief dusk. His high, thin cry was a mournful echo to my own sad spirit. This was not my place anymore.

The next day, I said goodbye to Salu and walked out of my house. Chabaila stood respectfully on the patio, his gentle face compassionate and understanding as we shook hands. I think he knew we would not meet again, and why. As the car drove away from the house, I did not look back.

We passed the derelict boat, still lying under its shabby old canvas cover and a layer of dead leaves and debris. The car swept up the lane and out to the main road. Right at the last, Gordon had told me he still had "things to do". I was to go alone and he would let me know when he could follow. It was symbolic of our lives that seemingly were destined to be apart.

We parted without emotion after I'd checked in at the airport. I sat in the departure lounge, my tired thoughts still drifting around what I was leaving. I believed Salu and Chabaila had come to Christ, as had many others. What was sound and lasting of any spiritual harvest was by the grace of God, and only time and heaven would reveal its true worth. My critics had accused me of being passive, judging our work as worthless. My friends had simply melted away. Though I had truly not known of the canker that had destroyed us from within, I was now embarked upon a journey of repentance and self-appraisal.

When my aircraft lifted off, I looked down at the beloved land as it passed beneath me. I had come to this rich, beautiful country in the early summer of my life, and now in its autumn I was leaving it eroded and dry with poverty, riddled with AIDS and torn apart from war.

CHAPTER TWENTY-FOUR

Backlash

My daughter was at London Gatwick to meet me. As her arms went round me, my tired spirit revived. I knew deep inside me that this was only the beginning of another phase. There were still so many lessons to be learned in compassion and forgiveness. We were survivors in the hands of a loving God and although we cannot know the length of it, grieving is for a season only. Even when sorrow remains there is hope in God's all-redeeming love.

Acquaintances, still on contract in Zambia, had offered us the use of their cottage in Wiltshire for a few months and it would be available from the beginning of October. It was good to feel we had a starting point. Meanwhile I went to stay with Grace in Croydon.

On the first Sunday in her church, someone sitting at the back stood up and brought a prophetic message in the Spirit. As soon as the interpretation began, I believed it was for me. Grace felt the same and later, when I was being introduced around, I met the woman and she confirmed it saying that she had also recognised it was for me as soon as we were introduced. The message had said, "My daughter, I know the year you have lived through. Do not fear what is ahead. The problems of the past will not be repeated. You have landed on the solid rock."

The language and the message was similar to those I'd received in Ely in 1984; it was startling but very encouraging. Gordon sent word he would arrive by the end of September and when he did, we went down to Wiltshire. God was very good to us. A friend from earlier days in

Lusaka, who had been vacationing in Europe, arranged for us to take over his car.

On the edge of Salisbury Plain, the village was so small it had no shops. The postmistress operated from her cottage and ran the post office from her front room in the afternoons. There was a pub and a twice-daily bus into Salisbury and back. The cottage was tiny, stone-built and thatched with three straw owls on the roof, and probably about three hundred years old. It was opposite the cemetery and a very small parish church surrounded by yew trees. On a busy day, one could encounter the odd horse and rider, a couple of cars, one or two pedestrians, a tractor rumbling by and a strolling cat. But it was God's gift to us, a haven of warmth and security, and in a very short time we found Christian fellowship in nearby Tisbury.

Winter was approaching and, as it turned out, it was a severe one. Fortunately, the woodshed was fully stocked with logs and we went to Salisbury's charity shops for some basic winter clothing, which was all our money allowed. Even with the roads deep in drifts, we were snug. Although I was not on any medication and generally feeling a great deal better, I remained unsure what to do and inhibited by my lack of money. I needed to be more settled within myself before I made any life-changing decisions.

Since it had only been possible to bring a tiny amount of money out, we had to find some means of support. We had no home or pensions in England, but fortunately we were both entitled to basic government social services income support and we carefully eked that out. At the back of our minds, we knew this was only a temporary measure; it wasn't possible to establish a new life under these conditions.

Gordon was a fair amateur photographer and thought he might be able to make some money at it. To this end he joined a photographic club and took a course. We settled into a life of rural walks and long evenings spent by the fire. Unbeknown to me, he also began enquiries into the training needed to become a non-stipendiary clergyman. Weeks later, when he'd found a sponsor among the local Christians for his training, he did tell me but wasn't happy when I pointed out the obvious: what was the sense in going after an unpaid job? He brushed that aside and remained uncommunicative. I was still waiting; come the spring, I had to have a plan.

He was restless and resumed his pattern of going off from time to time on his own and on outings with the photographic club. I began planning for Christmas. Grace was coming for a few days. Stuart would be coming from America, and John, his wife and baby from Sussex. It would be the first time in years we'd all be together. Even my family from Solihull planned to join us for Boxing Day.

Our farmhouse had been left just as it was, not packed up. Before leaving, Gordon had told me he'd arranged for it to be let to a friend who wanted to move out of town. We had packed two tea chests of personal effects, all that we were allowed to take out of the country. In one, knowing there'd be no money to set up a home when we first arrived in England, I packed bed linen, towels, a small amount of cutlery, a couple of sets of my Melamine dishes and so on. Gordon chose to pack books. By the time I left, with one of Grace's paintings as hand luggage, the boxes had been delivered to a freight depot to await instructions. We didn't have the money to send them then, but Gordon said he'd see to that before he finally left. In the end, he wasn't able to do it but made arrangements with the new tenant in our house to do so, the cost to be deducted from the first rent.

Christmas started off well and it was a joy to see my children, grown up as they were: Grace, a legal secretary with a prestigious firm in the centre of London; Stuart, full of stories about college life in America; and John, with his little family. I did my best to set my personal concerns aside but there were deep undercurrents. It was all too easy for a chance remark to be hurtful, a careless reference to spark a flash of anger. While Gordon urbanely coasted around the conversation, all the rest of us were struggling with difficult memories, frightened of upsetting one another. But in the grace of God it was, overall, a good time.

After I waved off my brother's car, I went indoors to find Gordon incensed that none of the rest of us wanted to spend a day visiting an acquaintance of his – naturally, we wanted to make the most of our short, precious time together. I'd only met the people Gordon was referring to once and our children didn't know them at all. He was mad because, as usual, he'd made arrangements without consulting me and insisted he'd lose face by cancelling. I thought they probably would understand – in any case, family came first – but he didn't like it.

Stuart and Grace left together and the winter closed in. A blizzard hit us at New Year and movement was restricted to chopping and hauling wood from the store shed to feed the big stone fireplace. It was a couple of days before we could get out to the main road and town to replenish our stores. Muffled to the eyebrows, we managed to go out walking a little each day and would stand briefly looking out across miles of countryside lying white and glittering under the bright sun. As far as the eye could see, the farmland was rendered almost featureless under its heavy cloak of snow and punctuated only by the occasional stark, leafless tree and the wisp of smoke from some half-hidden farmstead.

I was brought back to an urgent review of my situation with a jolt. Gordon was away for the day and I accidently came across undisputable evidence that he was conducting an illicit sexual affair again. I fought off waves of nausea, forcibly reminded again that there'd be no peace until I took action. My attempt to talk to him on his return failed, as did other attempts to confront him. He sensed at the onset what I was about and responded either in anger or by elusively slipping away.

I needed someone to talk to, but not knowing anyone there well enough, I phoned a retired pastor friend who lived not very far away, knowing he had a relative near us whom he visited from time to time. He kindly offered to come over as soon as convenient. As it turned out, when he came a few days later, Gordon was out and we were able to talk. It helped me a little but, of course, no one else could do anything. It was all up to me.

Our two tea chests arrived in late January. It was apparent that at some time, if not all the time, they had been left outside one on top of the other. The box of books was badly damaged by water seeping up from the bottom whereas my box was only damp at the top with no real damage at all.

February swept in with more snow and I succumbed to a virulent throat infection. It left me feeling as if I was trapped in some sort of time warp, drained and apathetic. I knew I had to get my head together and decide what to do but I was temporarily powerless to engage in the battle again. My mind swirled in an endless spiral, rehashing the sequence of events, wondering how I could have managed things better. Had I been that naïve, that passive, that stupid?

The events following the brethren's confrontation with Gordon and the attitude of people round me had left me with scars because I'd been so vulnerable. I knew our friend in Bethesda House had done his best in most trying circumstances and I was grateful. Before leaving, he'd come to me and apologized for his mistakes and we had parted well. Perhaps I was needlessly beating myself over the head about it all, but I still struggled to understand. What had kept me tied in that situation so long? Stateless for so long, Grace had been the string – and also my long-awaited hope for my husband and my belief in God's faithfulness. Though it cost me dear, I could not regret my choices.

I drifted through a few more weeks as the weather changed. Drifts of aconites and snowdrops appeared under the trees and cottage gardens were carpeted in primroses. Suddenly it was Easter. Grace came down for the weekend and I know she sensed I didn't know what to do or where to go. She urged me to move out and while I accepted the wisdom of her advice, I still struggled with the question of how. I tried not to worry her with the knowledge that I was having some distressing symptoms for which I had no explanation. From time to time I experienced a lump in my throat and could not swallow or breathe properly. Though I tried to make light of it, she could read in my face just what that long, drawn-out winter of tension and indecision had cost me.

With her alongside, I tried hard to whip up my flagging will to action, but I was penniless, still not strong and potentially homeless. I knew that I simply had to get away or the whole of the rest of my life would be ruined. My sense of failure was profound and I felt I was losing myself – the person I really was – and feared I would never be that person again.

The glorious weather continued. The weekend after Easter, Gordon decided we should pay a visit to his mother in Bath. It was Sunday so he decided we should leave early and go to morning service at a church in Salisbury first. Suddenly, at some point in the service, I was riveted to hear the minister giving a warning in his sermon, the words almost identical to those warnings Gordon had received at the farm. I looked sideways at him, half reaching out to touch him, but his face was fiercely set, rigid with such stony anger that I felt chilled and looked away swiftly. As I did so, my eyes alighted on a banner hanging against a pillar, lit with a shaft of sunlight from a window opposite. Its text, surrounded by bright embroidered spring flowers read, "You will go out in joy and be led forth in peace; the mountains and the hills will burst into song before you, and all the trees of the field will clap their hands."[11]

Returning to our car after the service, he looked a little more approachable so I resolved to make one last attempt to focus on the problem between us and his reluctance to be accountable and trust God. No sooner had I begun to speak than he adroitly sidestepped the issue. "Why do you want to talk about us? Why should we? Everything's fine." He smoothly dismissed my attempts with a smile and once again I was reduced to ineffectual shadowboxing with words. In no way would he let me get near, so we relapsed into silence.

At his suggestion, we broke our journey at Wells to visit the cathedral which I had never seen. While there, I became aware of an extraordinary phenomenon. It seemed as though a thick cloud had rolled between us like an encroaching fog. It was so real I looked around to see if other people around us were affected. But no, it seemed not, although the dark cloud looked real and almost solid to me.

A weight descended on my spirit. We walked for a while in the sunshine, and the weight and the shadow remained. Within, I was weeping; the burden of grief I had held at bay for so long struggled for expression as the last glimmer of hope died.

Resuming our journey, we went through the motions of visiting and taking tea and made our farewells without any discernible hitch in the politeness. Driving home, I gazed unseeing at the passing scenery in the twilight while my mind turned to a passage in Isaiah 52: "Depart, depart, go out from there! Touch no unclean thing! Come out from it and be pure, you who carry the vessels of the Lord. But you will not leave in haste or go in flight; for the Lord will go before you, the God of Israel will be your rear guard."

In my heart, by now, I had already separated, having in some indefinable moment cut the cord between us. My course was set. The question of how I could physically leave remained unanswered for the moment, but in the light of God's word, I felt I didn't have to fret about that. It would happen, provision would come, and I would be able to leave without fear of my husband's reaction.

---

[11] Isaiah 55:12

In the local fellowship we had met one couple who had become my friends. They were discerning and loving and had become aware of my problems long before I confided in them. A few days after Gordon and I returned home, the wife arrived at the cottage with a gift. She knew I did not have travel money nor the means to leave without incurring his anger, that I was afraid of a physical confrontation. This dear lady said she was glad to catch me on my own as she'd prayed my husband would be out when she arrived so we could talk privately. She pressed an envelope of money into my hand, assuring me the gift came with her husband's blessing also. She suggested I phone her when my opportunity came and she would drive over and take me to the station. So the door was poised to open and all I had to do was go through it. But at that time, I hadn't yet been able to decide where to go.

A family wedding invitation came to my aid. We accepted and I asked the groom's parents, my brother and sister-in-law, if I could stay with them and visit for a few days afterwards. They and Gordon agreed. So we drove to London together and I openly brought along a small suitcase and the spare key to the cottage.

I had won a small respite but was presented with another dilemma: how could I fully explain my leaving to his relatives, of whom I was very fond and who were being so kind to me? I really needed a neutral place in which I could figure out what to do next. I didn't feel it right to go to Grace, who only had a bed-sit, because I didn't know how Gordon would react when he knew I wasn't coming back. I didn't want to put her at risk of his possible violence. The problem consumed my thoughts and after one awful nightmare-filled night, I contacted her pastor and asked for his help. He arranged a room with a family in the church who had a large house and it was agreed I'd move the next day.

I decided not to tell my in-laws the true reasons and details of my complex situation, for fear of hurting them or causing a rift between the brothers. I wanted to be in a safe, neutral place before contacting Gordon to tell him I wasn't coming back, knowing his anger would erupt. However, in trying to protect them, I made a serious mistake. When they heard from Gordon, they accepted his version of what had happened. And, of course, I hurt them anyway because I'd left without a full explanation and they rightly felt used.

Once settled in the new household, I was offered a part-time job and, being used to working, I accepted. In hindsight, it might have been better to have rested and applied for Social Services financial aid, but I was not used to the English system and anxious to establish as near a normal life as possible. Before I started work, my friend from Wiltshire phoned to say that she had discovered Gordon was to be away for a while and if I would like to come down, she would meet my train and take me to the cottage to get the rest of my things. Once in Salisbury, I was back on the train within three hours with all my personal belongings and had posted the spare house key back through the letterbox.

Gordon's rage was monumental but I was away. Naturally, he was not prepared to accept my defection and harassed me a great deal. With all this happening, and getting to grips with a new job, I hadn't realized how great a strain I was under. I felt it but didn't realize its possible consequences. My hosts were kind and the pastor repeatedly asked me what I wanted to do, but I just didn't know. The dammed-up grief kept bursting through, and more than anything I needed time to settle. Nevertheless, I did what I could: paid what they suggested for my keep and contributed to the household by making new sitting room curtains, sewing repairs and working in their greenhouse.

Then several things combined to add those last few 'straws to the camel's back'. I didn't know quite what to do next. Instead of waiting till my overloaded emotions had settled down, I allowed myself to be pressured into action. My hosts and the pastor were well intentioned but the result was disastrous.

My hostess took me along to consult a female divorce lawyer who was aggressive and not at all to my taste. I suppose I'd gone along hoping for some general advice but she requested a written record of my reasons for divorce, and though I tried, it was too stressful. I began to be plagued by vivid nightmares culminating in a particularly awful one, a vision of my husband marooned on a moonscape of rejection and loneliness.

I went down to Sussex to see John and his wife and talk to them. On the return journey, crossing the over-rail bridge at the railway station, I tripped at the top of the flight of iron clad stairs and fell, seriously injuring my knee. My leg swelled alarmingly and was soon twice its size from ankle to thigh. The pain was considerable and I couldn't bend my leg or sit. Insidiously, the stress was building.

Then came the day when I became aware that I wasn't functioning properly and began to hallucinate. My hostess and a friend took me to her doctor and the next thing I was aware of was being in a strange hospital and not even sure of how I got there. What I didn't know, and had never been warned about, was that the effects of the prescription drug Ativan stayed in one's system for a long, long time. After almost two years of taking no medication at all, I was experiencing a full-blown backlash and was once more in a mental hospital. And this time the experience was vastly worse than before; not from the point of view of the effects of the medication I received, nor the length of stay, for that was very short, but because of the things that happened there.

Within a few days I was moved to a rehabilitation ward and allowed to go into town on a shopping trip. I had also been told I could go to a day-centre, where there were sewing facilities, for a further one week before being discharged. I bought some beautiful dress material but on the first day, when my back was turned, a fellow patient took shears and slashed my material to ribbons. I was sent flowers but another patient ripped them apart and threw them across the floor. In my emotionally fragile state, this was worse than anything I'd experienced in the Zambian hospital.

Yet there was a day when there was an accident in the kitchen adjacent to the dining room and, without thinking, I stepped forward to help. Moreover, I stayed to assist the domestic staff until the end of their shift. I suppose this was a good indicator of how well I was recovering but I didn't think about it in this way at the time; I just acted instinctively.

I had been going for daily walks in the hospital grounds and often came across an old decrepit 'bag lady' hanging round the gate. She had all her possessions bundled into black plastic garbage bags stuffed into an old shopping trolley. She was grubby and unkempt and very likely homeless. Every time I saw her, the enemy of my soul would hiss in my mind taunts that this was my destiny. Every walk became a spiritual battleground as I prayed and once more endeavoured to claim my life back.

This time there was a new dimension to my fight for total healing and restoration. I now had to fight fear itself. Knowing it was not of God, it nevertheless threatened my determination to make a way out. The doctors here now told me that this sort of episode would most likely reoccur and therefore I must prepare to live accordingly. Having previously been totally and joyously convinced of healing, this knowledge was hard to hear and I resolved not to take it on board.

God is faithful and true to his word. I latched on to the scripture, "...the one who is in you is greater than the one who is in the world."[12] I walked, prayed and laid claim to all that was mine in the here and now: family, friends, health, the ability to work and above all, the hope of an opportunity to embrace a renewed spiritual ministry. And in direct response to that awful figure at the gate, I reminded myself and the enemy of who and what I am: a daughter of The King, in neat clothes and good shoes, whose matching handbag held a cheque book and car keys. I was not going to live my life on the floor. This was no academic war of words; this was my fight to affirm all the practical outworking of what I believed and the future I wanted.

A few days after the kitchen incident, I was discharged; I went to stay with Grace for a short while and applied for Social Services aid. Fortunately, I was able to use a friend's bedsit on her landing that was vacant for three weeks. So I had that long to come to a decision of what to do next. Despite my grip on renewal, it was much harder to step out and make decisions this time; every step was a conscious battle. I still had the odd feeling of depersonalization, a feeling of being unreal in my body, no doubt a little leftover trace of the medication. But even with the knowledge it would fade in time, it was still disconcerting.

Everywhere I went, I tried to memorize the street names and house numbers and other details in an effort to stir my reluctant mind into action. I struggled with the irrational fear that I could no longer accomplish simple practical things, so immediately I forced myself to practise those very things whatever they were: cooking, typing, sewing, crosswords, card games, Scrabble or accounts. The list was long and I deliberately asked Grace's pastor and his wife if I could come to their house and do some domestic jobs for them in order to prove to myself my fears were groundless and I hadn't lost my skills. Someone else in the church also accepted my offer of domestic help and also a little secretarial work. Gradually, I built up my confidence and was thankful for their understanding.

---

[12] 1 John 4:4

I had a growing sense of homelessness. I went down to John's home in Sussex for a while and there took a temporary office job but I hadn't the computer skills needed and the job defeated me. I went back and found temporary lodgings with friends from Grace's church. The loss of my own home, that source of such quiet content, that pivotal core of my existence so hard won and joyfully shared, was a constant ache. The sense of being shut out and disposed overwhelmed me.

After a while, I accepted an invitation to stay with another family from Grace's church, but without work and a proper home, I still felt adrift and was still reaching for that necessary stability. While I was there my Canadian friend Mary came to stay with me for a couple of nights. My hosts were very kind and welcomed her generously. Mary was a breath of fresh air and I delighted in her company. We went up into central London for the day but the visit left me more sensitive to all I had lost, especially in the area of study and learning. I had neither the money nor the strength as yet to go out and seize what I instinctively knew I needed.

CHAPTER TWENTY-FIVE

Very Small Steps

The need to establish a proper new life for myself continued to drive my outlook; how to achieve it was the crux of the problem. I had to change lodgings again and this time I wasn't able to go to friends. Instead I found a place in a large house, the home of a non-Christian widow and her little girl, and where there were two other lodgers. She wanted someone to look after the house and was willing to forgo rent in favour of someone who could perform this service. This suited me very well because although I could have applied for a housing allowance, the last thing I wanted was to sit around. It was far better that I work, so I settled into a pattern of caring for the house in the mornings and not letting myself rest or watch TV till after lunch. The house was on the fringes of Croydon so I was still able to attend Grace's church.

Our former farm manager, who'd returned after the raid and trained for the Christian ministry, had kept in touch, and he and his new wife had kindly given me a television set so I didn't have to share with the others in the house. It wasn't a happy time but this interim period and its tasks did help.

The idea of having to find a job and going back to work was curiously daunting this late in life. No matter how extensive my knowledge, how competent my former abilities, psychologically my recent experiences had 'pulled the rug from under my feet' in how I felt about myself. I had managed a farming estate employing a large workforce but I had not been employed by someone else for over twenty years, in England for about thirty years. Times and technology had changed radically in that time and I knew that any prospective employer would not be interested in my struggles; they would only pay money for one to turn up and perform.

After three months, I resigned from the housekeeping and applied for housing benefit so I could pay rent. I signed up for two courses at Croydon College, an 'Introduction to Word Processing and Computing' and a refresher course, 'Women in Management'. In the latter there was little new for me, but it was valuable in bringing me up-to-date with UK business conditions and practices. I re-sat my UK driving test, which was no problem at all. My original UK driving licence had been lost in our fire. I found all this hugely enjoyable and my confidence grew as my uncertainties faded.

But one area of my life remained unsettled. The paperwork regarding my proposed divorce lay in a drawer of the desk in my room. From time to time that winter, I took the papers out, picked up my pen and put them back unsigned. I just wasn't ready to do it and I knew in my heart I hadn't reached the point of acceptance that it was the only way out. Periodically, the whole problem would rear its head and I'd have to chew it over again in my mind. But no amount of reviewing the situation changed a thing.

Nor, it has to be said, was I ready to cope with the necessary upheaval of the divorce until I was in a more stable position. My still fairly recent experience of the Ativan backlash had seriously compromised my emotional balance and I was extremely cautious. It was as if in rebuilding my life piece by piece, I dared not risk jeopardizing each small step, each hard-won victory, until I was sure that the next move would not overset what had gone before. I was determined I would never go through such a battle again and believed with all my heart that God would help me succeed. Also, I had no wish to involve or hurt my children further by implication or the broadcasting of sensitive details if Gordon fought the case. I had learned the hard way to distrust his reactions. It was already too late to simply use adultery as a reason.

Despite the setbacks, the ill-advised counselling and my drawn-out struggles, the church leadership had never wavered in their support. One of them had even accompanied me to Birmingham for a meeting with Gordon who had found work there. I had requested the meeting to discuss a legal separation to which he agreed, though he later reneged and refused to sign the papers.

However, now I had come so far in establishing myself, I was content to wait. It was time to address the problem of work and finding a proper place to live, ever mindful that I had no savings and no pension. There were still moves to make if I was to aim for a professional job. For instance, I reckoned it would be good to find a 'little job' in order to re-enter the workplace and gain confidence and, in any case, I had no suitable clothes yet. Also, I desperately needed somewhere decent to live, and didn't want to settle for anywhere dingy even for a short time.

Accordingly, I decided to return to the midlands, wondering if it would be possible to prepare for this next step from my brother's home, though there was little room as my mother lived there also. The biggest problem was, how long would it take for me to achieve my goal?

With the lack of money governing every practical step, a strange opportunity presented itself and, ever mindful of the pitfalls ahead, after prayer and thinking it through I accepted. I looked on it as a crutch to assist me to the next level. Shortly before, Gordon had reappeared and asked me to go back, but I would not. I was unsure of his real motives; perhaps they were connected with his new job as caretaker at a Christian College. He persisted though and I agreed to a discussion.

I made it plain that under no circumstances would I resume a marital relationship but would consider sharing his living quarters for a period. He stipulated that I'd have to pay all my own expenses, plus half the household bills and pay entirely for a telephone since I considered that a necessity. I agreed and he took an additional available room on the ground floor of the house.

Installed in this temporary symbiotic relationship, I went job-hunting. I'd been thinking along the lines of some part-time office job to start with and wasn't having any success. Then it came to my notice that there was a boys' boarding school in the same road, only a five-minute walk away, and they were advertising for a cook. Happily calling off my search for something grander, I went along and got the job.

I was to cook for breakfast and lunch each weekday, working from 7 am until 2 pm. There was no need for smart clothes as overalls were provided and a fair wage in school term time, half pay in the school holidays. There was no need to pay for public transport and the school was happy to have someone who could be relied upon to get there even in the worst of winter weather. It was a godsend and allowed me to ease back into the employer/employee and fellow worker roles. After nearly three months, I had gained much confidence and started to think about the next step.

It was far from easy being in such close proximity to Gordon again but no matter how odd it may have appeared to other people, or what he chose to tell them, the situation was clear from my point of view. During that time, he even agreed to take some counselling when a mutual friend urged him, and I supported him in this. But after a short time, he pulled out again. For those several winter weeks, the truce held until events combined to push me forwards again.

One dark February morning I went to work as usual and, shortly after breakfast was served, I tripped over a shallow unlit step in the basement storeroom. The fall shook me but not until the agony struck a bit later did I realize I'd sustained a serious injury. After several hours in the casualty ward of the local hospital, I was sent home with a torn ligament in my hip. For the next nine weeks, I could only hobble on crutches very short distances round the apartment when the power of my painkillers was at maximum strength.

Hardly settled into this new and practically house-bound routine, Gordon announced he was off to Zambia for an unspecified time. Apparently, the rent for the farmhouse had not been paid for a considerable period. Indeed, the tenant had left the house vacant and the whole place had been badly neglected. Attempting a comment on the subject by asking Gordon why the tenant had not been accountable to him or his agent in Lusaka so his fault would have been discovered sooner, I was told sharply, "Its none of your business," and for another six years I heard no further news of the farm.

My employers were not able to keep my job open beyond the end of the first month and I was not eligible for any sort of sick benefit. A telephone call in March to Social Services regarding this resulted in me receiving incorrect information, so I had no further income until I was fit enough to go to their offices in person. Then I had to wait another two weeks for the assistance to arrive. My one helper was a lovely Christian student who lived on the next floor and she drove me for treatment and to appointments. Another neighbour brought in shopping for me twice a week. Both these young women were a great blessing for which I was profoundly thankful.

While I was trapped in my inactive routine within the apartment, I delighted in watching the garden green up and the first daffodils appear. In myself, strengthening changes were being forged; on the one hand, by waiting on the Lord and asking the Holy Spirit to guide me in getting a better job as soon as my injury was healed, and on the other hand, by the knowledge I'd gained in this time.

Gordon had obtained a job as student accommodation maintenance man at this college. He'd found friends and local fellowship and was already prominent in a house group. He had laid down a foundation of half-truths, implying that I was mentally unfit, which even after my arrival no one questioned. A friend of his came to the door one day and when I answered the door and introduced myself, this person expressed intense surprise, saying that my husband had led her to believe I was still hospitalized. She wouldn't leave a message and left abruptly.

Maybe he said these things to gain the 'sympathy vote' with the local Christians – or was it pride to put himself in a good light? Who can tell? It was all too complex for me to fathom. When I first arrived, I thought that the people at the college seemed a little wary of me but had dismissed that idea as fanciful. He continued to use innuendo and half-truths and was very dismissive of me in public.

When he returned, the college was shut for the Easter vacation. My injury was almost healed. However, that same day he announced he was going away again to stay with friends. Out of interest to see what he'd say, I asked him if he could delay a few days until after my birthday so we could go out, since I'd been housebound for so long. He said no, his trip could not wait and he would be off the following morning. So I knew at once there would be no time for talk.

That night, when he went for a bath before bed, I noticed his briefcase left open on the table. The rubber-stamped address on the top half of a large brown envelope was showing above the pocket in the lid of the case. What drew my eye like a magnet was that it was the address of my doctor's office in Lusaka. Beginning to tremble, I drew it out carefully. It was bulky, with my husband's name handwritten across the front. Without compunction and with a pounding heart, I very carefully steamed it open, all the while listening with bated breath for any sound from the bathroom that would indicate my husband's return. There in my hand I held the complete record of my medical history in Zambia.

My mind grappled with the question, what was his motive in procuring these records? What was he planning to do with them? How had he managed to do that? With shaking hands, I hastily found and wadded sheets of approximately the same quantity of blank typing paper and put them in the envelope, re-sealed it as best I could and replaced the package in the briefcase. I hid the medical records under the carpet beneath the table. Then I called, "Goodnight!" in the direction of the bathroom and went to bed.

The next day after his departure, I called my support team, handed over the medical records for safekeeping and arranged for the team to come over to the apartment upon my husband's return. Suddenly I was in the clear, calm and sure of myself. I knew exactly what I was going to do. All doubts and uncertainties were laid to rest. It was time to finish it.

The day after his return, the support team came over and I was able at last to calmly explain my decision to leave for good. Arrangements were made for him to be away from the apartment the following day while I removed my things, then one of them drove me to my brother's house. Gordon never challenged me about the missing records and shortly after that my support team saw to it they were burned as a symbol of the past put behind me.

CHAPTER TWENTY-SIX

A New Beginning

The heap of black plastic bags that lay on my brother's garage floor was reminiscent of my earlier flights, but now it was different. It was not the end of anything, it was a beginning. Though my head was grappling with many practical problems, I could feel the sap rising in my heart and spirit.

Furnished with the best publication I could find for my purpose, I sat down and drew up a list on a large piece of paper. When I'd first arrived at my brother's house, I had thought to find a job – any job – as quickly as possible. But after praying about it, I realized now was the time to go about the task more carefully. If I was expecting to receive the fulfilment of those promises I believed were mine, then I must do all I could to put myself in the way, on the path of that possibility.

Accordingly, I drew up columns and listed what I needed, what I wanted, where I thought I should be, and why. Finally, alongside all this, I wrote out the specific words I had received from God.

It had to be a good job that offered enough salary to allow me to buy some pension, set up a proper home and establish a new life. Instead of just going anywhere where I knew no one, it made sense to be near one part of my family or the other. This furnished me with three options: Solihull, Sussex or Croydon. With this checklist now complete, I opened the publication and began to search the "situations vacant".

There I found the job that fitted all the criteria on my list. Applications had to be in within six days so I telephoned for an application form and learned that the job had already been advertised for some weeks, this being for the last time. Then I went out to find a secretarial agency that could prepare me a professional C.V. at short notice. As soon as I returned home, I phoned the two most likely people available that could give me references.

As soon as the form arrived, I carefully prepared my application and posted it back without delay. On the afternoon of the day applications closed, a telephone call from London advised me I was shortlisted and invited me to an interview the next Thursday morning at 11.30 am.

That evening I called Grace and arranged to sleep on her sofa the following Wednesday night, explaining why I wanted her to book me into her hairdresser early on Thursday. We had a lovely visit that Wednesday evening and while I pressed my one good dress and polished my shoes, I explained just where this job was: right in the next suburb.

The interview was held in a small lounge off a dining room that sat eighty people. Though I had no formal qualifications, I had a wealth of practical experience and felt calm and confident. After the interview, I was given a conducted tour of the place. I returned to Grace's flat, picked up my overnight bag and set off for the railway station for the return trip to Solihull. Four hours later, as I entered the house, my sister-in-law met me in the hall with the news that she had received a telephone message: the job was mine.

Getting the job was a great relief. There was a very nice unfurnished apartment that went with it which was newly decorated and carpeted. Stuart, who had returned from America, was living in another adjacent suburb so I could look forward to being near both of them for the foreseeable future. My cup was full.

When the euphoria had settled a little, I began to think of what I must do next. There was barely two weeks to go before taking up my appointment and I had almost no money. Reluctant to borrow from my family, I prayerfully made out another list of the very least of my needs and the estimated cost of the move itself.

Stuart hired a self-drive van on my behalf and drove my things down to my new place the following weekend. My mother gave me an old but comfortable arm chair and a television set. Fortunately, I had sufficient bedding, towels and so on. But I only had one good dress and the pair of shoes I'd worn to the interview, plus a good winter coat that was a gift from my family. All my other stuff had been bought at charity shops and was badly worn, not at all suitable for my new position.

Once again, I went to prayer, holding a piece of paper on which I had written my promises and the list of my needs side by side. This time the needs were more detailed. And all this was pinned to my job confirmation letter. I telephoned the bank in the city that I'd used when working at the school and where I'd left a few pounds just to keep the account open, and requested an appointment with the bank manager. Fortunately, she had an opening the following day.

Seated across from the bank manager, I explained my position and produced my letter of appointment which also stated my salary. Feeling steady, with a real sense of peace, I outlined my minimum needs: a bed, an iron, some more clothes and the need to keep myself until my first pay day. I then asked for a £300 overdraft and she said yes. In a very short time I was out in the street feeling very relieved and thankful.

My particular appointment, in a block of eighty-two flats for retired teachers, was that of Deputy Warden over sixty-two of those flats, the 'sheltered' section. That simply meant that the flats had safety features built in and the wardens (the managers) lived on site and were on call in case of an emergency. My job included the responsibility for catering, which meant I was able to take my main meal on duty; this helped enormously that first month. Grace brought me an ironing board so after the first week I didn't have to iron my clothes on the carpet. My bed had been the one big new purchase at the start, but soon I was able to add a few items, mostly from second-hand shops, and piece by piece, bit by bit, my new life began.

Divorce. It was a bereavement without dignity, a form of death without a body and a burial. No matter that the world found it commonplace, it grieved me deeply. In it, to my mind, there exists a strange dichotomy for a Christian. There is no hiding it and it signals some degree of failure, subtly altering other people's perception of one. In the end it happened very quietly, a mere exchange of documents between lawyers, ironically becoming final on Grace's birthday.

Holding my divorce papers, I wept again, grieving that I had been pushed into such a position. My husband had sworn he would see I never got a penny if I went through with it. With all his property and assets in Zambia, I knew it was futile to try. All I wanted, as I'd promised myself when I left Africa, was to find a way to bring about something good from my time there. I had come away with deep sorrow, with no fond farewells, no accolades or good wishes from friends or colleagues, just a lonely exit shadowed in shame.

At that time, in such dark circumstances, it had been difficult to remember all the good stuff. With so many reasons to put the past behind me, I was nevertheless very reluctant to see 'the baby' thrown out with 'the bathwater', the baby in this case being all the good and lovely things I had experienced at the hand of God, the joys and precious times I could rightly praise and thank him for, the hopes and dreams I had entrusted to him.

Before I left Africa, and for a long time after my return to England, I engaged in the humbling process of evaluating my past choices and decisions. Nevertheless, I remained unshaken in the conviction that my long fight had been worthwhile. I had learned the hard way that no amount of love, devotion, loyalty or prayer will move a man against his unrepentant will, and this was a devastating lesson. But however naïve and mistaken I may be judged to have been, I did not regret my choice to stay so long. What does it say in the marriage service, which after all is an oath taken before God? "...to love and to cherish... forsaking all others... for better or worse... till death do us part." Love had died a hard, lingering death while I tried to fulfil my half of the contract.

I had long accepted my struggles and disappointments in the marriage, knowing full well how imperfect I was, but adultery was a far cry from all I had learned much later. A greater, more damaging betrayal, that had destroyed so much, had been the crux of the matter; that I had been powerless to prevent it was my most bitter burden.

Yet how faithful our God is, how swift to reach out and restore us when we turn to him! How patient and ready he is to teach us how to rebuild! Though I wished with all my heart that we had never had to tread that dreaded path, I would not trade past anguish for what I learned about his grace.

Sometime in my childhood, my mother gave me a book and she wrote on the flyleaf, "This above all: to thine own self be true, and it must follow as the night the day, thou canst not then be false to any man."[13] How often these words echoed in my mind over the years,

---

[13] Shakespeare: Hamlet, Act 1

more epically as I had struggled to find my way through the mire of deceit, to become my own person once again.

What had God promised me? In 1984, at the height of my tribulation, he had spoken into my situation through godly counsellors, giving me the assurance that I was understood as well as loved, and the encouragement I had found in my knowledge of the scriptures had given me a solid base from which to rise. Although this Calvary journey had taken a long time, it had produced a far deeper understanding and a wider, more objective view of an era and a family, a purpose and its trials and, above all, the encompassing, never-failing strength of God's redeeming love.

Despite the defection of many friends in Zambia, I found myself reflecting on the many kindnesses I had received at the hand of other Christian friends and acquaintances elsewhere.

Looking back over the way God had led me, where I'd struggled and fought, sacrificed and at last capitulated, there had been no instant when my Lord had left me. After the fire which took all our material goods, only a small portion of undamaged brick wall was left standing. It was a mute testimony to: "The LORD is good, a refuge in times of trouble. He cares for those who trust in him..."[14]

I had learned that whatever my circumstances, he understood what I was going through and I could count on him for all that I needed. When the dour spirit of discouragement threatened to drag me down and the enemy whispered, "You're not going to make it," he gave me the courage I needed to fight back, to stand up again. God never said anything he could not back up, never promised anything he couldn't deliver. Though many answers took time, my Lord was with me in the waiting room.

Deep in my heart was the deposit left by the Holy Spirit in the prophetic messages brought to me at Ely in September 1984. They specifically spoke of healing, of a new way forward and of a new ministry. Throughout, I'd learned much about God's grace: that no matter what fraught shadow is cast by past events, it is possible to go forward in peace and hope knowing the best is yet to come.

---

[14] Nahum 1:7

Glossary (mainly Zambia Chinyanja)

Amoyo	life
Amakhulu	old grandmothers
Amayi	mother, older woman
Ba kulu!	salute to a great leader, an elder
Bambo	respected old gentleman
Bilharzia	African waterborne disease
Boma	enclosure for dwellings, name given to town municipal office
Bubezi	jackal
Bundu	bush land, wilderness
Bwana	boss
Bwelani	"Come!"
Bwelani kuno	"Come here!"
Bwino	good
Chabwino	"It is good."
Chibuku	native beer made from maize
Chitenje	length cotton with native design, also used as wrap-round dress
Dagga	cannabis
Dambo	open damp grassy area, swamp
Dona	polite form of address i.e. madam, lady (Portuguese)
Duka	small shop, country trading post
Faro	rhinoceros
Fundi	craftsman or expert
Fisi	hyena
Gundwane	cane rat
Hambe gahle	"Go in peace!"
Indaba	tribal council for airing opinions or giving judgements
Inde	"Yes!"
Inkosikaza	respected old lady
Kaingo	leopard
Khasu	garden hoe
Kalani bwino	"Stay well!" said in farewell
Kalani pansi	stay down, sit, stay or wait
Kanyoni	small birds of the bush
Kapenta	tiny lake fish
Kifaru, faru	rhinoceros

Kopje	small hill (Afrikaans)
Kraal	village or thorn fenced paddock for cattle
Kusanga	go to the bush
Kuyenda	to walk
Kyinu?	"And you?"
Lekker	wonderful, fantastic (Afrikaans slang)
Machete	large hacking blade, panga
Malondo	night watchman
Maluwa	flowers
Mansi	water
Matete	reeds
Mbile	the number 2
Miningi	many
Mipando	chair, stool
Munda	garden; munda wanga – my garden
Muti	medicine
Ndeke	aircraft
Ndio	relish (tomato-based vegetable mix)
Ndiri bwino	"I am well"
Ngombi	cattle
Nkumba	pig
Njoka	snake
Nkosi	king, used also as 'boss' in the sense of 'sir'
Nkosi-kazi	a term of high respect when addressing a wife
Njobu	elephant
Nkosi wanga	my wife
Nyama	meat, animal
Nyati	buffalo
Nyenyezi	stars
Nzou	elephant
Odi	"Excuse me!"
Phiri	hill
Rondaval	African round house, usually mud brick/pole and thatch
Stoep	veranda (Afrikaans)
Tackies	canvas gym shoes
Tengani	the command 'to bring'
Tiyende	"Let's go!"
Toto	child
Zikomo	thank you'
Zirombo	weeds

What Shall I Read Next?

Mary Something-Else

Author
ISBN 978-1-907509-92-6

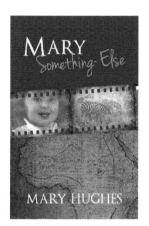

"I want something else!" demanded two-year-old Mary.

"Well, what do you want?" her mother asked. "A sweet?"

"Yes," she replied, grabbing the opportunity, "but I want something else!"

Mary's journey would take her to Africa and back, meeting many interesting people, looking for the 'something else' that would change her life forever...

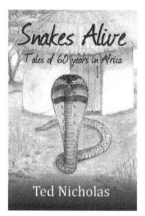

Snakes Alive

Ted Nicholas
ISBN 978-1-907509-61-2

Ted Nicholas, a former pioneering farmer, has brought up a family of five children, together with his wife, Margaret. After many years of successful agricultural business ventures in three continents, his life changed when a visiting preacher came to his local area in Africa. Attending the meeting for his children's benefit, he found himself making a deliberate and sincere commitment to the Lordship of Jesus Christ that would change his destiny.

In his work, he faced threats from witchdoctors, wild beasts, the environment and dangerous people. However, he found that time and time again God gave him the strength and boldness to become 'more than a conqueror' through Jesus.

Books available from your local Christian bookshop and from the publisher:

www.onwardsandupwards.org